TEILHARD DE CHARDIN
AND THE MYSTERY OF CHRIST

Pierre Teilhard de Chardin

CHRISTOPHER F. MOONEY, S.J.

TEILHARD DE CHARDIN AND THE MYSTERY OF CHRIST

HARPER & ROW, PUBLISHERS
NEW YORK

TO MY MOTHER AND THE MEMORY OF MY FATHER

Imprimi potest: John J. McGinty, S.J., November 27, 1964
Imprimatur: Richard Cardinal Cushing, Boston, August 5, 1965

FIRST EDITION

LIBRARY OF CONGRESS CATALOG CARD NUMBER: 66-15050

Foreword

The present study is an attempt to organize the theological thought of Pierre Teilhard de Chardin into a synthesis which he himself outlined a number of times but never actually made. One might compare it to an orchestrated musical chord composed of a large number of notes, many of which have already been sounded together frequently, but which have never been so arranged that they could all be sounded at once. Hence what is presented here is a reconstruction and interpretation, but one whose purpose has been first and foremost to have each individual note come through as clearly as possible.

Though by profession a geologist and palaeontologist, Teilhard de Chardin was preoccupied throughout his life with the larger question of the role of man in the universe. This he felt to be a question not for philosophy and theology alone but for science as well, and his own understanding of evolution was an attempt to enlarge the traditional boundaries of science so as to include a study of the human person in relationship to the material world. One cannot, however, fully understand his thought if one believes that his analysis of man as a phenomenon constitutes his total intellectual achievement. For as a Christian, a Catholic priest and a Jesuit, he was led to undertake a much more ambitious project: to rethink within his own distinctive evolutionary system the data of Christian revelation concerning the Person of Christ. This he tried to do primarily because he believed that Christ, as God Incarnate, revealed in himself not only the mystery of God but also the meaning of man, and therefore the ultimate meaning of that evolutionary process of which God is the cause and man the culmination.

Yet in addition to this he believed that the discovery of evolution

5

was in itself of immense theological importance, since it threw a totally new light upon a theological problem as old as the epistles of St. Paul, namely the relationship of the cosmos to Christ. A satisfactory answer to this problem in terms of evolution, Teilhard felt, could do much to bridge the chasm which exists today between Christians and non-Christians on the question of building the earth. For many a good Christian, he once noted,[1] the universe is transparent; it stands between himself and God but he does not see it at all. For the unbeliever, on the other hand, the universe is opaque and he can see nothing else. The Christian who feels himself secure in a certain avenue of escape to the next world, frequently sees no ultimate value to the progress that man makes in the present one. The results of human effort precisely as human tend to have little interest for him. The unbeliever is quick to sense this ambivalence. In his eyes the planning and shaping of the modern world are of supreme importance, and he reproaches the Christian, sometimes bitterly, for his apparent lack of interest in grappling with the grimy machinery of society and identifying himself with the city of man. 'Why is it that, nine times out of ten, a believing Christian is, as regards man, a "sceptic"? That is the great stumbling-block for the gentiles.'[2]

Hence Teilhard directs the following questions to both Christian and non-Christian, 'How can the man who believes in heaven and the Cross continue to believe seriously in the value of worldly occupations? How can the believer, in the name of everything that is most Christian in him, carry out his duty as man to the fullest extent and as whole-heartedly and freely as if he were on the direct road to God? That is what is not altogether clear at first sight; and in fact disturbs more minds than one thinks.' An answer to these questions will show to believer and unbeliever alike how 'the most traditional Christianity, expressed in baptism, the Cross and the Eucharist, can be interpreted so as to embrace all that is best in the aspirations which are characteristic of our age.'[3] The subject matter of the following pages is the theological analysis by which such an answer is obtained.

As far as possible Teilhard will be allowed to speak for himself.

All translations are those of the writer except where it was possible to make use of an official English translation. This has been modified, however, whenever it was judged necessary for greater accuracy or clarity; where such modification is substantial, this fact has been indicated in the Notes. As a general rule two peculiarities of Teilhard's highly personal French style have for the most part been eliminated. One is a tendency to capitalize all important nouns, which can be most distracting to the English reader; the other is a frequent use of italics for emphasis where such emphasis is already quite evident in English. There has also been an occasional modification in paragraph structure to conform with English usage. In all other respects the original texts have been followed as faithfully as possible.

The texts themselves may be divided into four general categories: those published by Teilhard himself; those prepared by him for publication but never published during his lifetime; those written as tentative formulations of his thought and circulated privately among theologians and friends; personal correspondence. His collected works already contain almost all items from the first category, with the source of publication noted, as well as a large number of items from the second category. In regard to the third category, it is fairly clear that certain items were never meant to be published as such; in other cases, however, one cannot say at the present stage of research whether a given essay belongs in this category or in the second. It is not intended, therefore, that the reader accept every text cited as of equal value. Each contributes in its own way towards a fuller understanding of Teilhard's mind, but it would be unfair to Teilhard to regard them all as equal expressions of that mind.

The extensive notes to this study have been added primarily to document as completely as possible the main argument. They also have as their secondary purpose to provide the student of Teilhard with further literature on related subjects as well as further precision on disputed questions. The general reader, however, who seeks simply an exposition of Teilhard's theological thought, would be advised to ignore them completely, and for this reason they have been kept well outside the body of the text. A list of abbreviations is included on the first page of the Notes.

The writer wishes to acknowledge a special debt of gratitude to Rev. Paul Henry, s.j., who directed the research for this study, Rev. René d'Ouince, s.j., Rev. Henri Bouillard, s.j., and Rev. Christian d'Armagnac, s.j., for their invaluable criticism, suggestions and constant encouragement. Acknowledgement must also be made to Rev. Maurice Giuliani, s.j., for making fully available the collection of Teilhard's unpublished writings at the Jesuit residence of *Etudes* in Paris; and to Mlle. Jeanne Mortier and M. Claude Cuénot for graciously providing several essays not to be found in the *Etudes* collection. Lastly the writer wishes to thank Rev. Thomas L. Sheridan, s.j., for his advice on a number of very difficult translations, and both him and Rev. Robert L. Faricy, s.j., for their assistance during the final stages of this work.

Contents

CONTENTS

CONTENTS

CHAPTER ONE

MODERN ANXIETY AND CHRISTIAN FAITH

TEILHARD'S LIFE AS A SEARCH FOR UNITY BETWEEN GOD AND THE WORLD

The thought of Pierre Teilhard de Chardin is an attempt at personal as well as intellectual synthesis. Fundamental to all his writings, even when concealed well beneath the surface, is a conviction of Christ's physical relationship through mankind to the universe as a whole. This fact, however, cannot be fully understood apart from an appreciation of the psychological orientation which gave that conviction birth. 'Knowledge has made its greatest advances when stimulated by some particular problem of life needing a solution; and its most sublime theories would always have drifted, rootless, on the flood of human thought if they had not been promptly incorporated into some way of mastering the world.'[1] What was Teilhard de Chardin's particular problem of life? Reduced to its simplest terms, it was the discontinuity he experienced between love of God and love of the world, between human achievement and the kingdom of Christ, between Christian detachment and personal self-development, between the data of revelation and scientific research. Hence the whole movement of his thought was a continuous search for unity, first in his own life, then in the lives of others. This is his fundamental preoccupation, the *leitmotiv* of his life. It alone enables the reader to find inner coherence in that vast maze of apparently unconnected writings, ranging from dull scientific reports to original theological enquiry, from research in palaeontology to a highly elaborated phenomenology of man's role in the universe.[2]

More accurately, perhaps, Teilhard's search was to *see* unity between God and the world. 'There are in reality two types of minds and two only, those who never get past the perception of multiplicity nor feel any need to do so, . . . and those for whom this same perception of multiplicity must necessarily resolve itself into some unity. The pluralists and the monists, those who see and those who do not.'[3] At the end of the first world war he wrote: 'I know it looks ridiculous and vain to play the part of being misunderstood. And yet (without the least vanity, I think), I honestly believe that I see something and I wish that something to be seen. You have no idea how intensely I feel regarding this whole matter.'[4] Whatever corrections, more or less broad, had to be made to the solution of his life's problem, 'there is one point no one will contest, and that is my preoccupation to unify an interior vision.' . . . 'It is a terribly painful thing not to be able to see enough!'[5] *The Divine Milieu* was written 'to teach how to see God everywhere, to see him in all that was most hidden, most solid, and most ultimate in the world. These pages put forward no more than a practical attitude—or, more exactly perhaps, a way of teaching how to see.'[6]

Seeing. We might say the whole of life lies in that verb—if not ultimately, at least essentially. Fuller being in closer union; such is the kernel and conclusion of this book. But, let us emphasize the point: union increases only through an increase in consciousness, that is to say in vision. And that, doubtless, is why the history of the living world can be summarized as the elaboration of ever more perfect eyes within a cosmos in which there is always something more to be seen. . . . To try to see more and better is not a matter of whim or curiosity or self-indulgence. To see or to perish is the very condition laid upon everything that makes up the universe, by reason of the mysterious gift of existence. . . . I repeat that my only aim in these pages, my whole driving power, is to try to see; that is to say, to try to develop a homogeneous and coherent perspective of our general experience extended to man. A whole which unfolds.[7]

The almost mystic quality of these lines from *The Phenomenon of Man* runs like a thread through all he wrote, knitting together the multi-coloured fabric of his thought. Nor is it at all surprising to learn that such a passionate search for unity should have been born of a very deep Christian faith. What is surprising and not at all sufficiently recognized in the case of Teilhard, is that this search was equally and simultaneously the product of an intense sense of anxiety before the mystery and apparent futility of human life. So true is this that the all important influence of Christian faith upon his thought can only be understood in terms of his experience of anxiety. The evident optimism of his later years was in no way the result of a pleasant disposition or a happy unconcern for the harsh realities of life. It was in every sense a victory of faith, and the price he paid was high.[8] Consequently to appreciate Teilhard's personal search for unity, it is necessary for us to document the simultaneous interplay in his life of anxiety and Christian faith.

I

'The one fault he detested, the one he would have nothing to do with, was the deliberate acceptance and delight in disgust with life, contempt for the works of man, fear of the human effort.'[9] This judgment of one of Teilhard's colleagues and friends is accurate but misleading, for it tends to convey a quite false impression that Teilhard himself neither felt nor sympathized with modern man's acute experience of the world's hostility. Consider, for example, the following reactions to death. 'With Boussac [a very close friend killed at the front in 1916] one of the pillars of my future is gone. At first I could see myself rejecting with spite everything I had ever worshipped. Instead of working for the improvement and conquest of the earth . . . wouldn't it be better to abandon to its own sort of suicide this absurd world which destroys its own best productions, and preoccupy oneself with the supernatural alone, chanting a paean of praise on the ruins of everything on earth that is beautiful and precious?'[10] Some twenty years later there was the death of Davidson Black, director of China's Geological Service: 'Black was the companion of my mind and heart, and it was with him that I envisioned my work. But there is more in it than that.

I mean a sharp and concrete realization of the utter vanity of human effort unless there exists a way out for the universe, natural as well as supernatural, towards some immortal consciousness. In my distress . . . I swore to myself on the body of my dead friend, to fight more vigorously than ever to give hope to man's work and enquiry.' He writes again in connection with Black's death: 'But what an absurd thing life is, looked at superficially! It is so absurd that you feel yourself thrown back upon a stubborn, desperate faith in the reality of spirit and its survival. Otherwise (if there were no such thing as spirit, I mean) we should have to be idiots not to call off the whole human effort.'[11]

It is indeed a paradox that this man who so loved the world and who has been accused of centring the whole of Christianity here on earth, could feel throughout his life that same world's power to discourage and oppress. 'You have to have felt the shadow of death pass over you,' he wrote at the end of the first world war, 'to realize all that is lonely in man's advance towards the future, all that is hazardous and frightful in starting out again. . . . Those who have never barely escaped death have no idea what is ahead of them.' . . . 'I felt pressing upon me the weight of an isolation that was final and definitive, the affliction of those who have gone all round their prison and found no way out . . . the moment they look up at the total shape of the world and see themselves shut in!'[12] In letters from China in 1923 he said he felt the world to be more and more 'a great and terrible thing', unable of itself to bring any light or offer any way out of man's fundamental problems. 'What a strange and sad thing life is, isn't it? We have to face the fact that nothing we are able to touch is the real consistency we are searching for, while what does seem to us to be the real consistency of the world we are unable to touch.'[13] Five years later the same sentiments appear in *The Divine Milieu*: '. . . on certain days the world seems a terrifying thing: huge, blind and brutal. It buffets us about, drags us along, kills us with complete indifference, . . . sweeps away in one moment what we had laboriously built up and beautified with all our intelligence and all our love.'[14]

There are more objective passages also, such as these lines from

16

The Phenomenon of Man: 'The whole psychology of modern disquiet is linked with the sudden confrontation with space-time. . . . Conscious or not, anguish—a fundamental anguish of being—despite our smiles, strikes in the depths of our hearts and is the undertone of all our conversations. . . . In the first and most widespread degree, the 'malady of space-time' manifests itself as a rule by a feeling of futility, of being crushed by the enormities of the cosmos. . . . Sickness of the dead end—the anguish of feeling shut in.'[15] This analysis, made in 1940, is reproduced almost verbatim in a prayer composed ten years later: 'The more the years pass, Lord, the more I recognize in myself and around me, the great secret preoccupation of modern man: it is much less to dispute possession of the world than to find some means to escape from it. The anguish of feeling, inside this bubble of the cosmos, not just spatially but ontologically shut in!'[16] There is a final recording of this same experience a year before he died: 'Fear of being lost in a world so vast . . . that man seems to have lost all significance. Fear of being reduced to immobility. Fear of being unable to find a way out.'[17]

Before proceeding further we must underline the significance of something unusual in the passages just cited, and that is Teilhard's use of the French word *issue*. It has been translated as 'a way out,' and this is its most common meaning for him. Yet the same word recurs countless times in his writings in the most unexpected places and when some synonym would be quite natural. Thus it is used in the sense of 'end', 'outcome', 'escape', 'opening', 'outlet', 'solution'. These are all legitimate meanings for *issue*, yet its continual repetition in very different contexts would seem to indicate a fundamental orientation of Teilhard's whole psychology. A 'way out'—but for what precisely? An answer to this question will bring us to the heart of the anxiety which caused him disquiet.

Let us imagine, he wrote towards the end of his life, that a group of miners are trapped through an accident deep down in the earth. For these miners to summon up the courage needed for the difficult struggle to climb back up the shaft, they have to presuppose two things: some opening exists at the other end, and when that opening is reached there will be air to breathe again and light to see. Now this is the case with our own generation. They are confronted with the realization that it is they themselves who are responsible for the march of mankind, an enterprise of staggering proportions, demanding long and painful labour, the end of which seems infinitely far away. It is useless to urge modern man to throw his energy behind such an effort if there is the least possible suspicion that the world is either hermetically closed, or that the opening at the other end leads to what is inhuman or subhuman. A death which is total, into which our whole earthly achievement disappears forever; or, what comes to the same thing, a survival which is humanly deformed and on a level lower than the noblest aspirations of man: either one of these dismal prospects would be enough of itself to inject into the marrow of man's action the incurable poison of weariness, discouragement and fear. The 'taste for life' would be stifled and 'the magnificent *élan* of humanity would eventually come to an end.'[18]

The third part of *The Phenomenon of Man* is permeated with a similar concern for this *élan* of humanity. Teilhard sees both science and mankind marking time at present because men's minds are reluctant to recognize that the development of man has a precise orientation and a privileged axis. 'Weakened by this fundamental doubt, the forces of research are scattered and there is no determination to build the earth.'[19] Like sons who have grown up, men are discovering that something is developing in the world by means of them, perhaps at their expense. In the great game being played 'we are the players as well as being the cards and the stakes. Nothing can go on if we leave the table. Neither can any power force us to remain. Is the game worth the candle, or are we simply its dupes? The danger today is that the elements of the world should refuse to serve the world—because they think. They will never bend their backs to the task unless convinced that the effort demanded has a chance of succeeding. 'Man will never take a step in a direction he knows to be blocked. There lies precisely the ill that causes our disquiet.'[20]

Now the answer to this uneasiness becomes clear as soon as we formulate the dilemma which the motivation inherent in human action has forced upon us. Either nature is closed to our demands for future existence, in which case thought, the fruit of millions of years of effort, is stifled, still-born in a self-abortive and absurd universe, or else an opening exists, a way out. Nor can we stop and wait at this crossroads, for we are being pushed forward by life and obliged to adopt an attitude if we want to go on doing anything whatsoever. To determine man's choice in his famous wager, Pascal loaded the dice with the lure of boundless gain. Here one of the alternatives is weighted with logic and, in a sense, by the promise of a whole world. 'In the last analysis the best guarantee that a thing should happen is that it appears to us as vitally necessary.'[21]

Hence a total death, an unscalable wall, on which consciousness would crash and then forever disappear, simply cannot be reconciled with the mechanism of reflection, which would immediately break its mainspring. Some absolute has to be implied in the very play of man's operative activity. Critical minds 'can go on saying as much as they like that the new generation, less ingenuous than their elders, no longer believes in a future and in a perfecting of the world. Has it ever occurred to those who write and repeat these things that if they were right all spiritual movement on earth would be virtually brought to a stop?... Without the taste for life, mankind would soon stop inventing and constructing for a work it knew to be doomed in advance. And, stricken at the very source of the impetus which sustains it, it would disintegrate from nausea or revolt and crumble into dust.'[22]

In the last of his famous Sorbonne lectures in 1949 Teilhard insisted again that it was this 'taste for life' which had to be strengthened today in the depths of the human soul; and that this meant fostering a sense of some future *issue* through which our most precious achievements could escape forever the threat of total death.[23] A widely discussed article published just before these lectures concentrated also on this 'will to survive': it is psychologically impossible to take part for any length of time in the struggle of life unless there is some way for the best of our achievements to escape total destruction. 'This is the whole problem of action.' Applied to an individual, the idea of total death may not shock at first; extended to humanity as a whole, it does violence to man's intelligence and brings nausea.[24] The celebrated book of the English astronomer Sir James Jeans, *The Universe Around Us*, came in for strong criticism from Teilhard precisely because it offered as hope to man the fact that life on earth would still go on for millions of years: 'as if in the face of a death which was absolute and sure, there was any difference to our taste for life between one year and a million million years!'[25]

This appeal to the motivation of human action, so evident throughout the texts we have been dealing with, owes much of its force to the philosophy of Maurice Blondel. Teilhard was in fact considerably influenced by Blondel and in two of his essays went out of his way to attach his conviction of man's need of an absolute to Blondel's metaphysical analysis.[26] Yet such philosophical reasoning, however helpful and convincing it might be for Teilhard's readers, was not of first importance for him personally. This he made clear as early as 1918 in an essay which sought to separate the essential character of his vision 'from the philosophical veneer I have provisionally given to it for want of something better.' This essential character, this 'axis of my interior life', was from his earliest years a spontaneous reaching out for some absolute. 'I do not believe I would ever have had the courage to act for any other objective.'[27] He wrote again in 1924 that before any explanation whatsoever of the impossibility of total contingence, he believed in it. There *must* be a successful outcome for man's earthly achievement. 'I believe this through inference. . . . I believe this through personal need. . . . Most of all perhaps, I believe this through love, for I love the world around me too much not to have confidence in it.'[28]

The Divine Milieu is no less explicit on this interior need for an absolute. Certainly it is a very great thing to know that, by virtue of the pure intention which motivates us ('the golden key which unlocks our interior world to the presence of God'), something of our inner activity will never be lost for eternity. But will not the work itself of our minds, our hearts, our hands—that is to say, our achievements, what we bring into being—will not this too in some sense be eternalized and saved? 'Indeed, Lord, it will be—by virtue of a need which you yourself have implanted at the very centre of my will! I desire and need that it should be. . . . If I believed that these things were to wither away forever, should I have given them life? The more I examine myself, the more I discover this psychological truth: . . . It requires no less than the pull of what men call the Absolute, no less than you yourself, to set in motion the frail liberty which you have given us. And that being so, everything which diminishes my explicit faith in the heavenly value of the *results* of my endeavour, diminishes irremediably my power to act.'[29]

Perhaps the clearest statement of Teilhard's own psychological independence of any philosophical system occurs in the last of his autobiographical essays. 'As far back as I go into my childhood, nothing appears to me more characteristic or familiar in my interior make-up than the taste or irresistible need for something all sufficient and all necessary. To be really satisfied and completely happy meant for me a knowing that something "essential" exists, of which all else is merely addition or ornament.' If over the years he has succeeded in discovering and remaining true to himself, the reason is that he has followed the direction of this particular inclination and relish. 'Once it is experienced, if ever so little, it is quite impossible to confuse it with any other emotion or desire, neither with the joy of knowing, nor the joy of discovery, nor the joy of creation, nor the joy of loving; not so much because it is different from these emotions, but because it is of a higher order and in a sense contains them all.'[30]

The treatment we have attempted here of Teilhard de Chardin's sense of anxiety would seem to warrant the following conclusions. The sampling of texts cited, taken over the years from his religious as well as from his scientific and philosophical writings, points to an interplay of two psychological forces. On the one hand there was an almost mystic attraction for some absolute in life, present from his earliest childhood; on the other hand, a very deep personal insight into the apparent futility of human effort, initially provoked by the shock of the war, yet remaining as an integral part of his outlook up to the time of his death. The juxtaposition of these two internal experiences was in large part responsible for what we saw to have been the fundamental anxiety of his life, namely the felt need of modern man, and first of all himself, for some certitude regarding an ultimate 'way out' for the flower of his earthly achievement, a certitude without which 'the magnificent *élan* of humanity would eventually come to an end.' As we shall see in the following chapter, the context within which this disquiet developed and eventually worked itself out was that of cosmic and organic evolution. It was through evolution that he eventually attained certitude on the natural level through his 'law of complexity-consciousness', his placing of man at the summit of the evolutionary process and his insistence that the cosmos is held together by spirit, not matter, and converges towards persons, not things. What concerns us here, however, is not the content of Teilhard's system but the psychological orientation of the man himself, the motivation of his drive for unity in the Christian life. And this leads us to consider a source of certitude which he possessed of an entirely different order. To complete the picture we are sketching, we must turn now to that other 'axis of my interior life', the dominant influence of Christian faith.

II

Teilhard de Chardin's deep conviction that man's human achievements would 'in some sense be eternalized and saved', was, as we have seen, less the result of philosophical analysis than of an attraction for the absolute deeply imbedded in his personality. He called this attraction at various times a 'cosmic sense', a 'sense of plenitude', a 'human sense', a 'sense of fulfilment'.[31] Now *pari passu* with the evolution in me of this innate cosmic sense . . . another process begun by education, never ceased to follow its course in my mind and heart: I mean the awakening of a certain Christic sense. . . . Cosmic sense and Christic sense: in me two axes apparently

22

independent of each other at birth; yet only after much time and effort did I at last grasp . . . their connection, their convergence and finally their ultimate identity.'[32] What was this 'Christic' sense, called by Teilhard 'a gift from heaven, supernatural',[33] and how precisely is it related to his cosmic sense? In seeking an answer we shall find ourselves face to face with that conflict in his life which became for him the source and motivation for much of his theological writing.

The movement which drew me into its current based itself upon a point, upon a person, myself. . . . But very soon I found this same self of mine caught up in another direction. Along with everything around me I experienced a sense of being seized by a movement of a higher order, which shuffled all the elements of my universe and re-grouped them in a new sequence. And when it was given me to see where this dazzling trail was leading, . . . I discovered that everything was again centred upon a Point, upon a Person, and this Person was you, Jesus! . . . From the moment that you said 'This is my Body', not only the bread on the altar, but to a certain extent everything in the universe became yours that nourishes in our souls the life of grace and the spirit.[34]

These lines, written at the front in 1917, suggest the distinctive character of Teilhard's devotion to the Person of Christ. This same special quality comes through again a year later: 'All my ideas and inclinations seem more and more to reduce themselves to a point, to an attitude, which is extremely simple and rich. . . . A prayer I now like to say sums up quite well what I mean: *"Jesu, sis mihi mundus verus.* May the chosen part of the world extend your influence over me and become more you through my effort".'[35] That same year he realized that it was within his knowledge and love of God that he had been developing his knowledge and love of the world, an unconscious result perhaps of his personal need to find for this world some absolute principle of unity and fulfilment. 'I think I have an inkling today, a feeling, how these two foci of man's love invoke each other in wondrous manner and are each other's mutual completion, God making use of the world to reach us as well as to come within our grasp, . . . and the world in its turn depending upon God to escape its contingence and plurality.'[36] On the occasion of his final vows in 1918 he summarized in a remarkably terse sentence this unity he perceived between God and creation: 'Christ loves himself as a Person and imposes himself as a World.'[37]

It is not difficult to see here the functioning of a fundamental law of the spiritual life, whereby God adapts himself always to the psychology of the individual soul. In Teilhard's case this involved a personal need to adore the Absolute through what was tangible and concrete, a need which provided, on the natural level, the foundation for the supremely important role in his life of the cult of the Heart of Christ. It was this which enabled him to see unity between his two 'senses', the two foci of his interior life. 'The entire physical reality of Christ gathered itself up before my eyes in a solid, fixed object where every accidental and restrictive peculiarity vanished away.' In the Heart of Christ there was a 'materialization' of God's love, at once spiritual and tangible, and yet at one and the same time an 'energizing' of that same love. 'Under the symbol of the " Sacred Heart" the divine assumed for me the form, the strength and the properties of an Energy, of a Fire. . . . Through its power to become universal, this Fire proved able to invade and impregnate with love the whole atmosphere of the world in which I lived.'[38]

The judgment of Henri de Lubac is that this relationship of Teilhard to the Person of Christ, based upon reasons which had nothing to do with his particular system of thought, secretly supported that whole intellectual effort, though the system as such, along with its premises and conclusions, can stand independent scrutiny and be judged alone.[39] In *The Phenomenon of Man* Teilhard admits explicitly that it was Christ who inspired him to elaborate his conception of the Omega Point. 'Doubtless I should never have ventured to envisage the latter or formulate the hypothesis rationally if, in my consciousness as a believer, I had not found not only its speculative model but also its living reality.'[40] Ten years later he says again that for him the ultimate focus of man's evolutionary movement is 'the figure of Christ wrapped in the mystery of his Resurrection and Parousia.'[41] And a month before he died there is the same admission: 'In short, this pole Omega is reached only by extrapolation; it remains by nature an assumption and a conjecture.' When however we accept 'the evidence that the Christ of revelation is identical with the Omega of evolution,' then 'a way out begins to shine through in the most distant future. In a world certainly open at its summit *in Christo Jesu*, we no longer risk dying of suffocation!'[42]

The certitude that there exists a 'way out'. Here is the point of contact between Teilhard's Christic and cosmic sense. That which ultimately made life bearable for him was a certitude that came from Christian faith, and it was primarily the support from this supernatural guarantee which enabled him to elaborate what he felt to be a natural guarantee based on reason and scientific research. 'If Christ vanishes, then what on earth have we left to justify the development of our taste for being and for life?'[43] Without faith in Christ the world would become 'unbreathable' for him, 'hopelessly shut in by a total death ahead, and also deprived forever of any warm living reality capable of breathing life into its frightful machinery.'[44] During the years of the first world war it was the consciousness he had of the world's need for purification which 'forces me to fall back absolutely, almost desperately, on Our Lord's power.' . . . 'The world is a heavy thing indeed for someone who is welded to it yet unable to give any life to its mass! Who is going to cure us of this pain of loneliness? Clearly Christ Our Lord alone.' . . . 'We believers have the strength and glory of having a faith in God more profound than our faith in the world: and that faith in God re-emerges and persists even if our faith in the world should be crushed by the impact of events.'[45]

This same insistence on faith became one of the dominant themes of *The Divine Milieu*. Teilhard's dignity as a man forbade him to close his eyes to the mystery of evil, 'that vast and horrible thing', and he could only escape the temptation to curse the universe by praying for light to see Christ concealed within it. 'O Lord, repeat to me the great liberating words, the words which at once reveal and are operative: *Hoc est Corpus Meum*. In truth, the huge and dark thing, the phantom, the storm—if we want it to be so, is you! *Ego sum, nolite timere*. . . . We have only to believe. And the more threatening and irreducible reality appears, the more firmly and desperately must we believe. Then, little by little, we shall see the universal horror unbend, and then smile upon us, and take us in its more than human arms. . . . The immense hazard and the immense blindness of the world are only an illusion for him who believes.'[46] From this absolute reliance upon faith there follows a conclusion of far reaching importance, and Teilhard gave expression to it as early as 1917: 'What delights me is obviously not the inferior portion of the world. . . . The true earth for me is that portion of the universe which is chosen, which is still spread out almost everywhere, but which is in process of . . . finding in Christ its true measure and substance.'[47]

Teilhard's frequent use of the word *élu*, 'chosen', when speaking of Christ's relationship to the material world, confronts us with a conviction which was eventually to be of paramount importance in his theological speculation. 'The love of Christ,' he says, 'is an energy into which all the chosen elements of creation are fused without losing their identity.'[48] The same Christian faith which made him certain of an *issue* for mankind in and through the Person of Christ, brought him certitude also that 'along with light and air, there comes down from this opening love. . . . Christ comes to modern man . . . not only to save him from legitimate revolt against a life with the least threat or suspicion of total death, but also to bring him the greatest possible stimulus, without which living thought on our planet could surely never reach its final destiny.'[49] Under the eye of faith this final destiny ceases for Teilhard to be purely natural and becomes divine; unless man's effort on earth is aided in its upward ascent by a gratuitous downward coming of Christ, it is quite capable of ending up in something less than human. 'The more I try with sympathy and understanding to measure as a palaeontologist the vast movements of life in the past, the more I am convinced that this gigantic development . . . will reach its goal only by becoming Christianized.'[50] This explains the significance he sees in the Church: 'I believe in and I love the Church as the mediatrix between God and the world,' he wrote in 1925.[51] Much later he said that 'in order to succeed, the *élan* of the earth needs to be synthesized and put into resonance with the *élan* of Christianity.' If he himself had not been born a Christian, his work as a scientist would most likely have forced him to become one 'in order to be completely a man.'[52]

In Teilhard's mind, therefore, the entire movement of mankind towards some *issue* up ahead is to be attributed less to a thrust from below than to an attraction from on high. We have seen already that his most fundamental anxiety was not so much to find a way out *from* the world as some way out *for* the world, for the flower of human endeavour and achievement, since here was 'the whole problem of action.' Now Teilhard became convinced that unless these achievements of man were somehow united to the Person of Christ, they were incapable of reaching their ultimate *human* fulfilment. 'Christ gives himself to us through a world which is to reach completion even on the natural level by reason of its relationship to him. You should note this well: I attribute no final or absolute value whatsoever to the varied achievements of man. . . . What I delight in is not their particular form but their function, which is mysteriously to build up, first what is to be divinized, and then, through the grace of Christ coming down upon our endeavour, that which is divine.'[53] And in *The Phenomenon of Man* he could state categorically that for the Christian 'the final success of hominization (and thus cosmic coiling) is positively guaranteed by the power of restoring to life which belongs to God incarnate in his creation.'[54]

This conviction that a 'chosen' part of the world and mankind could reach natural fulfilment only through supernatural union with Christ, occasioned for Teilhard a succession of theological enquiries which eventually constituted his nascent Christology. However, side by side with this conviction, motivating it continually, yet in a sense caused by it, was a psychological conflict which developed in the man himself, and this is what concerns us here. It will be remembered that the cult of the Heart of Christ enabled Teilhard to 'materialize' what was divine, to bring into a single concrete focus both his attraction for matter and his adoration of the Person of Christ. Now it was precisely the 'juncture of these two complementary currents, one originating in heaven, the other on earth', which was responsible 'for the progress and, I must honestly add, for the struggles in my interior life. . . . The intimate relationship between my Christic and cosmic sense and their definitive coexistence in my heart, produced in the depths of my soul a conflict between the God of the "Upward" and a new type God of the "Forward".'[55] In a letter to one of his closest friends he admitted that 'this has always been the problem of my life.' This letter, written in 1916, deserves to be quoted at length.

What I mean is the reconciliation of progress and detachment, —of a passionate and legitimate love for this great earth and unique pursuit of the kingdom of heaven. How is one to be more fully a Christian than anyone and at the same time more fully a man? It is all very well to study science, philosophy, sociology to please God and to fulfil an assigned task. But this is not enough; unless I recognize in the midst of study and toil the possibility of loving my work; unless I see that I must give myself to it completely, that I consolidate my progress towards an absolute by reason of the conquests themselves (and not just by the moral value of my efforts); unless the world appears to me not merely as an occasion for gaining merit but as a κτῆμα ἐς ἀεί to build up and to refine, —then I shall remain uncommitted among my fellow men, and because of my religion they will regard me as a deserter who is only half a man.

Consequently, for my own satisfaction and to put some 'system' into my interior life, I have been trying to discover what there could be that is divine and predestined within the matter itself of our cosmos, our humanity and our progress. Indeed, I find myself drawn by the study of all those currents and connecting links which are *in nobis sine nobis*, which sweep us along, channel us, become objects of our instinctive adoration, which we fight against yet which in their entirety constitute our life in the cosmos. For it is there that God must be hiding himself. . . . Once again, cannot the object, the matter itself, of our human love be transfigured, transferred into the absolute and, in short, into the divine? . . . I want to love Christ with all my strength in the very act of loving the universe. Can this be absurdity, blasphemy? Besides communion with God and communion with the earth, is there not also communion with God in and through the earth? I should like it to be so, for myself and for many others . . . but I do not know.[56]

Almost four years later there is another letter which insists that the difficulty with Christian renunciation conceived as a rupture with the world is that it does not provide a workable solution to the problem of sanctity for the human race as a whole. In the case of the vast majority of men, an immense part of their lives is devoted to purely human activity imposed by circumstances beyond their control. Yet this purely human effort has a spiritualizing power of the first order, not only through the moral 'training' it gives, 'but also by the positive results of the work itself. . . . There is in the life of every man and in the history of the human race as a whole, an enormous capacity for positive achievement and this must not be allowed to stagnate. It is absolutely necessary that Christ be as large as my life, my whole life. I must have an awareness of growing in him, not only by asceticism and the painful wrench of suffering . . . but also by whatever positive effort I am capable of, whatever is naturally perfective in my human achievement. I must have this awareness, I say, otherwise Christianity would be robbing me of the courage to act.'[57]

The spiritual conflict described in the above letters appears again in *The Divine Milieu*. How often, says Teilhard, does the Christian read or hear that perfection consists in detachment, that the world around us is vanity and ashes? How is he to reconcile this with that other counsel which tells him that as a Christian he must be an example to the world in energy and leadership in performing the duties of his state in life? 'There is a type of mind . . . for whom this difficulty takes the form and importance of a constant and paralyzing perplexity. Such minds, set upon interior unity, become the victims of a veritable spiritual dualism.' In the most spiritual layers of their being they experience a tension between the drawing power of two rival stars which are apparently opposed: God and the world. In the majority of cases the Christian will give up any attempt to make sense of his situation. 'He will never belong wholly to God, nor ever wholly to things; imperfect in his own eyes, and insincere in the eyes of men, he will become resigned to leading a double life. I am speaking, it should not be forgotten, from experience.'⁵⁸

At the time he wrote *The Divine Milieu* in 1927, Teilhard was able to give a theoretical solution to this conflict between his Christic and his cosmic sense, but the practical problem of daily reconciliation remained with him more or less up to the end of his life. Five years before his death he still witnessed to it. 'Today I encounter still the risks to which he is exposed who finds himself compelled by inner constraint to leave the well beaten track of a certain traditional type of asceticism not fully human, in order to search out a way to heaven along which the whole dynamism of matter and flesh can pass by way of synthesis into the birth of spirit. . . . To synthesize the "Upward" and the "Forward". . . . To reach heaven by bringing earth to perfection. To Christify matter. There is the whole adventure of my life, a great and magnificent adventure, during which I am still often afraid, but to which it was impossible not to have committed myself.'⁵⁹ This same combination of uncertainty, confidence and sense of vocation had appeared many years before in a letter following the defence of his doctoral thesis: 'The Lord has led me along such unexpected paths that I rely on him to use me best for his glory. If only I could be of some little service to that noble cause,—the only one I have really set my heart on,—I mean the explicit fusion of Christian life with the natural sap of the universe.'⁶⁰

There is one final element in Teilhard de Chardin's psychological orientation, and it is the one which summarizes perhaps better than any other the simultaneous interplay in his life of anxiety and Christian faith: his preoccupation with the future. 'I am a pilgrim of the future on my way back from a journey made entirely in the past,' he wrote from China in 1923. 'The world holds no interest for me unless I look forward, but when my eyes are on the future it is full of excitement.' Twelve years later there is the same sentiment: 'The past has revealed to me how the future is built, and preoccupation with the future tends to sweep everything else aside.' And again in 1948: 'I now experience a kind of repugnance for study of the past.'[61] The significance of this concentration upon the future should become immediately evident if we recall that Teilhard's anxiety for some *issue* for mankind could be resolved only 'up ahead'.[62] The juncture of the 'Upward' and the 'Forward', towards which he projected his interior search for unity, was an event of the future. 'My views, as you know, hardly change, but they simplify themselves and interlock with such an increase of intensity—in the interplay (so wonderfully contrived) of what I call the two lines of curvature (or convergence), the cosmic ("natural") and the Christic ("supernatural").'[63]

More concretely, therefore, the future which preoccupied him was the point where the cosmic and the Christic converged. Belief that such a convergence was not only possible but inevitable, explained for Teilhard why his experience of the world of nature was always 'so much more disturbing than satisfying'. Nature is the base of something, and this something is the figure of Someone who is hidden. Man can find satisfaction in nature only by going straight to its ultimate term. What we are doing by our analyses and observations of the world is moving down towards a base and therefore in the direction of divergence, and this is why the ultimate explanation of things keeps slipping through our fingers. It is an illusion to look for the secret of things in their origins. The meaning of the natural world is to be looked for at its summit, in a spiritual principle of attraction and convergence. We can accept a nature that disturbs and disquiets us only because we know by faith that we are, as it were, at the base of a cone. 'I can still see only one *issue*: to keep pressing forward in ever-increasing faith. May the Lord only preserve in me a passionate taste for the world.'[64]

It is this conception of the world of nature as a cone with an *issue* at its apex which fostered in Teilhard the expectation of a very great event: 'The discovery of a synthesized act of adoration, in which an ardent desire to conquer the world, and an ardent desire to unite ourselves to God, will unite and catch fire from each other: the vital act, specifically new, corresponding to a new terrestrial age.'[65] The exact nature of this event he made quite clear in *The Divine Milieu*. It is the Second Coming of Christ, the Parousia. He saw that one day the tension gradually accumulating between humanity and God would touch the limits prescribed by the possibilities of the world, and this would bring an end to time. 'Then the presence of Christ . . . breaking through all the barriers within which the veil of matter and the water-tightness of souls have seemingly kept it confined, will invade the face of the earth. . . . Like lightning, like a conflagration, like a flood, the attraction exerted by the Son of Man will lay hold of all the whirling elements in the universe so as to reunite them or subject them to his Body. . . . Such will be the consummation of the divine Milieu.' And Teilhard adds what is probably the most perfect description of his own state of soul: 'Expectation—anxious, collective and operative expectation of an end of the world, that is to say of an *issue* for the world— that is perhaps the supreme Christian function and the most distinctive characteristic of our religion.'[66]

On this description of Christian hope we may end our enquiry into Teilhard de Chardin's 'particular problem of life'. In the course of our study we have, in one form or another, touched upon all the major themes of his theological thought. His overriding concern was, as we have seen, to create a living unity between the movement of supernatural faith in God which rises upwards and the movement of natural faith in man which advances forward. This involved him in turn in the delicate problem of the natural and the supernatural, or more precisely, the relationship between Christ, mankind and the material world, made concrete for him in the mystery of the Incarnation and the Eucharist. Hinging directly upon this relationship was his vision of the Omega Point, God's entire creation converging through time towards the Person of Christ 'wrapped in the mystery of his Resurrection and Parousia'.

Hence came the emphasis he placed on the ambiguity of all temporal progress when separated from the redemptive love of Christ. Hence too his emphasis on the mystery of death, death of the individual and death of the world, the moment of maximum excentration and reversal to Christ. Ultimately it is the unitive force of Christian charity which alone can conquer death, and it is this conviction which leads Teilhard to insist upon the central importance of the Church as a 'phylum of love' inserted into the evolutionary process. He sought indeed to unify all these themes into some intellectual synthesis, but at a deeper level it was unity for his own life which he sought. 'All my joy and success, O my God, my whole justification for living and my very taste for life, are suspended from this fundamental vision I have of your conjunction with the universe.'[67] Over the years the interplay of anxiety and faith in his life fostered this effort to see, this vision, and what he saw in the end was the accomplishment of a single great mystery.

CHAPTER TWO

CHRISTIANITY AND THE OUTCOME OF EVOLUTION

THE HYPOTHESIS OF A CONVERGING UNIVERSE AS A CHRISTOLOGICAL PROBLEM

In 1936 Teilhard de Chardin summarized in the short space of a few paragraphs the broad lines of his whole life's work. The passage deserves to be quoted in its entirety, since it is perhaps the clearest statement of the triple direction taken by his thought in its search for unity in the Christian life.

If we want to reach the modern religious current at its deepest level and change its course, three steps seem to me to be necessary, each linked to the other.

  a A first step would consist in developing (along the lines of the 'perennial philosophy': primacy of being, act and potency) a correct physics and metaphysics of evolution. I am convinced that an honest interpretation of the recent achievements of scientific thought justifiably leads not to a materialistic but to a spiritualistic interpretation of evolution:—the world we know is not developing by chance, but is structurally controlled by a personal Centre of universal convergence.

  b The second step concerns dogmatic theology and would consist in articulating a Christology which would be in keeping with the dimensions of the universe as we know them today. This would mean a recognition that, along with those strictly human and divine attributes chiefly considered by theologians up to now, Christ possesses, by virtue of the mechanism of the Incarnation, attributes which are universal and cosmic, and it is these which constitute him that personal Centre hypothetically invoked by the physics and metaphysics of evolution. Such a perspective is in striking harmony with the most fundamental texts of St. John and St. Paul, and with the theology of the Greek Fathers.

c A third step concerns the spiritual life and would consist in developing an evangelism of human conquest. This third step follows automatically from the second, since it is indeed impossible for Christians to have a clearer vision of Christ as the summit of the world's evolution without at the same time appreciating more deeply the supernatural value of human effort carried out *in Christo Jesu.* The universal Christ enables us to understand that the most direct way to heaven is not to let go of earth as quickly as possible, as could sometimes appear, but to bring this earth to fulfilment, since we see it now as a much vaster thing, more unfinished than we ever suspected. In this way fundamental Christian attitudes would thrive and move ahead forcefully, without in the least deviating from their traditional course.[1]

In subsequent chapters we shall have to deal at length with the second step above, and to some extent also with the third, since the two are so closely connected. Our concern in this present chapter, however, is the precise connection between step one and step two, between Teilhard's hypothesis regarding the outcome of the evolutionary process, and the Christological problem which he proposes as a result of this hypothesis. The problem arises, as we shall see, not within the sphere of Christian revelation itself, but rather at that point where the theology of the Incarnation confronts modern man's understanding of the world in which he lives. 'As long as the universe was considered a static system, whose stuff was without genetic development, the entrance into it of the kingdom of God raised no structural difficulty at all. . . . However, and this is the essential point, the moment the universe is defined not in terms of "cosmos" but of "cosmogenesis", the problem of the Incarnation becomes complicated, since from now on there is question of reconciling two axes, which are different and partially autonomous, that of anthropo- and that of Christo-genesis. Hence the importance, or rather the necessity, of a Christology in which there

is a correspondence between the human point of planetary maturation and the Christic point of the Parousia.'[2] To appreciate the full
import of this last sentence we shall first have to attempt a summary
of Teilhard's analysis of cosmic and organic evolution. We shall
then be in a position to appreciate the relationship he wishes to
establish between this analysis and traditional Christian thought.

I

For purposes of summary we may divide into two successive stages
Teilhard's 'generalized physics' of evolution,—or 'hyperphysics'
as he calls it in The Phenomenon of Man.[3] The first stage is a
phenomenological analysis of the process of evolution from its
beginnings up to the coming of life and the birth of thought. At
the outset it is important to recall that Teilhard was initiated into
the world of science as a geologist and palaeontologist, that is to say,
through the study of the various layers in the earth's crust and of the
petrified remains or 'fossils' to be found at these layers, whether
these be of plants, animals or men. This fact is significant because
it accounts in large part for Teilhard's tenacious commitment to
the truth of evolution. Although the idea of an evolution between
species arose in the last century as a result of discoveries in com-
parative anatomy, in our own time it has been the study of fossil
forms from various geological periods which has provided the most
convincing evidence for its support. Palaeontology has shown that
animal and plant organisms have succeeded each other in a certain
order, an order in which a higher degree of fossil organization has
almost always been found at a later point in geological time. In
spite of those multiple lacunae in the genetic line of organisms still
so perplexing to biologists, nothing has yet been discovered to
disturb this basic order in the appearance of animal and plant forms.
Teilhard was trained to observe this gradual movement of life
imbedded in successive layers of the earth, and he began very early
to search for its sense and direction. It is this sense and direction
which he wishes to demonstrate in this first stage of his study.[4]

It cannot be emphasized too strongly that Teilhard is restricting himself to what he insists is a phenomenological analysis. As a consequence, what is most striking in this first stage is his attempt to find on a purely scientific plane a common ground of discussion between 'materialists and upholders of a spiritual interpretation, between finalists and determinists.' One group insists on talking about objects as though they only consisted of external actions in impermanent relationships, the other group is obstinately determined not to go outside a kind of solitary introspection in which things are only looked upon as being shut in upon themselves in their 'immanent' working. Both these groups see only half the problem. 'I am convinced that the two points of view require to be brought into union, and that they will soon unite in a kind of phenomenology or generalized physics in which the internal aspect of things as well as the external aspect of the world will be taken into account. Otherwise, so it seems to me, it is impossible to cover the totality of the cosmic phenomenon by one coherent explanation such as science must try to construct.'[5]

This plan for an enlarged science faithful to its phenomenal character is at the heart of Teilhard's whole analysis of evolution. In regard to man especially, he never ceased pointing to a modern anomaly in the academic world: both the 'materialists' and the 'spiritualists' have managed to shut their eyes to the intimate connection between man and the concrete material world, 'one group from fear of falling into metaphysics, the other from dread of profaning "the soul" by treating it as a mere object of physics.' The result is that man, 'in so far as he has something special to reveal for our experience, that is to say, in those characteristic qualities which we call "spiritual", is still excluded from our general constructions of the world. Hence the paradox: a science of the universe without man. We have knowledge of man on the fringe of the universe, but still no science of the universe including man as such. Present day physics (using the word in the broad Greek sense of "a systematic comprehension of all nature") as yet makes no place for thought; which means it is still constructed wholly apart from the most remarkable of all phenomena provided by nature for our observation.'[6]

Teilhard therefore is going to use what he feels to be a purely external method to discover that which is interior. It is this methodology, cutting as it does across boundaries long established between intellectual disciplines, which leads him to insist that all matter, living or not, has a 'within' as well as a 'without', that is, a 'psychic' as well as a physical aspect. This 'psychic' aspect Teilhard also calls 'consciousness', but it should be carefully noted that this word is never used as a synonym for 'thought' but is related to thought rather as the whole is to the part. 'The term "consciousness" is taken in its widest sense to indicate every kind of psychism from the most rudimentary forms of interior perception imaginable to the human phenomenon of reflective thought.'[7] This postulate of a 'within' to things is of capital importance for Teilhard's subsequent study of evolution, since by it he immediately eliminates a sharp dualism between matter and 'consciousness', and situates them not in two separate realms of being, but as part of one and the same pattern for the universe. Such an approach to matter could be considered an attempt on Teilhard's part to reconcile what others consider irreconcilable, in this case the theories of Darwin and Lamarck. The 'within' would correspond to a Lamarckian inner principle, while the 'without' of things would be Darwinian. In reality, however, this attempt to reconcile opposites is a reflection of a much deeper drive in Teilhard's psychological make-up. What he sought to grasp was nothing less than the whole of reality. In evolution he saw not simply a scientific hypothesis, but an experimental affirmation of the coherence of being. He was convinced that being *had* to be coherent and therefore intelligible, and that the only possible way to arrive at any constructive explanation of the universe was to treat it, throughout space and time, as if it were one.

In this same extraordinary second chapter of *The Phenomenon of Man* Teilhard notes that between this 'within' and 'without' of things the interdependence of energy is incontestable, a fact which up to now science has provisionally decided to ignore. He assumed all energy in the world to be psychic,[8] although this manifests itself in two different tendencies which he calls respectively radial and tangential energy. Radial energy tends to draw an element forward into structures of greater complexity; tangential energy on the contrary tends to link an element to other elements on the same level of organization. In the early stages of the earth it was radial energy which led to the production of larger and more 'centred' molecules, until such time as the first 'critical point' of evolution was reached and there was the sudden appearance of life. 'Critical points' are of great importance in Teilhard's thinking, for they always mark a profound change in nature by which something totally new is produced. The mechanism involved in this sudden transfer to a higher level may be imagined by comparing it, for example, to the sudden and tumultuous expansion of vaporized molecules whenever water is heated to boiling point under normal pressure. The same injection of energy at a given point suddenly results in an altogether unpredictable reaction, the change of liquid into gas. 'In every domain, when anything exceeds a certain measurement, it suddenly changes its aspect, condition or nature. The curve doubles back, the surface contracts to a point, the solid disintegrates, the liquid boils, the germ cell divides, intuition suddenly bursts on the piled-up facts. Critical points have been reached, rungs on the ladder, involving a change of state—jumps of all sorts in the course of development.'[9]

This presence in nature of critical points finds its most startling application in the case of 'hominization', the instantaneous leap from instinct to thought. Tangential energy had, in the slow course of geological time, continued to cause living cells to reproduce themselves on the same level, but radial energy began immediately to take the form of biological evolution, drawing life forward towards a new critical point. Teilhard insists that the parameter for measuring the relationship between these two energies is the law of complexity-consciousness. For him this means that a more developed consciousness will always correspond experimentally to a more complex organic structure of greater internal unity and concentration. On the phenomenological level life acts as if it were 'a process of "coiling", and represents, as a whole, a sort of vortex (the movement of the vortex being towards "arrangement")—

consciousness continuously growing (as a temperature) in the core of the vortex, according to the greater tightness of the coiling, that is, to the higher degree of internal organization.'[10]

The direction of evolution can be judged, therefore, by following 'Ariadne's thread', the line of growing complexity, a line which has gradually made its way through only one zoological group or 'phylum', that of the vertebrates, moving through mammals and primates up to man. In the primates, Teilhard notes, evolution went straight to work on the brain, neglecting everything else. In their case, consequently, an increase of consciousness is always found to be in direct proportion to the degree of 'cerebralization', that is, to the increase in complexity of the nervous system and brain. Through this phenomenon of cerebralization the ascending advance of life was slowly directed towards the critical point *par excellence*, the threshold of reflection. 'Because the specific orthogenesis of the primates (urging them towards increasing cerebralization) coincides with the axial orthogenesis of organized matter (urging all living things towards a higher consciousness), man, appearing at the heart of the primates, flourishes on the leading shoot of zoological evolution.'[11]

It should be carefully noted that in applying the law of complexity-consciousness to the first appearance of man, Teilhard is in no sense asserting a relationship of strict efficient causality. This point must be insisted upon, since it has been the subject of frequent misunderstanding. 'Need I repeat that I confine myself here to phenomena, i.e. to the experimental relations between consciousness and complexity, without prejudging the deeper causes which govern the whole issue? . . . It is only, it seems, *under the appearances* of a critical point that we can grasp experimentally the "hominizing" (spiritualizing) step to reflection. . . . There is nothing to prevent the thinker who adopts a spiritual explanation from positing (for reasons of a higher order and at a later stage of his dialectic) whatever "creative" operation or "special intervention" he likes *under the phenomenal veil* of a revolutionary transformation.'[12] God's intervention as efficient cause of the human soul in no way prevents the child from being considered the natural result of his parents' act of generation. In the same way man may be considered the end and purpose of evolution, in the sense that the whole process is oriented towards that end and constitutes a pattern which would be empty and meaningless unless it culminated in man. 'For Christian transformism,' wrote Teilhard in a more explicit passage, 'God's creative action is no longer conceived as abruptly inserting its work into the midst of pre-existent beings, but rather as *causing to come to birth* in the depths of things the successive terminations of its activity. It is not on this account any less essential, any less universal, nor above all any less intimate to things.' In a more succinct formula: 'God . . . makes things make themselves.'[13]

What Teilhard is affirming, then, in this first stage of his analysis, is that the world is a coherent unity, that a single pattern runs through the whole of the universe, and that the dominant orientation of this pattern is towards man. Far from being an exception to biological evolution, man is in reality the key to the entire process, for this process 'is no more than a movement of consciousness veiled by morphology.'[14] For Teilhard it would be utterly absurd to think of evolution suddenly going off in a direction other than that running from the primates to *homo sapiens*. In this sense evolution is irreversible, though this irreversibility is obviously not absolute, but conditioned on whether or not mankind continues in existence. If it does, then evolution must also continue its upward 'coiling' towards complexity and greater consciousness. Consequently to consider man as anything else but the principal aim of cosmic development is unthinkable, not only because he comes at the end of a progressive interiorization of matter moving upward along the axis of complexity, but much more because the phenomenon of reflective consciousness is of its very nature totally unlike any other event in the evolutionary series. Looked at superficially, the psychic make-up of various species in the proximity of man seems to reach right up to the borders of intelligence. In reality, however, the crossing of that threshold was a unique event, of an order quite different from that of non-reflective consciousness, 'a mutation from zero to everything'.[15]

The whole sense of evolution, therefore, must reside in the fact that it is an ascent towards 'personality'. To use Teilhard's own phrase, we are living in 'a personalistic universe'. Man alone in the material world can say 'I'. He alone is a 'person', able to communicate with other persons on the level of spirit. Teilhard returned to this point constantly. 'By the capital event of hominization the most "advanced" part of the cosmos found itself personalized.' . . . 'The true evolution of the world takes place in the souls of men and in their mutual union. Its inmost agents are not mechanistic but psychological and moral.' . . . 'It is not the rigid determinism of matter and of large numbers, but the subtle combinations of spirit, that give the universe its consistency.' . . . 'People usually speak of person as if it represented some quantitative reduction or qualitative diminishment of total reality. Exactly the opposite is the way we shall have to understand person. The "personal" is the highest state in which we are privileged to grasp the stuff of the universe. . . . The only way to express in a phrase the fact that the world is continually moving forward without loss, is to say that the quantity and quality of the personal must constantly go on increasing.'[16]

Moreover, this advent of thought represents not merely a turning point for the individual or even for the species, but marks a transformation which affects life itself in its organic totality. Properly speaking, from now on the evolutionary process continues its development not so much in the sphere of life, the 'biosphere', as in the sphere of mind and spirit, the 'noosphere', the 'thinking layer', which since its germination at the end of the tertiary period has spread over and above the world of plants and animals. 'Even from the most dispassionate point of view possible, the phenomenon of man represents nothing less than a general transformation of the earth, through the establishment on its surface of a new envelope, the thinking envelope.' . . . 'This sudden deluge of cerebralization, this biological invasion of a new animal type which gradually eliminates or subjects all forms of life that are not human, this irresistible tide of fields and factories, this immense and growing edifice of matter and ideas—all these signs that we look at day in, day out—seem to proclaim that there has been a change on the earth and a change of planetary magnitude. . . . The greatest revelation open to science today is to perceive that everything precious, active and progressive originally contained in the cosmic fragment from which our world emerged, is now concentrated in and crowned by the noosphere.'[17]

In this first stage of his phenomenological analysis Teilhard has been concerned, as we have seen, with the meaning which evolution gives to man. We may now describe the second stage as a concern for the meaning which man gives to evolution. For it is of the very essence of Teilhard's thought that the world is still in process of development. There is no reason whatsoever to suppose that the evolutionary forces at work for millions of years should suddenly have ceased to operate once the threshold of reflection had been crossed. The crucial difference, however, is that henceforth the principal development of these forces must take place on the other side of this threshold, in the noosphere. 'How could we imagine a cosmogenesis reaching right up to mind without being thereby confronted with a noogenesis? . . . *The social phenomenon is the culmination and not the attenuation of the biological phenomenon.*'[18] 'Noogenesis' will therefore be spiritual and social, that is to say, it will concern itself with the development of individuals as persons and with society on the level of interpersonal relationships. This is 'socialization' in Teilhard's sense of the term, a slow process of 'collective cerebralization' within which the law of complexity-consciousness operates in the same way as it formerly did in the case of individual cerebralization before the coming of thought.

By their very nature, and at every level of complexity, the elements of the world are able to influence and mutually to penetrate each other by their 'within' so as to combine their radial energies in 'bundles'. While no more than conjecture in atoms and molecules, this psychic interpenetrability grows and becomes directly perceptible in the case of organized beings. Finally in man, in whom the effects of consciousness attain the present maximum found in nature, it reaches a high degree everywhere. It is written all over the social phenomenon and is of course felt by us directly. But at the same time, in this case also, it operates only in virtue of the tangential energies of arrangement, and thus under certain conditions of spatial juxtaposition.[19]

This mention of 'certain conditions of spatial juxtaposition' brings us to the central significance which Teilhard saw in the roundness of the earth. Let us imagine, he says, that a pulsation enters a sphere at the south pole and spreads out inside the sphere in the direction of the north pole. From the very beginning the movement of this wave is one of convergence, in which two principal phases can be distinguished, one of expansion from the south pole to the equator, the other of contraction from the equator to the north pole. Now there is no better image than this to illustrate the development that has taken place in the noosphere, as well as the crisis of growth through which mankind is passing at this very moment.[20] For about thirty thousand years humanity had been expanding more or less freely, with nothing to prevent it from slowly covering more and more of the uninhabited earth. The result of this lack of pressure was that for centuries the advance of socialization was extremely slow. There was a gradual branching out into the various races, and nations and peoples multiplied easily. Indeed, if such expansion had not taken place over a globe, but had spread out indefinitely on an unlimited surface, man today would be quite different from what he is, since on an unlimited surface the relationship between radial and tangential energy would not have been the same.

As it was, however, all the available space on the earth was gradually occupied and the human waves of socialization started to recoil upon themselves and to interpenetrate. Mankind began to pack together more tightly. Under pressure of a constant increase of numbers in more confined areas, men found themselves sharing each other's thoughts to a greater and greater degree, and at the same time extending little by little the radius of their individual influence. This is what led to the modern technological revolution, with its extraordinary speed of movement, as well as to the prodigious biological event represented by the discovery of electro-magnetic waves, by which each individual finds himself able to be simultaneously present over land and sea in every part of the earth. The result has been that in our own age we have come to constitute an almost solid mass of humanity within which the totality of thinking units are always tending towards greater personal interiorization and greater interpersonal communion. In other words, the law of complexity-consciousness continues to be operative; through technology tangential energy produces a more complex exterior organization of humanity, a kind of 'mega-synthesis', while at the same time radial energy fosters a correlative spiritualization, a further intensification of the psychic temperature of the noosphere. What we have been experiencing for some time now, without being aware of it, is in reality the beginning of the second phase of noogenesis, the phase of contraction. Humanity has already crossed the equator and is engaged in a movement of convergence towards some future pole. The socialization of which Teilhard has spoken is gradually developing into a 'planetization', a coiling up of the human phylum around the surface of the earth, a completely new mode of 'phylogenesis'. 'Because it contains and engenders consciousness, space-time is necessarily of a convergent nature. Accordingly its enormous layers, followed in the right direction, must somewhere ahead coil themselves up to a point which we might call "Omega", which fuses and consumes them integrally in itself.'[21]

Here we should note again that we are still, in Teilhard's mind, on the level of phenomena. It is no departure from scientific method to recognize the direction which a trajectory *should* take if it continues to follow a course whose past has already been charted. Teilhard believes he has found a single evolutionary pattern up to the present, and he would seem to be justified in deducing from this the mode of its future development. Evolution has been seen as essentially an ascent towards man and reflective consciousness. The formation and deployment of the noosphere continues this ascent. Unless the movement ceases altogether, therefore, it must advance in the direction of some supreme consciousness, some ultimate manifestation of radial energy's tendency to bring greater unity from greater complexity. The universe would thus be converging towards some ultimate centre, since all consciousness is of its very nature a 'centring', and a supreme consciousness would be something like a supreme centre. Or, if the image of the sphere is to be retained, the universe is converging towards some pole, still millions of years away, at which all the radii of human energy will eventually gather themselves together. This centre, this pole, this point of convergence, Teilhard provisionally calls 'Omega', since it would come at the very end of the whole evolutionary series.

Moreover, it is quite possible that the human race, in reaching this harmonized collectivity of consciousness, should pass through another 'critical point', a second threshold of reflection, analogous to that of hominization. But here again we should note Teilhard's insistence that such a threshold to complete 'totalization' of humanity must necessarily mean the perfection of all the personal elements of the world precisely in so far as they are persons. 'It is only towards hyper-reflection—that is to say, hyper-personalization—that thought can extrapolate itself. . . . It is therefore a mistake to look for the extension of our being or of the noosphere in the impersonal. . . . In any domain—whether it be the cells of a body, the members of a society or the elements of a spiritual synthesis—*union differentiates*. In every organized whole the parts perfect themselves and fulfil themselves.' The dichotomy between totalization and personalization is the result of confusing individuality with personality. 'The peak of ourselves, the acme of our originality, is not our individuality but our person; and according to the evolutionary structure of the world, we can only find our person by uniting together.' . . . 'Totalization and personalization are the two expressions of a single movement.' . . . 'Socialization means not the end but rather the beginning of the Era of the Person.'[22]

As we end this second stage of Teilhard's phenomenological study of man, we should carefully underline two facts. First, Teilhard does not envisage the outcome of the natural evolutionary process to be some sort of human super-person, a kind of Nietzschian superman, resulting from a union of individual persons, an hypothesis which would hardly make any sense. It is true that he frequently uses the prefix 'super', but this 'is employed to indicate not a difference of *nature*, but a *degree* of more advanced realization and perception.'[23] What Teilhard has in mind, therefore, when he speaks of 'the planetary maturation of mankind', is a certain collective act of reflection, something which is quite credible if we once concede his analysis of evolution and admit his law of complexity-consciousness. He himself is clear on this point. 'We are faced,' he says, 'with a harmonized collectivity of consciousness equivalent to a sort of super-consciousness. The idea is that of the earth not only becoming covered by myriads of grains of thought, but becoming enclosed in a single thinking envelope so as to form, functionally, no more than a single vast grain of thought on the sidereal scale, the plurality of individual reflections grouping themselves together and reinforcing one another in the act of a single unanimous reflection. This is the general form in which, by analogy and in symmetry with the past, we are led scientifically to envisage the future of mankind.'[24]

The second fact to be recognized is that we have been dealing up to now with an hypothesis regarding the *probability* of convergence. The pattern which Teilhard has discovered is, as we have seen, irreversible, but this irreversibility is external and relative. The cosmic coiling of noogenesis must indeed continue towards some supreme consciousness, but only on condition that it continue at all. And on the level of phenomena we have absolutely no way of knowing whether or not this condition is to be fulfilled. As a phenomenological law, the pattern of complexity-consciousness is unable to tell us if the universe is in reality destined in and through man to reach a terminus in some ultimate pole or centre, and concerning the so-called 'Omega Point' we can know almost nothing at this stage, since by Teilhard's own reckoning it will not be attained for some hundreds of thousands or even millions of years. He believes his study of man has shown that evolution is moving across humanity to a kind of 'super-humanity', but by this term 'I mean the biologically superior state which humanity *appears* destined to achieve *if* it succeeds in totalizing itself completely upon itself, body and soul, by pushing to the end the movement of which it is the historical culmination.'[25]

This second fact is extremely important, for as we shall see in a moment, Teilhard is about to advance from this hypothesis of probability, based on the experimental law of complexity-consciousness, to an hypothesis of *actual* convergence, that is to say, to a study of the conditions required in order for mankind to know that here and now it is *actually* converging towards a supreme centre. This change of perspective is going to force him to leave the level of strictly observable phenomena, and this is what he himself announces at the end of the third book of *The Phenomenon of Man*. 'Either nature is closed to our demands for futurity, in which case thought, the fruit of millions of years of effort, is stifled, still-born in a self-abortive and absurd universe. Or else an opening exists— that of a supersoul above our souls. . . . On neither side is there any tangible evidence to produce. Only, in support of hope, there are rational invitations to an act of faith.'[26] 'Faith' in this context has nothing to do with Christian revelation. It concerns faith in the world's future and is a common Teilhardian synonym for 'intellectual synthesis'. In the present text it means accepting the intellectual perspective he is about to propose in which an ultimate failure of evolution becomes a completely unacceptable possibility. Moreover, and this is of paramount significance for us here, it is this new perspective which will finally enable him to give to his hypothesis of a converging universe the dimensions of a Christological problem.

II

Teilhard de Chardin's ultimate purpose in developing the 'hyperphysics' of evolution we have just summarized was in no sense exclusively scientific. He was a man who, as we have already noted, experienced a very acute sense of anxiety before the mystery and apparent futility of human life. Up to his very last year he was acutely aware of the world's power to discourage and oppress, and it is this awareness which to a large extent conditioned his own personal search for unity between God and the world. Hence the frequent references to modern anxiety in *The Phenomenon of Man*, for Teilhard was convinced that his own experience was typical of twentieth century man. 'In all my work I am conscious of being merely a sounding-board, amplifying what people around me are thinking.'[27]

In addition to this sense of anxiety there was his almost mystic attraction for some absolute, present as we have seen from his earliest childhood, and this made it imperative that the evolutionary pattern to which he had committed himself as a scientist, should also be related intrinsically to some absolute. On the strict level of the physical sciences this was obviously impossible, since by its very nature evolution is relative. This explains Teilhard's constant preoccupation with the future, the end of the process, the terminus where all the radii converge at the Omega Point. Here it was possible for him to locate an absolute for cosmogenesis which, though itself outside the process, would provide that assurance of ultimate success which was alone capable, in his mind, of assuaging the anxiety and fear of modern man. Consequently he continues his analysis of evolution into convictions 'strictly undemonstrable to science, . . . faith in progress, . . . faith in unity, . . . faith in a centre of personality exerting an infallible attraction.'[28] Again, what we shall attempt here is the barest summary.[29] The following text will serve as our point of departure and also help avoid any misconception about what he is going to do:

On the strictly psychological plane . . . I mean by 'faith' any adherence of our intelligence to a general view of the universe. . . . The essential note of the psychological act of faith is, in my opinion, to see as possible and to accept as more probable a conclusion which, because it envelopes so much in space and time, goes far beyond all its analytical premises. *To believe is to achieve an intellectual synthesis.*[30]

Teilhard begins his 'act of faith' with two factors, two phenomena, which have profoundly changed the whole character of noogenesis. The first is modern man's sudden awareness of what is taking place in him and by means of him. This awareness of evolution is indeed the specific effect of the process peculiar to our present age. *The Phenomenon of Man* links the whole psychology of modern disquiet with the confrontation of space-time. 'What has made us in four or five generations so different from our forebears (in spite of all that may be said), so ambitious too, and so worried, is not merely that we have discovered and mastered other forms of nature. In the final analysis it is, if I am not mistaken, that we have become conscious of the movement which is carrying us along, and have thereby realized the formidable problems set us by this reflective exercise of human effort. . . . What makes and classifies modern man . . . is having become capable of seeing in terms not of space and time alone, but also of duration, . . . and above all of having become incapable of seeing anything otherwise—anything—not even himself . . .—the definitive access of consciousness to a scale of new dimensions.'[31] The result is the 'malady of space-time', the feeling of both anxiety and futility, the sense of being crushed by the enormities of the cosmos.

Far more decisive, however, is the second factor, that of human freedom. For it is not only *in* man that the movement of evolution is now carried on, but *by* man. It is man who invents and discovers and who has, by taking into his own hands the direction of the world, gradually replaced nature in the progress of life. Through man evolution has not only become conscious of itself but free to dispose of itself,—it can give itself or refuse itself. Upon man therefore falls the awful responsibility for his future on earth. In the great game being played 'we are the players as well as being the cards and the stakes. Nothing can go on if we leave the table. Neither can any power force us to remain. Is the game worth the candle, or are we simply its dupes? The question has hardly been formulated as yet in man's heart, accustomed for hundreds of centuries to toe the line; it is a question, however, whose mere murmur, already audible, infallibly predicts future rumblings. The last century witnessed the first systematic strikes in industry; the next will surely not pass without the threat of strikes in the noosphere. . . . If progress is a myth, that is to say, if faced with the work involved we can say "What's the good of it all?" [then] the whole of evolution will come to a halt—*because we are evolution.*'[32]

Teilhard's first assurance to modern man is to point to the pattern he has uncovered through his generalized physics of evolution. Time and space are terrifying only if they are thought to be motionless and blind; they immediately become humanized as soon as a definite movement appears which gives them a physiognomy and shows them to be part of a developing whole. 'What matters the giddy plurality of the stars and their fantastic spread, if that immensity (symmetrical with the infinitesimal) has no other function but to equilibrate the intermediary layer where, and where only in the medium range of size, life can build itself up chemically? What matters the millions of years and milliards of beings that have gone before, if those countless drops form a current which carries us along?'[33] In Teilhard's mind we are not simply face to face with 'change' in the world but with 'genesis', which is something quite different. It should be noted that the French word *genèse* is much wider in meaning and more common in usage than the English 'genesis'. It applies to any form of production involving successive stages oriented towards some goal. The law of complexity-consciousness is thus an assurance that there has been 'genesis', that the universe has been pursuing an aim, that a single pattern has thus been running through the whole and that this pattern has been oriented towards man. Man is the key to the whole biological process, since it was through him and him alone that evolution crossed the threshold of reflection into the mysterious realm of the person.

But Teilhard sees clearly that what the present generation needs most is assurance not about the past but about the future of evolution. The universe has always been in motion and at this moment continues to be in motion. But will it be in motion tomorrow? 'Tomorrow? But who can guarantee us a tomorrow anyway? And without assurance that this tomorrow exists, can we really go on living, we to whom has been given—perhaps for the first time in the whole history of the universe—the terrible gift of foresight?... What disconcerts the modern world at its roots is not being sure, and not seeing how it ever could be sure, that there is an outcome—*the right outcome*—to this evolution.'[34] He then asks a question which could never legitimately have been asked on the strict level of phenomena. 'What should the future be like in order to give us the strength or even the joy to accept the prospect of it and to bear its weight? ... In the last analysis the best guarantee that a thing should happen is that it appears to us as vitally necessary.'[35]

There is an important qualification, however. Such a guarantee must be given in the context of human freedom; it cannot come from an order imposed by coercion or sustained by fear. In Teilhard's mind this is precisely the reason for the world's present discouragement with the whole human aspiration towards unity. Up to now every gigantic effort to reduce the multitude of mankind to some order seems to have ended by stifling the human person. Communism, nazism, fascism have produced the most ghastly fetters; men hoped for brotherhood and found only ant hills. 'Instead of the upsurge of consciousness which we expected, it is mechanization that seems to emerge inevitably from totalization.' Yet what men forget is that, monstrous though it is, modern totalitarianism is really a distortion of something magnificent, and thus quite near the truth. When an energy runs amok, the engineer, far from questioning the power itself, simply works out his calculations afresh to see how it can better be brought under control. And in our modern world what has gone wrong is that we have neglected those forces of freedom which emerge from the depths of the human person and therefore constitute a unitive force which is interior, a force based not upon coercion or fear but upon love.[36]

Love is the only energy in the world that is capable of personalizing by totalizing. It is consequently the highest form of that energy which Teilhard has called 'radial'. It alone unites human beings in such a way as to complete and fulfil them, for it alone joins them to what is deepest in themselves. On the strictly phenomenological level this is a fact of daily experience, not only in the sexual love between man and wife,[37] but also in the love of parents for children, the love between friends, and even to a certain extent love for one's country. In order therefore for men to continue in freedom towards that unity in the noosphere which is their destiny, their power of loving must gradually develop until it is capable of embracing the whole of mankind and the whole of the earth. In other words, what Teilhard has called 'planetization' (intensification of the noosphere's psychic temperature from man's tighter contraction around the surface of the earth), must eventually become an 'amorization'. A common objection against such an idea is that man's capacity to love does not carry beyond the radius of a select few, that to love all is contradictory, a false gesture which will lead in the end to loving no one. 'To this I would answer that if, as you claim, a universal love is impossible, how can we account for that irresistible instinct in our hearts which leads us towards unity whenever and in whatever direction our deepest emotions are stirred? A sense of the universe, a sense of the whole, . . . cosmic affinity and hence cosmic sense. A universal love is not only psychologically possible, it is the only complete and final way in which we are able to love.'[38] At this level, then, the law of complexity-consciousness has been transformed into a law of growing amorization.

But how then are we to explain the appearance all around us of growing repulsion and hatred? If such a strong potency is really besieging us from within and urging us to unite, what prevents it from passing into act? One thing only: 'that we should overcome the "anti-personalist" complex which paralyzes us, and make up our minds to accept the possibility, indeed the reality, of some source of love and object of love at the summit of the world above our heads. So long as it absorbs or appears to absorb the person, the collectivity kills the love that is trying to come to birth.' Unless the modern impetus towards union is leading us towards 'Someone', it must certainly end up by plunging us back into matter. In order to turn this failure that threatens us into success, what we must do is to recognize 'not only some vague future existence, but also, as I must now stress, the radiation *as a present reality* of that mysterious Centre of our centres I have called Omega.'[39]

This sudden change in the mode of conceiving Omega is indicated also in the last of Teilhard's Sorbonne lectures for 1949. 'Under pain of being unable to act as keystone of the vault for the noosphere, "Omega" can only be conceived as the point of encounter between the universe, once it has reached the limits of centration, and another Centre deeper still—one which is self-subsistent, an absolutely ultimate principle of irreversibility and personalization: the only *real* Omega.'[40] We have here perhaps the clearest expression of Teilhard's distinction between the term 'Omega' as applied to a state of collective reflection at the end of the evolutionary process, and the same term as applied to the supreme personal Being here and now responsible for the process itself. An hypothesis therefore of *actual* convergence would demand that the ultimate terminus of evolution be already in existence, and especially that it be personal, 'loving and lovable at this very moment'. Love energy, the only force capable of moving free men towards unity, must have something to draw it. 'Love dies with contact with the impersonal and the anonymous. With equal infallibility it becomes impoverished with remoteness in space—and still more, much more, with remoteness in time. For love to be possible there must be co-existence. . . . A real and present noosphere goes with a real and present Centre,' the supreme source and the supreme object of man's love.[41]

Such an absolute and indestructible Centre must likewise be postulated by the very play of man's operative activity, for men will never bend their backs to the task of unity unless convinced that the effort demanded has a chance of succeeding. The prospect of a total death on which consciousness would crash and forever disappear would certainly doom the whole evolutionary ascent. 'No consideration of any kind could rightfully authorize us to take the least step forward if we did not know that the rising road leads to some summit from which life will never again descend.'[42] In no sense therefore can the *real* Omega be the end product of natural evolution. 'To satisfy the ultimate requirements of our action, Omega must be independent of the collapse of forces with which evolution is woven. . . . While being the last term of its [evolution's] series, it is also outside all series. . . . If by its very nature it did not escape from time and space which it gathers together, it would not be Omega.'[43] While by its action Omega influences directly the movement of each element in the noosphere, its own nature must be truly transcendent, capable of being present at the beginning as well as at the end of the evolutionary process.

There now follows a conclusion which represents Teilhard's final understanding of cosmic evolution and which will ultimately determine his line of approach to Christian revelation. It is summarized in the terse expression, 'Everything holds together from above.'[44] 'Contrary to appearances still accepted by physics, the great stability is not at the bottom in the infra-elementary sphere, but at the top in the ultra-synthetic sphere. It is thus solely by its tangential envelope that the world goes on dissipating itself in a chance way into matter. By its radial nucleus it finds its shape and its natural consistency in gravitating against the tide of probability towards a divine focus of spirit which draws it onwards.' Omega is thus seen as the 'Prime Mover ahead . . . the principle which at one and the same time makes this [cosmic] coiling irreversible and moves and collects it.'[45] The entire ascent towards life, that of life towards spirit and of spirit towards Omega, this whole movement of radial energy is due not to some mechanical thrust from below, but to an *attraction* from above. It is 'an inverse form of gravitation'.[46]

For Teilhard, therefore, what evolution ultimately depends upon is not its point of departure but its point of *arrival*. The influence here of biology is not difficult to recognize. It is not from an embryo that a biologist understands an adult form of life; rather it is the full expansion of the adult which makes the embryo intelligible, along with all its stages of development. 'Not a single thing in our changing world is really understandable except in so far as it has reached its terminus.'[47] At the end of the second stage of his 'hyperphysics' Teilhard had discovered a universe whose convergence was so far in the future and whose outcome so problematical that it could provide no guarantee, no *issue* at all for mankind. The principal axis of zoological evolution had now passed from the realm of brute nature into the realm of the human person, and whether or not radial energy would continue its advance towards higher consciousness had come to depend entirely upon the free decisions of men. /More concretely, the future of the noosphere now hinged upon the growth of amorization, the free circulation over the surface of the earth of that highest form of radial energy, love. Such amorization would in turn depend upon belief in a personal source and object of love who alone could motivate progress and conquer man's tendency towards repulsion and isolation.

This Teilhard has now provided for. 'To make room for thought in the world I have had to "interiorize" matter; to imagine an energetics of mind; to conceive a noogenesis rising upstream against the flow of entropy; to provide evolution with a direction, a line of advance and critical points. Finally I have had to make all things double back upon "Someone".'[48] Through his 'act of faith' he has now given to evolutionary convergence a stability it could never otherwise have had, for he now demands for its very existence a real attraction from a real supreme Being, 'loving and lovable at this very moment'. 'Since Aristotle we have never ceased to fashion our "models" of God after an extrinsic Prime Mover acting *a retro*. But since a consciousness of evolution has developed, we are no longer physically able either to conceive or adore anything but a God who is an organic Prime Mover *ab ante*.'[49] For Teilhard, therefore, the ultimate explanation of life's movement is that the universe is converging upon God, '—God reflecting himself personally upon the organized sum of thinking monads, to guarantee an outcome for their hesitant activities which is certain and guided by exact laws.'[50] In order completely to understand the dynamism of evolution in his system of thought, we are thus forced in the end to recognize the primacy of being over becoming, of act over potency—which is indeed, as Teilhard himself noted in the text with which we began, 'along the lines of the "perennial philosophy".'

Now it is this final hypothesis of convergence, that of an already existing personal Centre able to activate the love energy of the world, which constitutes the background, the framework, the stage for Teilhard's whole theological enquiry. For he is quite well aware that his act of intellectual 'faith' in the existence of a divine Omega, however clearly demanded by his analysis of love energy, must necessarily remain fragile and insecure. The God he has discovered is a faceless God, the God of a philosophical speculation. 'Does not the success of anthropogenesis, depending as it does on our making contact with the supracosmic, . . . conceal deep within itself an irreducible element of indetermination and incertitude?' . . . 'This pole Omega is reached only by extrapolation; it remains of its nature an assumption and a conjecture . . . which nourishes our hope on traits that are vague and ethereal.' There is need therefore 'to support our muddled extrapolations with some positive facts.'[51] His motivation here, be it noted, remains unchanged. Intellectually it is 'to reach the modern religious current at its deepest level and change its course.' But on the personal level it is still anxiety, his own as well as that of modern man, for some way out, some *issue*, not so much *from* the world as *for* the world, for the flower of human achievement in the noosphere. 'Who can guarantee us a tomorrow . . . ?'[52]

This guarantee, this ultimate successful outcome for evolution, Teilhard now proposes to find in the data of Christian revelation. 'Far from overshadowing Christ,' he writes, 'the universe can find only in him the guarantee of its stability.' What preoccupies him is 'a more and more intense concentration on this basic question of the relations between Christ and "hominization". It has become for me a question of "to be or not to be".'[53] By appealing to Christian revelation he believes he can at last bridge the gap between a philosophical hypothesis and an historical fact. 'In place of the vague focus of convergence demanded as a terminus for evolution, we now have the well-defined personal reality of the Incarnate Word, in whom all things hold together.'[54] If we accept 'the evidence that the Christ of revelation is identical with the Omega of evolution, [then] a way out begins to shine through in the most distant future. In a world certainly open at its summit *in Christo Jesu*, we no longer risk dying of suffocation!' For 'when we look ahead towards a superior pole of humanization and personalization, no matter what the extent of our conjecture, it is in fact towards Christ that our gaze is directed.' . . . 'Christ is perfectly comparable to the Omega Point which our theory made us anticipate (provided he is disclosed in the full realism of his Incarnation), and he tends to produce exactly the spiritual totalization we were waiting for.' . . . 'Without him the human sense and everything it hopes to achieve can only miscarry.'[55] Consequently 'for a Christian believer . . . the final success of hominization (and thus cosmic coiling) is positively guaranteed by the power of restoring to life which belongs to God incarnate in his creation. But this takes us beyond the plane of phenomena.'[56] The newness of this dimension 'beyond the plane of phenomena' becomes still more precise in the following text, published in 1948, which will deserve our close attention:

For a Christian (on condition, of course, that his Christology recognizes in the collective consummation of humanity on earth not an indifferent or hostile event, but a preliminary condition [necessary though insufficient] for the establishment of God's kingdom at the Parousia),—for such a Christian, I say, the final biological success of man on earth is not a simple probability but a certitude: for Christ (and in him, virtually, the world) is already risen. This certitude, however, belongs to a supra-phenomenal realm and proceeds from an act of faith which is 'supernatural'.[57]

The above passage is rather remarkable in that it sketches the broad lines of Teilhard's Christology and at one and the same time indicates the method of his theological enquiry. Let us briefly treat the question of methodology first, in order better to appreciate the problem which is about to be raised. What is immediately significant in the text just cited is the clear distinction drawn between the two sources of knowledge, one natural on the level of phenomena, the other supernatural on the level of revelation. Teilhard was in fact continually trying to avoid the charge that he was establishing a single epistemological line running from a scientific knowledge of evolution to a philosophical hypothesis of a personal Omega, which in turn demanded that this Centre of centres be none other than the Person of Christ. There is indeed a single epistemological line up to his hypothesis of a personal Omega, but what Teilhard does at the beginning of his theological enquiry is not to prolong this line of thought, but rather to break it off and confront it with a totally different line of thought drawn from a totally different source of knowledge. Here is the reason, as Henri de Lubac has noted, [58] that the section in *The Phenomenon of Man* dealing with 'The Christian Phenomenon' is entitled an epilogue and not a further chapter or a conclusion. This brief analysis of Christianity is indeed that of a phenomenon in our world, but all its elements are new, recognized as such, and in no sense either inferred or deduced from what has gone before.

Two texts will serve to bring this out more clearly. In the epilogue just mentioned there is the following statement: 'To confirm the presence at the summit of the world of what we have called the Omega Point, do we not find here [in Christianity] the very cross-check we were waiting for?' This is then corrected in a footnote: 'To be more exact, to confirm the presence at the summit of the world of something in line with but still more elevated than the Omega Point. This in deference to the theological concept of the "supernatural", according to which the unitive contact between God and the world, *hic et nunc* already begun, reaches a super-intimacy, and therefore a super-gratuity, of which man can have no inkling and to which he can lay no claim by reason of the exigencies of his nature alone.'[59] This same point is made in the second text, written eight years later: 'It is under the illuminative influence of grace that our mind recognizes, in the unitive character of the Christian phenomenon, a manifestation (reflection) of Omega upon the human consciousness, and it identifies the Omega of reason with the universal Christ of revelation.'[60]

Consequently there is no attempt whatsoever at a facile concordism which would confuse these two sources of knowledge, either deducing God's plan of salvation from purely natural reasoning, or finding in the data of Christian revelation a scientific explanation of the world. 'Far be it from me,' said Teilhard in a 1921 lecture, 'to think of deducing Christian dogmas from a mere inspection of those qualities which, according to the light of reason, characterize the structure of the world. . . . Science alone cannot discover Christ, but Christ fulfils the desires which spring up in our hearts from the teachings of science.'[61] Over twenty-five years later he was more explicit: 'Concordism must not be confused with coherence. Religion and science obviously represent two different meridians on the sphere of our minds, and it would be wrong not to keep them separate (which is the concordist error). But these meridians must necessarily meet somewhere at a pole of common vision (which is the meaning of coherence). Otherwise our whole intellectual and cognitive enterprise collapses.'[62] Again that same year: 'The essential test of truth, its specific mark, is to be able to develop indefinitely, not only without ever developing an internal contradiction, but especially in forming a positively constructed whole, in which all the parts are mutually supporting and complement each other in ever more perfect ways. On a sphere it would be absurd (concordism) to confuse the meridians at the equator; but at the pole (coherence) they ought to rejoin each other by structural necessity.'[63]

The last sentence throws a flood of light on Teilhard's methodology. He is not trying here and now to cast into a single mould the data of revelation and that of science as we know it today. Not only would such a juncture be hazardous and premature, but it would tend to stifle the spirit of independent research, which, in the case of both science and theology, is carried on by modes of investigation quite different and distinct. Rather, what he proposes to do at present is to confront the respective movements of each meridian and to examine them critically for signs of their *future* juncture. His presupposition is of course that a pole of truth already exists and that here and now the two lines of thought are dealing with one and the same objective reality, 'otherwise our whole intellectual and cognitive enterprise collapses.' Yet his clear distinction between meridians makes ample allowance for the partial nature of each intellectual discipline as well as for the gratuitous and transcendent character of Christian revelation. All the more striking therefore is the extraordinary *rapprochement* which Teilhard believes he has found between this revelation two thousand years old and his inductive vision of the world drawn from cosmic and organic evolution. The result is in fact a single great anticipation of that moment when, within the human mind, the two meridians reach their pole and the two sources of knowledge are perfectly harmonized. It is of this moment that he wrote shortly before he died: 'Science and revelation can continue to perform their proper functions only within that movement which carries them closer towards each other.'[64]

But there is a condition, and this brings us to consider the Christological problem as Teilhard has come to understand it. In the passage a few pages back which led us to a discussion of methodology, Teilhard states that the dogmatic foundation for his theological enquiry is the Resurrection of Christ, in which all humanity is destined to participate by reason of Christ's union with human nature at the Incarnation. He was well aware, however, that what the Incarnation and Resurrection guarantee is the success of a *supernatural* consummation of mankind in the final Plenitude of Christ at the end of time. He was aware too that Christian revelation as such does not directly concern that *natural* process by which mankind makes progress on earth, which up to now has been the principal object of his phenomenological study. Hence what he is about to do is to construct a theology, or more accurately a Christology (that is to say, a reflection upon the data of revelation regarding the Person of Christ), in which he can postulate a connection between this natural process and the supernatural consummation of mankind. This is what he means when he says, in that same passage, that in order to find in Christianity a positive guarantee of evolution's success, one must be ready to accept the collective consummation of humanity on earth as a necessary though insufficient condition for the coming of the Parousia.

Teilhard was in fact preoccupied all his life with this relationship between the culmination of evolution and the Parousia of Christ. As early as 1920 he wrote: 'Without biological evolution which produced the brain, there would be no sanctified souls; similarly, without the evolution of collective thought which alone can realize on earth the fullness of human consciousness, could there be a consummated Christ? In other words, without the constant striving of every human cell to unite with all the others, would the Parousia be physically possible?'[65] A more highly concentrated formulation appears in 1934: 'Christ needs to find a summit of the world for

his consummation just as he needed to find a woman for his conception.'⁶⁶ Fourteen years later he is again speaking of the relationship 'between what I have called "the critical point of human
maturation" on the one hand, and on the other the point of
Parousia (or second coming of Christ in triumph), with which the
Christian horizon comes to a close at the end of time. In structure
the two points inevitably coincide, in the sense that the perfection
of hominization through ultra-reflection appears as a preliminary
condition, necessary [but not sufficient], for its "divinization".'⁶⁷
These texts are merely a sampling of numerous references to the
Parousia.

Yet the Christological problem with which Teilhard was
grappling goes deeper than this. It has already been hinted at in the
text which appeared at the start of our enquiry: 'As long as the
universe was considered a static system, whose stuff was without
genetic development, the entrance into it of the kingdom of God
raised no structural difficulty at all. . . . However, and this is the
essential point, the moment the universe is defined not in terms of
"cosmos" but of "cosmogenesis", the problem of the Incarnation
becomes complicated, since from now on there is question of
reconciling two axes which are different and partially autonomous,
that of anthropo- and that of Christo-genesis. Hence the
importance, or rather the necessity, of a Christology in which
there is a correspondence between the human point of planetary
maturation and the Christic point of the Parousia.'⁶⁸ Teilhard is
indeed preoccupied with the 'correspondence between the human
point of planetary maturation and the Christic point of the
Parousia.' But note carefully the reason for such preoccupation,
namely the complication which is introduced into the problem of
the *Incarnation* as soon as the universe is defined in terms of 'cosmogenesis'. To express this complication Teilhard coined the term
'Christogenesis', and in so doing he stated with admirable terseness
the Christological problem as he had come to understand it.

For ultimately what Teilhard wants to do in the realm of theology
is to rethink the *total* mystery of Christ in terms of *genèse*. 'Lately,'
he wrote in 1951, 'I have once more become aware that the whole

nucleus of my interior outlook depends entirely upon and can be reduced to a simple transposition into dimensions of "cosmogenesis" of the vision which is traditionally expressed in terms of "cosmos". Creation, spirit, evil, God (and, more specifically, original sin, the Cross, the Resurrection, the Parousia, charity . . .), all these ideas, transferred to the dimension of "genesis", become coherent and clear in a way which is astounding.'[69] If the Parousia assumes such importance, it is because it represents the final maturation of God's salvific plan for the human race, and so corresponds immediately to Teilhard's first understanding of Omega as man's planetary maturation on earth. But Omega, as we have seen, is not merely the name for the state of collective reflection at the end of time; it is also and more fundamentally the name for that supreme personal Being here and now responsible for the time process itself, the real Omega, the Prime Mover ahead, who not only is, but has always been. If therefore the Christ of revelation is to be identified with the Omega of evolution (and this is Teilhard's initial supposition), then that which is responsible for relating the Parousia to mankind's planetary maturation must somehow already be present in the life, death and Resurrection of Jesus of Nazareth. For in the Person of Jesus the real Omega took flesh and became part of that evolutionary current for which he himself is responsible. His whole work of salvation thus became rooted in space-time and destined to continue in the material world up to its final fulfilment. Hence all the great Christological events must somehow be obedient to evolution's most fundamental law. Somehow we must be able to speak of a genesis which is Christic as well as a genesis which is cosmic, and in some sense we must be able to speak of them both as ultimately one and the same. It is precisely to speak in such a way, while yet remaining faithful to the testimony of revelation, which is the aim of Teilhard de Chardin's Christology.

In elaborating such a Christology it is natural that he should make use of his own system of thought. Such an approach has frequently been compared to the use which St. Thomas made of the system of Aristotle. What should be insisted upon, however, is that in Teilhard's case the theological effort is far more modest and contained. His concern is not with the whole of revelation, but only with those areas in which a theology of the Incarnation confronts modern man's understanding of the world in which he lives. His exclusive interest is in 'the marvellous and liberating harmony between a religion which is Christ-centred and an evolution which is convergent.'[70] In examining the data of revelation he will naturally pass over much in order to concentrate his attention on those aspects which correspond to his hypothesis of convergence. But in no sense does he try, as some have supposed, to dilute the Christian message of salvation to a mere supporting structure for the discoveries of modern science; nor does he attempt to reduce this message of eternal life to a message regarding some future life on earth. Rather, the point he is making is that within the total Christian message there are to be found affirmations regarding the cosmic grandeur of Christ which do in fact support beyond all natural expectations the needs and aspirations of modern man. 'If the world is convergent and if Christ occupies its centre, then the Christogenesis of St. Paul and St. John is nothing else and nothing less than the extension, both awaited and unhoped for, of that noogenesis in which we experience the culmination of cosmogenesis.'[71]

Consequently the development of Teilhard's theological thought will move in three main directions. The first is speculation concerning the physical relationship between the Body of Christ, mankind and the material world, a speculation based primarily on the cosmic vision of St. Paul in Colossians and Ephesians, and embracing the mysteries of the Incarnation and the Eucharist. The second is speculation regarding the meaning of death and the oppressive enigma of evil, both moral evil and physical evil, when seen in the context of cosmogenesis, a speculation involving the mystery of Christ's redemptive death and Resurrection. Finally there is speculation concerning the relationship between cosmic history and salvation history, between God's continuous creation in time and the gradual growth of the final Plenitude of Christ, a speculation embracing the mysteries of the Church and Parousia. It is these three large areas of speculation which constitute Teilhard's

Christological legacy, and they will accordingly provide the subject matter for the three chapters which are to follow. Such a theological enterprise hardly meets at all points with equal success. It would indeed be surprising if it did. The extraordinary thing is not that it does not fully succeed but that it should ever have been thought of at all.

We may conclude this chapter by noting once again that in the thought of Teilhard de Chardin there are three different levels or strata, each dependent upon the other two and therefore not always clearly distinguished. The first is his hyperphysics, a phenomeno-logical analysis of the evolutionary process based on scientific data. This results in an hypothesis that the human species, if it continues to develop according to the pattern of complexity-consciousness, should in all probability converge after hundreds of thousands or even millions of years upon a point of planetary maturation, provisionally called Omega, at which mankind would cross a second threshold of reflection and enter into a single collectivity of consciousness that would bring to perfection all personal elements precisely in so far as they are persons. This first stratum then merges with a second, which is Teilhard's 'psychological act of faith' in an Omega which is personal and which *must* be personal, 'loving and lovable at this very moment,' if it is to activate the love energy of the world.[72] Fundamental to this philosophic 'option', as Teilhard calls it,[73] is his conviction that true evolutionary progress resides not in the forces of tangential energy, now moving inevitably towards an ever greater technical mastery of mind over matter, but rather in the forces of radial energy, which in man have become 'psychosocial',[74] urging him forward towards ever higher forms of inter-personal communion. Because man today has suddenly become conscious of what is taking place in him, it follows that the successful outcome of evolution now depends upon his free decision to co-operate with these forces of radial energy. Hence Teilhard's insistence upon a divine Omega who, as personal source and object of love, can not only motivate this free decision by giving certitude of eventual success, but also conquer man's native tendency towards repulsion and isolation.

These first two strata follow a single epistemological line. The third stratum, however, is based upon a totally different source of knowledge, namely Teilhard's faith in Christian revelation, and it is through this third stratum that he seeks to move from a philosophical hypothesis to an historical fact. Towards the end of *The Phenomenon of Man* he admits that his concept of a personal Omega was in fact motivated by the knowledge he had through faith of the Person of Christ.[75] Christ is the true Omega of evolution through whom mankind is destined to achieve its ultimate unity on a new plane of being. Fully to understand evolution, therefore, means to see as its goal and centre of convergence 'the figure of Christ wrapped in the mystery of his Resurrection and Parousia.'[76] Teilhard's third stratum of thought thus completes and complements the other two. His phenomenological analysis and his psychological act of faith merge with the data of revelation to become a Christology in which the Prime Mover of creation actuates all the energies of the universe. 'More urgently than ever I feel that the great question in the depths of my being is one of a faith, a "Christology", that will give the fullest possible stimulation to the forces of hominization in us—or, which comes to the same thing, the forces of adoration.'[77] What Teilhard was searching for always was an approach to the mystery of man which would enable him to dispense with looking at the human person alternately from a scientific, philosophic and theological point of view. He wanted to be able to pass in a single movement from one mode of knowledge to another, from the data of reason on its various levels to the data of Christian revelation, and to do so with ease and without confusion. He may indeed have failed. Even to dream of such an achievement may in itself be a chimera. Yet his intuitions are none the less germinal, in the fullest sense of that word, and in the end they are quite capable of infusing a new life into traditional Christian thought.

CHAPTER THREE

THE INCARNATION AND THE EUCHARIST

THE BODY OF CHRIST AS A PHYSICAL CENTRE FOR MANKIND AND THE MATERIAL WORLD

For Teilhard de Chardin modern man's most pressing psychological need is, as we have seen, an assurance that some successful outcome exists for that progress on earth for which he knows himself to be responsible. Unless such guarantee is given, that is to say, unless the prospect of a total death ahead can be eliminated, then there is serious danger that progress will flounder and the whole human enterprise come to a halt. The three strata of Teilhard's thought, of which we spoke at the end of chapter two, are an effort to elaborate such a guarantee on the three levels of science, philosophy and theology. His first assurance to modern man is to point to the pattern of the past which he has uncovered through his hyperphysics, or phenomenological analysis of evolution. Through his law of complexity-consciousness he believes he has shown that up till now there has been not simply change in the cosmos but 'genesis', which for Teilhard means that the universe has been pursuing an aim, that a single pattern has been running through the whole, and that this pattern has been oriented towards man. Man is the key to the whole biological process, since it was through man that evolution crossed the threshold of reflection into the 'noosphere', the mysterious realm of the person. 'How could we imagine a cosmogenesis reaching right up to the mind without being thereby confronted with a noogenesis?'[1]

Teilhard's second assurance is to point to the fact that in the noosphere this law of complexity-consciousness must operate on the level of spirit, and consequently, because of the steady growth of human socialization, there is reason to believe that the law itself will eventually be transformed by man's freedom into a law of growing amorization. For in Teilhard's system it is the free circulation of love energy between persons which is alone capable of totalizing humanity and of centring it upon that ultimate Pole of convergence called Omega. For this to happen, however, for modern man freely to foster this union with other men through love, it is first necessary to believe that this Centre of centres is a present reality, and above all that it is personal, 'loving and lovable at this very moment'. In other words man must believe in a divine Omega, here and now engaged in drawing human persons to himself by radiating and activating the love energy of the world. Omega is thus the Prime Mover ahead who began the evolutionary process in time and who is himself the guarantee of its ultimate successful conclusion.

But there is a third assurance, on the level not of natural reason but of supernatural faith, and it is this third assurance which gives rise to what Teilhard sees as the modern Christological problem. For Omega in his system of thought is reached only by extrapolation from phenomena; it remains of its nature an assumption and a conjecture, and cannot in the end provide the necessary guarantee for cosmogenesis. Consequently Teilhard appeals to Christian revelation in order to bridge this gap between a philosophical hypothesis and historical fact. He identifies the Christ of revelation with the Omega of evolution, and by so doing gives to cosmogenesis, 'in place of the vague focus of convergence, . . . the well-defined reality of the Incarnate Word, in whom all things hold together.'[2] He thereby postulates a connection between the natural evolutionary process and the supernatural consummation of mankind, and it is this postulate which explains the frequent references to the Parousia in much of his religious writing. The problem, however, goes deeper than this. For if there is to be a connection between cosmogenesis and the Person of Christ, then not only the Parousia but all the great Christological events must be able to be spoken of in terms of *genèse*. Hence the term 'Christogenesis', which Teilhard coined to indicate not only the problem but also the line of approach he would take in seeking a solution.

Such a solution, however, presupposes a very close connection between one's outlook on the world and one's method of dealing with the data of revelation. Of itself this data is transcendent and limited to no specific human culture. A theology, on the other hand, which is man's reflection upon this data, his attempt to understand it as an organized whole, is necessarily linked to the culture in which it was born, since it depends for its expression on the resources of human philosophy, and these in turn are always inspired by the *Weltanschauung* of any given historical period. In an article published in 1939 Teilhard made this point clearly:

By the Incarnation God entered into nature to give it supernatural life and lead it back to himself: that is the substance of Christian dogma. Of itself this dogma can be accommodated to any number of images of the experiential world. For example, while the human spirit saw in the universe only a fixed arrangement of finished elements, the Christian found no serious difficulty in situating within this static order the mysterious process of his sanctification. But was this not to some extent a makeshift accommodation? Is a fundamental cosmic immobility really the most favourable setting one could think of for the great spiritual metamorphosis represented by the coming of the kingdom of God? . . . A universe whose structure evolves—as long as one correctly understands the direction of such a movement—could well be, after all, the milieu most favourable for developing a great and homogeneous understanding of the Incarnation. Christianity found itself stifled by materialistic evolution. But within the large perspectives which are developing of a universe being drawn upward towards spirit, does it not find a most suitable climate? What better than an ascending anthropogenesis to serve as a background and foundation for the descending illuminations of a Christogenesis?[3]

To what extent, then, is it legitimate, while remaining faithful to the testimony of revelation, to speak of a genesis which is Christic as well as one which is cosmic? And to what extent can the two movements be considered one and the same? While

the term 'Christogenesis' was not coined until 1939, the relationship
it expresses between Christ and the evolutionary process had always
been one of Teilhard's master ideas. Hence it is not surprising to
find that, long before the development of his own system enabled
him to formulate the problem so precisely, he was already laying
the foundation of an answer. This foundation gradually crystallized
itself into the assertion that the Body of Christ forms a physical
Centre for mankind and the whole material world. It is this
fundamental assertion of Teilhard's nascent Christology which is
the subject of this present chapter.

Significantly enough, the relationship between Christ and the
universe was a preoccupation of his first theological essay in 1916.
The following passage is interesting for a number of reasons and it
will serve well as our point of departure:

Minds who are timid in their conceptions or filled with
individualistic prejudice, who try always to see relations
between beings as moral and logical, are quite content to think
of the Body of Christ by analogy with aggregates of men. For
them it is much more like a social assembly than a natural
organism. These minds dangerously weaken scriptural thought
and render it incomprehensible or banal to people enthusiastic
over interconnections that are physical and relationships
properly cosmic. They unduly diminish Christ as well as the
profoundly realistic mystery of his Flesh. No, the Body of
Christ must be understood boldly, as it was seen and loved
by St. John, St. Paul and the Fathers. It forms in nature a world
which is new, an organism moving and alive in which we are
all united physically, biologically. . . .

It is first by the Incarnation and next by the Eucharist that
[Christ] organizes us for himself and imposes himself upon
us. . . . Although he has come above all for souls, uniquely
for souls, he could not join them together and bring them life
without assuming and animating along with them all the rest
of the world. By his Incarnation he inserted himself not just
into humanity but into the universe which supports humanity,
and he did so not simply as another connected element, but with

the dignity and function of a directing principle, of a Centre towards which everything converges in harmony and in love.[4]

Teilhard's appeal to Scripture in the above passage is not unusual. Frequently in his theological writings he repeats that what he is doing is simply transposing into an evolutionary framework the great cosmic affirmations of St. Paul regarding the Person of Christ. Perhaps, therefore, we can best disengage the various elements in Teilhard's approach to the Body of Christ by first treating his thought on the Incarnation and the Eucharist, and then trying to determine the extent to which this thought can be supported by the teaching of St. Paul. Teilhard's appeal to St. John and the Fathers will have to be considered at some other time, for to add even the briefest treatment of these two large areas would hopelessly lengthen the present study and render it more than justifiably superficial.

I

Teilhard's central affirmations regarding the Body of Christ may be reduced to three, namely that it is the Body-Person of Jesus of Nazareth, that it here and now forms a personal Centre for mankind and the material world, and that this personal Centre is a 'physical' Centre. His understanding of the mystery of the Holy Eucharist serves to clarify and bring into sharper focus the meaning of 'physical' and consequently to underline again both the organic and the personal aspects of his thought. In this first part of our study we shall consider in turn each of these affirmations.

That the Body of Christ is the Body-Person of Jesus of Nazareth who lived and died at a certain point in history, is a truth which is essential to Teilhard's whole theological enquiry. Christ for him is always the Person of Jesus. The impression continues to persist, however, that he somehow looked upon Christ as an idealistic symbol for humanity. Usually the reason for this is a simple misunderstanding of the radically incomplete presentation of the subject in The Phenomenon of Man. Another reason, however, is the fact that for Teilhard the historical Incarnation had always the

71

aspect of a *beginning*, and beginnings of any type at all had far less interest for him than developments and terminations. Consequently, while the Christ he is speaking of is always the Christ of the Gospels, it is rare that his life *in* the Gospels becomes a subject of discussion. Limiting oneself intellectually and spiritually to the daily life of Christ on earth, Teilhard felt, was not the way to understand the Incarnation or grasp its ultimate meaning. 'Not a single thing in our changing world is really understandable except in so far as it has reached its terminus. . . . Hence if we want to form a correct idea of the Incarnation, it is not at its beginnings that we must situate ourselves (Annunciation, Nativity, even the Passion), but as far as possible at its definitive terminus.'5

A number of texts from various periods in Teilhard's life will bring this outlook into relief. 'Christianity,' he writes in *The Divine Milieu*, 'unveils to our eyes and hearts the moving and unfathomable reality of the historical Christ in whom the exemplary life of an individual man conceals this mysterious drama: the Master of the world leading, like an element of the world, not only an elemental life, but (in addition to this and because of it) leading the total life of the universe, which he has shouldered and assimilated by experiencing it himself.'6 If the historical reality of Christ is suppressed, then the divine omnipresence would become uncertain, vague and conventional. 'The mystical Christ, the universal Christ of St. Paul, has neither meaning nor value in our eyes except as an expansion of the Christ who was born of Mary and who died on the Cross. . . . However far we may be drawn into the divine spaces opened to us by Christian mysticism, we never depart from the Jesus of the Gospels.'7

These last lines were written in 1927. During the following decade Teilhard is again insisting that 'the universal Christ, where my personal faith finds satisfaction, is nothing else than an authentic expression of the Christ of the Gospels.'. . . 'The extraordinary power of spiritual development which we find in Christianity is inextricably bound up with the idea that Christ is historical. If we take away this nucleus, Christianity becomes nothing but a "philosophy" like any other: its whole force and vitality is lost.'. . . 'The universal Christ is a development and extension of the Heart of Jesus, and would simply vanish were it not for the historical reality of his human nature.'[8] In 1944 he is still making the same point: 'Concretely and historically it is incontestable that the living and conquering idea of the universal Christ appeared and developed in the Christian consciousness when Jesus the Man was recognized and adored as God. It is the same today. To suppress the historicity of Christ (i.e. the divinity of the historical Christ [sic]) would be to make disappear into the unreal all the spiritual energy accumulated for two thousand years in the Christian phylum. Christ born of the Virgin and Christ risen from the dead: the two form one single inseparable bloc.'[9]

Teilhard was in fact continually answering the objection that the human reality of Jesus seemed to be disappearing in his effort to link the data of revelation with that of scientific research. Frequently the root of such a misunderstanding is the common practice of modern intellectual disciplines to speak separately of the human body and the human person. A discussion of one does not usually involve or even imply a discussion of the other. When Teilhard speaks of man, however, it is always concrete man, a body-person. Just as he never uses the word 'spirit' in the metaphysical sense of 'pure spirit' but always in relation to the matter it animates, so his use of the word 'body' when applied to man always includes the idea of 'person'. Consequently when he speaks of the Body of Christ he always means the concrete Body-Person of the historical Jesus. 'The more I reflect upon the profound laws of evolution, the more I am convinced that the universal Christ would be unable to appear at the end of time at the world's summit, unless he had previously inserted himself into the course of the world's movement *by way of birth* in the form of an element. If it is really by Christ-Omega that the world is held in movement, then, for our own experience, it is from his concrete source, the Man of Nazareth, that Christ-Omega draws (theoretically and historically) his whole stability.'[10] Five years before his death he is emphasizing this once again: 'Because of those very characteristics which would seem at first to particularize him too much, a God incarnate historically is the only one who can satisfy the inflexible laws of a universe where nothing is produced or appears except *by way of birth*.'[11]

It is Jesus of Nazareth, therefore, whom Teilhard has always in mind when he identifies the Christ of revelation with the Omega of evolution. Such an identification, however, leads him to his second affirmation concerning the Body of Christ, namely that it forms a personal Centre for mankind and the whole material world. Here again we should note carefully that Teilhard's dialectic is continually making use of two sources of knowledge. From reason comes his hypothesis of a converging universe, which demands the existence of a transcendent personal Centre capable of drawing evolution to its ultimate conclusion by here and now activating the love energy of the world. From Christian revelation, especially (as we shall see) from the letters of St. Paul, comes belief in a cosmic function for the Person of Christ by which he is Lord over all of creation. While Teilhard is well aware that the data of one source of knowledge is not the data of the other, he is likewise convinced that the two lines of thought are ultimately dealing with one and the same reality. Hence his conclusion that in the present concrete order, granting of course his hypothesis of a converging universe, Christ must fulfil the function of Omega, which is to be a personal Centre radiating its influence upon the whole evolutionary process.

In bringing home this second affirmation, moreover, Teilhard is not only eager to keep separate these two sources of knowledge but also to safeguard the gratuity of the present supernatural order. Two early essays show his concern in this matter. 'Christ is, of course,' he wrote in 1917, 'not the Centre which all things here below could naturally aim at embracing. Being destined for Christ is a favour of the Creator, unexpected and gratuitous. It nonetheless remains true that the Incarnation has so recast the universe in the supernatural that, concretely speaking, we are no longer able either to seek or imagine the centre towards which the elements of this world would gravitate without the elevation of grace.'[12] This concern of his comes to the fore again in 1924. 'In any hypothesis the world has to be centred in order to be thinkable. Consequently the presence of an Omega at its head has nothing to do with its "supernatural elevation". What gives the character of "gratuity" to the world is precisely the fact that the function of universal Centre has not been given to some supreme intermediary between God and the universe, but has been assumed by God himself, who in this way has introduced us into the depths of his immanent Trinitarian action. I say this to clarify my theological position.'[13]

Consequently it would be an error to distinguish in man as he exists in the present concrete order two distinct attractions, 'one towards a hypothetical natural end for the cosmos, the other towards an end which was supernatural.' There is in the universe 'one Centre only, at the same time natural and supernatural, which activates the whole of creation along one and the same line, first towards the greatest possible consciousness, then towards the highest degree of sanctity, and this Centre is Christ Jesus, personal as well as cosmic.' In 1920 he wrote to a close friend of the 'impossibility of understanding a Christ who would be organically *central* in the supernatural universe and physically *juxtaposed* in the natural universe.' And in a letter to Maurice Blondel during the same period he says: 'The supernatural Plenitude of Christ receives support from the natural plenitude of the world, . . . the supernatural is continually being formed by a new creation of the natural. . . . Christ gives himself to us through a world which is to reach completion even on the natural level by reason of its relationship to him.'[14] In a real but analogical sense Christ has become a constitutive part of our universe, though ultimate solidification in Christ is still in abeyance, still in the process of 'becoming'. This is the reason we are able mentally to stop the process and to imagine the world sustaining itself naturally, independently of Christ. But in the real order such a separation does not exist.

Sometimes I have thought of mitigating the absolute nature of this conception of mine, at first sight so improbable. I used to picture the world as separate from Christ, with some primal existence all its own, its own natural order and its own sphere where human progress took place. Those who held fast to Jesus Christ by faith and a good intention, and those only, would go beyond this first sphere and enter, along with their world, into that other sphere of Christ's divinizing power. Thus in the objective order there would be two distinct compartments in the universe, the created world and the world of Christ, the latter gradually absorbing the former. But such a mitigation of my thought seemed illogical to me, at variance with the identity of God the Creator and God the Redeemer, at variance also with the elevation of the natural order in its entirety. . . . For grace does not force man to enter another universe; it introduces him into an extension of our own universe.[15]

Hence what Teilhard is insisting upon in this second affirmation is that, in this concrete supernatural order, created reality has been elevated in its entirety, and that whatever God has brought into being, whether natural or supernatural, has been destined to constitute a single unity whose Centre is the Incarnate Word. This is why he believes that ultimately there can be no natural end for true evolutionary progress, that is to say, for that movement of radial energy towards higher spiritual consciousness and interpersonal communion. Only tangential energy, moving inevitably towards a technical mastery over matter, can reach ends which are purely natural. It should be remembered, moreover, that such progress in tangential energy is simply meant to provide greater material organization for radial energy so that the latter may move forward towards higher consciousness. The distinction therefore between 'natural' and 'supernatural' remains, but it cannot mean that something has been created which is unconnected with the supernatural destiny of mankind and which would be without reference to the final Plenitude of Christ.

'Christ is the term even of the natural evolution of beings,' writes Teilhard in 1916. In 1918 he says that 'the characteristics which Scripture attributes to the Incarnate Word and which the Church has magnificently collated in the Litany of the Sacred Heart, are quite formal in asserting that to Christ belongs the function of binding together into a unity the totality of creation. The world, i.e. our substance, is centred upon God *in Christo Jesu.*' A decade later he insists that 'the world can no more have two summits than a circumference can have two centres.' A few years afterwards there is the same emphasis: 'Concretely speaking, there is only a single process of synthesis going on from the top to the bottom of the universe,' and 'no element or movement could exist at any stage of the world without the "informing" action of the principal Centre of everything.'[16] These early statements are echoed in 1943: 'You can turn things around again and again as you like, but the universe cannot have two heads, —it cannot be "bicephalous". . . . A Christic Centre for the universe fixed by theology, a cosmic centre postulated by anthropogenesis: in the end these two foci necessarily coincide (or at least overlap) in the historical order in which we find ourselves. Christ would not be the sole moving force, the unique *Issue* of the universe, if the universe in some way, even at a lower level, could gather itself together independently of him.'[17] Finally in 1951 there is a last formulation: 'In order to incorporate all things into himself (to use St. Paul's expression) and then, bearing the world with him, to return to the bosom of the Father, it is not enough, as we perhaps thought, for Christ to sanctify supernaturally a harvest of souls; it is also necessary for him to exert his creative power to bring cosmic noogenesis to the term of its natural maturity.'[18]

From this second affirmation concerning the Body of Christ there immediately follows the third. In the present supernatural order, Teilhard has just said, Christ must correspond to Omega and fulfil the function of personal Centre for the universe, for all that is natural and all that is supernatural. What he now adds and insists upon in his third affirmation is that, as a consequence, Christ must somehow be a *physical* Centre. 'Christ is an organic Centre for the whole universe; organic Centre, i.e. on whom all development, even what is natural, is suspended finally and physically.'[19] The use of the word 'physical' in this context, as well as its synonym 'organic', may strike one as strange at first, though it is a perfectly logical conclusion from Teilhard's understanding of the evolutionary process and its significance. Within his system of thought one *should* be able to say that Christ is in some sense a physical Centre. Yes, but in what sense?

77

In seeking our answer we should note three facts. First of all there is Teilhard's conviction that the word 'physical' is absolutely necessary. While his training in experimental science is an obvious explanation for this, a deeper reason is the strongly emotional reaction he experienced against the 'juridical' approach to Christology to which he was exposed as a seminarian in the early part of the century. These early studies left their mark, and in 1934 his feelings are still strong. 'As long as the Incarnation is described and discussed in juridical terms, it appears as a simple phenomenon, superimposable upon any type of world at all. Whether the universe be big or small, static or evolving, it is just as simple for God to *give* it to his Son, since the only thing involved is a declaration.' The whole situation changes, however, as soon as the Incarnation is looked upon from an organic point of view, since now 'in order to be Saviour and Life of souls in their supernatural prolongation, Christ first has to satisfy certain conditions vis-à-vis the world considered in its natural and experiential reality.'[20] A decade later he wrote a criticism which is quite unfair to many theologians of the period, as well as to a whole segment of Christian tradition, but which emphasizes again Teilhard's unchanging point of view:

In spite of the repeated affirmations of St. Paul and the Greek Fathers, the universal power of Christ over creation has been considered by theologians up to now chiefly under an aspect that is extrinsic and juridical. 'Jesus is King of the world because his Father has *declared* him to be such. He is master of all because all has been given to him.' . . . With the exception of the mystery of 'sanctifying grace', the organic side of the Incarnation and therefore the physical conditions to be presupposed have been left in the dark, —all the more readily since the recent and frightening enlargement of the universe around us (in volume, direction and number) would seem to render quite unimaginable any physical control by the Person of Christ over the totality of the cosmos.[21]

The second fact to note is that, though Teilhard insisted upon the word 'physical,' he had continual difficulty in giving it a positive content when he applied it to the relationship between the universe and the Body of Christ. The ambiguity of his early essays prompted Maurice Blondel to remark in a 1919 letter that 'a supernaturalism which is purely physical is nonsense.' Teilhard accepted this criticism and several letters later brought their brief correspondence to a close with the admission that 'in regard to the extent to which the divine fire is "physical" and the precise mode of its transforming action, I am conscious of having again broached this difficult problem without really coming to grips with it. . . . I too speak with the greatest hesitation, especially in giving my opinion on this final point which separates us.'[22] Nevertheless, there are two texts from this early period which are significant in the light of what Teilhard will say later on. The first is from 1917; it describes the cosmic Body of Christ, 'whose principal attributes are sketched by St. Paul,' as 'the Point towards which [beings] converge or just as equally the Milieu in which they are immersed.'[23] The second text, written a year later, is the following:

There is nothing strange about there being a universal physical element in Christ. Each one of us, if we but reflect, is enveloped, aureoled, by an extension of his being as vast as the universe. What we are aware of is only the nucleus which is ourselves. But the interaction of monads would be incomprehensible if an 'aura' did not extend from one to the other, i.e. something proper to each one and common to all. How then are we to imagine the constitution of Christ as cosmic Centre of creation ? Simply as an extension, a transformation, brought about in the humanity of Jesus, of that 'aura' which surrounds every human monad.[24]

Whatever meaning 'physical' is to have, therefore, it will have to be situated in the realm of the human and the personal. Teilhard is not going to 'confuse naively the planes of reality and make of Christ a physical agent of *the same order* as organic life or the ether. That is what is blamable and ridiculous.' This is simply to become a visionary, whose 'real error . . . is to confuse the different planes of the world and consequently to mix up their activities.'[25] Accordingly, in 1924, Christ's 'supremely physical influence over the total reality of the cosmos' begins for the first time explicitly to assume in his mind the aspect of a *personal presence*. 'The presence of the Word Incarnate penetrates everything as a universal Element. At the heart of all things it shines as a Centre infinitely intimate and yet at the same time (because it coincides with the consummation of the universe) infinitely far away. . . . Everything around us is physically "Christified" and can become so more and more.' Some pages later in a footnote he takes pains to be precise: 'The only difference, but an essential one, between these considerations and the usual speculation which is current concerning the presence of God, is that, from the point of view adopted here, the presence of God reaches the elements of the world only through (and in) the Body of Christ.'[26]

It is not, however, until *The Divine Milieu* three years later that 'Body of Christ', 'physical Centre', and 'personal presence' become definitively united and dealt with at length. 'Omnipresence' is indeed the central theme of the whole work, and the title itself is a synonym for the presence of Christ, who 'through his humanity' is the active Centre radiating all those energies which lead the universe back to God. 'However vast the divine Milieu may be, it is in reality a Centre. It therefore has the properties of a centre, and above all the absolute and final power to unite (and consequently to complete) all beings within its breast. In the divine Milieu all the elements of the universe touch each other by that which is most inward and ultimate in them.' In this divine Milieu 'we recognize an omnipresence which acts upon us by assimilating us to itself *in unitate Corporis Christi*. As a consequence of the Incarnation, the divine immensity has transformed itself for us into the omnipresence of Christification. All the good that I can do, *opus et operatio*, is physically gathered together, by something of itself, into the reality of the consummated Christ.' The great mystery of Christianity is not exactly the appearance, but the transparence of God in the universe: 'not only your Epiphany, Jesus, but your diaphany.' This is why at the end of time 'the presence of Christ' will have 'silently grown in things'.[27] For by his Incarnation he 'became coextensive with the physical immensities of duration and space, without losing the preciseness of his humanity.'[28]

It is important to note here that at the time he wrote *The Divine Milieu* Teilhard was beginning to develop the paramount role which the human person was to play in his own distinctive system of thought. This explains why even now he is explicitly trying 'to avoid the perverse pantheism and materialism which lie in wait for our thought whenever it applies to its mystical concepts the powerful but dangerous resources of analogies drawn from organic life.' The physical relationship therefore between mankind and the Incarnate Word must be affirmed 'without rejecting anything of the forces of freedom and of consciousness which form the physical reality proper to the human soil.' Union with the Body of Christ must preserve in harmony 'all that is most flexible in human combinations and all that is most intransigent in organic structures.' To designate such a union he wishes to retain the term 'mystical', but only on condition that it 'mean the strengthening and purification of what is contained really and immediately in the most powerful connections which we see in every order of the physical and human world.'[29]

Besides Teilhard's insistence upon the word 'physical' and his difficulty in giving it a positive content, there is also a third fact to note. What eventually brings some measure of clarity to the meaning of 'physical Centre' is a line of thought which seems to have begun independently of the problem we are now discussing. This new line of thought is Teilhard's approach to the mystery of the Holy Eucharist. For him the Eucharistic presence is the symbol and concrete sign that Christ's 'kenosis into matter', as he called the historical Incarnation,[30] is in fact extended throughout the universe and so constitutes a promise of its eventual transfiguration. But here again we find development. Until 1923 the concept explicitly linked to the Eucharist is not 'physical Centre' but 'universal Centre'. In a poetic meditation on the Blessed Sacrament written at the Front in 1916 and running to eighteen pages in the published text, the word 'physical' does not occur once. Teilhard's emphasis falls upon the 'mysterious expansion of the Host' by which 'the world had become incandescent, resembling in its totality a single great Host. . . . A transformation was going on in the sphere of love, expanding, purifying, capturing all the power of loving contained in the universe.'[31] The same thought appears in another essay the following year, and two years later it completely dominates a highly devotional prose poem called *The Priest*. Here Teilhard sees Christ prolonging his Incarnation when he descends to replace the bread and wine at Mass, but without restricting his action to the material species alone. 'The transubstantiation is aureoled by a real though limited divinization of the whole universe. From the cosmic element into which he inserts himself, the Word acts to subjugate all else and assimilate it to himself.'[32]

Early in the year 1923 the word 'physical' begins to be linked for the first time to this 'universal presence' of Christ in the Eucharist. Teilhard writes that when Christ comes sacramentally to each of the faithful, 'it is not only to hold conversation with him. It is to join him more and more to himself, physically, and to all other faithful in the growing unity of the world. When he says through the priest "This is my Body", . . . the priestly action extends beyond the transubstantiated Host to the cosmos itself, which the still unfinished Incarnation gradually transforms in the course of the passing centuries.'[33] In the summer of the same year, on a scientific expedition to the Ordos desert in China, Teilhard found it impossible to say Mass, and this occasioned the composition of the beautiful *Mass on the World*, one of the finest examples of his spiritual writing. Again the universe is 'an immense Host' and Christ is 'the physical focus of creation', as well as 'an Energy *quae possit sibi omnia subjicere*', 'an influence secretly present in the depths of matter and a dazzling Centre'.[34] A year later Teilhard is once more speaking of these 'real physical extensions of the Eucharistic presence'. While the 'primary Body of Christ is limited to the species of bread and wine', still Christ can find 'his organic fullness only by assimilating all that surrounds him in a way that is mystical (a term which we said must have the sense of hyperphysical).' The whole world 'transforms itself into him who animates it. The Eucharistic Bread is stronger than our flesh, says

St. Gregory of Nyssa; this is why he assimilates us when we receive him instead of we assimilating him.'[35]

It is *The Divine Milieu*, however, which in 1927 finally presents a synthesis between this thought on the Eucharist and that other block of speculation which has revolved around the terms 'physical Centre' and 'omnipresence'. Some readers may feel, says Teilhard, that the explanation he has given of the physical presence of Christ strains in too realistic a sense the meaning of Body of Christ—'in spite of the decisive expressions of St. Paul.' Actually what he has done, he continues, is simply to take 'another path to rejoin the great highway opened up in the Church by the onrush of the cult of the Holy Eucharist.' From the beginning of the Messianic preparation up to the Parousia, passing through the historic mani-festation of Jesus and the phases of growth of his Church, 'a single event has been developing in the world: the Incarnation, realized in each individual through the Eucharist. . . . All the communions of all men, present, past and future, are one communion. Have we ever sufficiently considered the physical immensity of man, and his extraordinary relations with the universe, in order to realize in our minds the formidable implications of this elementary truth?'[36] He then goes on to spell out some of these implications, and it will be worth our while to hear him out at length.

If, then, the Eucharist is a sovereign influence upon our human natures, then its energy necessarily extends, owing to the effects of continuity, into the less luminous regions that sustain us. . . . At every moment the Eucharistic Christ controls—from the point of view of the organization of the Pleroma (which is the only true point of view from which the world can be under-stood)—the whole movement of the universe: Christ *per quem omnia, Domine, semper creas, vivificas et praestas nobis.*

The control of which we are speaking is, at the minimum, a final refinement, a final purification, a final harnessing, of all the elements which can be used in the construction of the New Earth. But how can we avoid going further and believing that the sacramental action of Christ, precisely because it sanctifies matter, extends its influence, on this side of the pure supernatural, over all that makes up the internal and external environment of the faithful, that is to say that it sets its mark upon everything which we call 'our Providence'?

If this is the case, then we find ourselves (by simply having followed the 'extensions' of the Eucharist) plunged once again precisely into our divine Milieu. . . . Christ is discovered in every single reality around us, and shines like an ultimate determination, like a Centre, one might almost say like a universal Element. Through our humanity assimilating the material world and the Host assimilating our humanity, the Eucharistic transformation goes beyond and completes the transubstantiation of the bread on the altar. . . . In a secondary and generalized sense, but in a true sense, the sacramental species are formed by the totality of the world and the duration of creation is needed for its consecration. *In Christo vivimus, movemur et sumus.*[37]

The above passage brings to a close the intellectual effort of a decade. In it Teilhard comes as close as he ever will to giving a positive content to his concept of Christ as 'physical Centre', a concept which in the end he is never able fully to clarify. Yet he does indicate clearly, without perhaps realizing it at the time, why such an understanding of the Incarnation is essential if the mystery of Christ is to be rethought in terms of *genèse*. We may summarize his thought briefly as follows. He has come to see the Body of Christ as a physical Centre for mankind and the material world, not in the primary sense in which Christ is present in the Eucharist, but in the secondary and generalized sense in which each individual man, as a body-person, is a centre for his own limited environment. In the case of Christ, however, the environment is beyond limitation, since he is able through the Eucharist to unite himself as a Body-Person to all the faithful in any time and place. This particular mode of omnipresence enables Christ likewise to be present to all persons and things which make up the internal and external environment of the faithful. Christ thus becomes 'physically' a universal Element, a Milieu and a Centre who controls in and through the extension of his Eucharistic presence the whole movement of the universe. Ultimately the purpose of such control is the salvation of mankind, that is, the gradual organization of Christ's Plenitude at the end of time and the construction of a New Earth. Yet in exercising this control Christ must at the same time and in some way sanctify matter itself, and in so doing bring to it a promise of eventual transfiguration.

In Teilhard's system of thought all created reality is 'physical' and 'organic', and he applies these words equally, though analogously, to the material and the personal as well as to the natural and the supernatural. Their application to the omnipresence of Christ, far from excluding a personal and hence supernatural influence, really presupposes it, since it is precisely in and through his Body that the Person of the Word unites himself to his creation. 'Precisely because he is the Centre, he fills the whole sphere. The divine omnipresence is simply the effect of its own extreme spirituality, and is exactly the contrary of that deceptive ubiquity which matter seems to possess by reason of its extreme dissociation.'[38] The nature of Omega, moreover, as well as the dominant role of the personal in Teilhard's thinking, makes it quite impossible for him to conceive the influence of Christ on the universe in any other than personalistic terms. Perhaps the closest equivalent to Teilhard's 'physical' in current theological usage is the word 'ontological,' which may be applied to whatever has existence in the present concrete order of things. 'Physical' is thus opposed to all that is juridical, abstract, extrinsic to reality. This is what is meant by saying that, as a consequence of the Incarnation, the divine immensity transforms itself into a physical 'omnipresence of Christification'. For Teilhard such omnipresence is a real prolonging of Eucharistic transubstantiation, and this is why he can say, 'in a secondary and generalized but true sense', that the sacramental species are formed by the totality of the world and that the duration of creation is needed for its consecration.

Years later in *The Phenomenon of Man*, when Teilhard calls the Incarnation 'a prodigious biological operation', it is precisely his own understanding of 'physical' and 'organic' which he has in the back of his mind. Here once more we find a weaving together of material and personal, natural and supernatural. 'As early as in St. Paul and St. John,' he writes, 'we read that to create, to fulfil and to purify the world is, for God, to unify it by uniting it organically with himself. How does he unify it? By partially immersing himself in things, by becoming an "element" and then, from this vantage point in the heart of matter, assuming control and leadership of what we now call evolution. Christ, principle of universal vitality because sprung up as man among men, put himself in the position (maintained ever since) to subdue under himself, to purify, to direct and to give supernatural life to the general ascent of consciousness into which he inserted himself. By a continual act of communion and sublimation, he incorporates into himself the total psychism of the earth.' . . . 'He invests himself organically with the very majesty of his creation.'[39]

We may conclude this first part of our study with two texts on the Eucharist, one from 1944, the other from 1955, the only occasions after 1927 when Teilhard writes of the subject. Both texts are significant because they explicitly link the Eucharist with what Teilhard has now come to designate as 'Christogenesis'. All the sacraments, he says in the first essay, are ultimately referred to the Eucharist because 'through it passes directly the axis of the Incarnation, that is to say the axis of creation.' In its ultimate operation the Eucharist 'is but the expression and manifestation of the divine unifying energy applying itself little by little to every spiritual atom of the universe. To unite ourselves to Christ in the Eucharist, therefore, is *ipso facto* inevitably to incorporate ourselves little by little into a Christogenesis which is itself the soul of universal cosmogenesis.'[40] The second mention of the Eucharist occurs in an essay written only a few weeks before his death, and here, significantly enough, the emphasis falls again upon that early theme of Christ's presence extended to the whole of creation through a prolonging of transubstantiation:

Supposing Christ to be identified with the Omega of evolution, it becomes conceivable that he should radiate physically over the bewildering totality of things; but still more is it inevitable that such radiation should reach a maximum of

86

penetration and activation. Raised up to be the Prime Mover of the evolving movement of complexity-consciousness, the cosmic Christ . . . *ipso facto* acquires and develops in the fullest sense a real omnipresence of transformation. . . . And here it is precisely the Eucharistic mystery itself which, before the astonished gaze of the believer, extends itself into the infinite through a truly universal 'transubstantiation', where the words of consecration fall not only upon the sacrificial bread and wine, but also on the totality of joys and sorrows occasioned in the course of progress by the convergence of the world.[41]

It will not be out of place to note once more that the designation of Christ as 'physical Centre' becomes necessary, in Teilhard's mind, as soon as the universe is seen to be in the state of genesis and to be converging upon an ultimate Pole of attraction. In a static universe, so he believed, the question of Christ as physical Centre would never arise at all, since his Kingship and primacy over creation would be sufficiently established by declarations of a juridical nature. It is therefore modern man's understanding of the world in which he lives which demands a re-examination of the organic relationship between Christ, mankind and the material world. 'Is the Christ of the Gospels,' Teilhard once asked, 'imagined and loved within the dimensions of a Mediterranean world, still capable of embracing and forming the Centre of our prodigiously expanded universe? . . . Without daring, perhaps, to admit to this anxiety yet, there are many (as I know from having come across them all over the world) who nevertheless feel it deep within them. It is for those that I am writing.'[42]

II

Teilhard's Christological enterprise is, as we have seen, an effort to explain how the Christ of revelation may be identified with the Omega of evolution—or, to use his own terminology, how there can be a Christogenesis as well as a cosmogenesis. His foundation and point of departure for such a Christology is his assertion that

Jesus of Nazareth forms a physical Centre for both mankind and the material world, an assertion which he insists is simply another way of expressing the cosmic function attributed to Christ in the epistles of St. Paul. Indeed, his appeals to St. Paul are so frequent and insistent that they tend to create the impression that he is quite illegitimately projecting into the data of revelation the elements of his own cosmological system. Such a facile concordism was in fact far from Teilhard's mind, as we saw at the end of the previous chapter. Yet in spite of his clear affirmations to the contrary, the impression remains, and continues to be a source of criticism and confusion.[43]

There are two reasons for such a misunderstanding. The first is that, in speaking of St. Paul, Teilhard almost always neglects to state explicitly one of the steps in his reasoning process. For example, he will say that what is important for him is Paul's assertion of 'the universal domination of the Incarnate Word over the cosmos', then add that such supremacy corresponds exactly to the function of Omega in his own system of thought. But since this system is founded upon the key concept of cosmogenesis, he is naturally led to discuss Christ's domination over evolution and to use such expressions as 'the Christogenesis of St. Paul'. At this point, however, he usually neglects to inform the reader that what he is now dealing with is no longer the thought of St. Paul, but the thought of St. Paul incorporated into his own hypothesis of a converging universe. In other words, he is again making simultaneous use of two sources of knowledge, one from phenomena and the other from revelation, without bothering to distinguish between them. In his mind this is a perfectly legitimate thing for the Christian to do. It might be said that St. Thomas himself did the same in rethinking revelation in Aristotelian categories. Reality is one as well as our knowledge of it, since faith and reason exist in the same intellect, and Teilhard's interest in any case is centred always upon the object of knowledge and not its psychological process. As for Paul, Teilhard would be the last to claim that the Apostle ever thought of Christ's dominion over the cosmos in present day scientific categories, or could have had the least inkling of modern man's knowledge of a universe in the process of change.

But there is a second reason, deeper and more fundamental, for misunderstanding these appeals to St. Paul. What Teilhard is seeking to do is to incorporate into his own system an aspect of Paul's thought which itself has received relatively little attention and almost no development since the time of the Greek Fathers. The whole question of the relationship between Christ and the cosmos, while never denied, was in the course of time relegated to the background of western theological tradition, and it is only in recent years that the so-called 'cosmic texts' of St. Paul have emerged as subjects of discussion and debate.[44] Teilhard, moreover, compounds the problem by simply referring to these texts, often rather vaguely, with little or no exegesis and hardly a mention of the psychological barrier awaiting someone unacquainted with their cosmic implications. Because such implications are usually presupposed, the unwary reader may well find himself suddenly being led without further ado from one unknown into another unknown, from an aspect of Paul's thought of which he may be ignorant or ill-informed, into an explanation of its relationship to Teilhard's own system, which itself can be as difficult as it is totally new. Consequently it is necessary that we ask at this point what these cosmic texts of Paul can mean and to what extent they support Teilhard's understanding of Christ as physical Centre of the universe. Consider for example the following passage, which is not only typical of Teilhard's approach to Scripture, but is also unusually explicit in the quotation of texts. The year is 1924, when the concept of 'physical Centre' was receiving its first clarification.

The Christ of revelation is quite simply Omega. To demonstrate this fundamental proposition, I need only refer to the long series of Joannine and especially Pauline texts where the physical supremacy of Christ over the universe is affirmed in terms which are magnificent.[45] I cannot enumerate them here. They all come down to these two essential affirmations: 'In eo omnia constant' (Col. 1:17) and 'Ipse est qui replet omnia' (Col. 2:10—cf. Eph. 4:9), so that 'Omnia in omnibus Christus' (Col. 3:11). There we have the very definition of Omega.[46]

The significance of this passage is that it clearly underlines the two main points upon which Teilhard bases his *rapprochement* between Scripture and his hypothesis of a converging universe, namely that in Paul's thought there exists a relationship between Christ and mankind which is 'physical', and that Paul extends such a relationship to the whole of creation, including therefore all that is material. Let us briefly examine these two central affirmations.

Paul's thought on the 'physical' relationship between Christ and mankind has received increased attention in recent years due to the modern trend towards a strong realism in explaining his use of the term 'Body of Christ'. Far from interpreting it as a metaphor signifying the collectivity of Christians as an organization, Pauline scholars, Catholic and Protestant alike, explain it as a literal designation of the risen Christ in all his concrete reality. Lucien Cerfaux affirms again and again that for Paul the faithful do not belong to a 'moral body', 'a mystical Christ', but rather belong to the real organism of his risen Person. Essentially the same position is held by Pierre Benoit, J. A. T. Robinson and many others.[47] In fact, the only objection today to this realistic thesis seems to be from those who argue not from exegesis but from the apparent lack of harmony between such an understanding of Paul and the fuller theological development in some of the Fathers and especially in the encyclical *Mystici Corporis*. These objections, however, seem to be an example of what has already occurred often enough, a simple misunderstanding on the part of theologians of thought patterns discovered by the exegetes.[48]

There are three sources for this realistic thinking of Paul. First of all, because he is a Hebrew writing on religious themes, Paul uses the word 'body' not as a neutral element in the body-soul composite of Greek anthropology, but rather as an animated and corporeal person, whose thoughts and desires are contained and revealed under the sensible aspect of bodily experience. Or to look at it from another viewpoint, because Paul is a Hebrew, 'he cannot imagine a man without his body, and therefore associates the body with the whole work of man's ultimate salvation.'[49] Using the word 'body' in a religious context, the Hebrew mentality includes in that term the whole person, with emphasis on what is sensible and somatic.

The second concept influencing Paul's thought, one quite familiar to the Old Testament, is that of the corporate personality. It is now generally accepted that the Semites conceived their nation or community, including its past, present and future members, as a single individual, who could be represented in turn by any one member of the nation. As a result there was frequently a natural oscillation in speech between group and individual, as can be seen for example in the Servant Songs of Deutero-Isaiah. Originating most probably from the role of the chief in Israel's tribal life, this concept is most important for understanding Paul's presentation of Christ as the new Adam who died and rose again with vicarious efficacy.[50]

Finally there is the influence upon Paul's thought from the Eucharistic Body of Christ. In I Corinthians 10:17 he directly bases the unity of the faithful on the Eucharist: 'The one bread makes us one body, though we are many in number, because we all partake of the same bread.' A realistic interpretation would understand Paul to say here that in so far as the community *feeds* on the Eucharist, it actually *becomes* the glorified Body of the risen and ascended Christ. Such a jump from 'feeding on' to 'becoming' is taken by no other New Testament writer, all of whom must have been as familiar with the words of institution as Paul himself, and it would therefore seem to demand some prior experience on Paul's part. One exegete has speculated that this experience must have been the encounter on the Damascus road. 'The appearance on which Paul's whole faith and apostleship was founded was the revelation of the resurrection Body of Christ, not as an individual but as the Christian community.'[51]

Along with this wide agreement on the realism of Paul's thought regarding the Body of Christ, there is also general acceptance of the fact that this thought itself underwent a significant development between the time he wrote Romans, probably in the winter of 57-8, and his arrival in Rome in the spring of 61, where he was to write the captivity epistles. At the end of the major epistles, says Lucien Cerfaux, the thought of Paul is that all Christians as a group, in so far as they are a spiritual organism, are mystically identified with the Body of Christ. It would go beyond the bounds of Paul's thought in these letters, he continues, either to identify this organism with the Person of Christ or to speak of a 'Mystical Body'. In the key texts of I Corinthians 12 and Romans 12 Paul concentrates on the fact that every Christian is united really and corporally to the risen Body of Christ. Within this limited thought pattern Paul can only say that all Christians together must be the Body of Christ. How this is possible is simply not his concern at this point.[52] In the captivity epistles, however, there appear quite suddenly two new dimensions. First there is the use of the word 'Church' to designate all those united to the Body of Christ, and secondly there is an emphasis upon their collective unity which Paul begins to vest more and more with the attributes of a living person.

Until now the word 'Church' has served almost always as a designation for local communities. In the major epistles it had almost never appeared in the ecumenical meaning we take for granted today, that of universal Church, the entire assembly of Christians.[53] Originally linked in Paul's mind with the Old Testament concept of 'God's People', the term 'Church of God' had gradually been applied by him to the individual Churches he had founded. Not until Colossians 1:18 did it suddenly take on a strong ecumenical sense, and it did so there as a result of a synthesis of the themes of Head and Body which seem hitherto to have undergone separate developments in Paul's mind.

The Head theme, for example, when it appeared in I Corinthians 11:2-4, was used to express not the union of Christians with or in Christ but a certain hierarchy of subordination: 'head' in the sense of 'superior'. Thus in I Corinthians 12:21 the 'head' is simply a member of the body and is not identified with Christ at all. The Body theme, on the other hand, had always been used to express the idea of unity which was central to Paul's concept of salvation. Through physical contact with the physical Body-Person of Christ in baptism and the Eucharist, the Christian received as through a

92

channel the life of the Spirit, and so in a very real sense became Christ, his members, his Body. The linking of these two themes of Head and Body, therefore, was natural enough when it occurred for the first time in Colossians 1:18. Paul was emphasizing the superiority of Christ as Head of the heavenly powers, and there was an easy passage from the use of 'head' in the sense of 'superior' to its use in the physical sense as Christ himself, Head of his Body the Church. The word 'head', moreover, when applied to the body, already contained the idea of vital principle and source of nourishment.[54]

It is in the fourth chapter of Ephesians, however, that one finds the full implications of this linking of the three concepts of Head, Body and Church. At the start of the chapter Paul affirms the collective unity of Christians along with their organic diversity (vv. 3-11), followed by an emphasis on the new idea that the Body of Christ grows and perfects itself. What enables Paul to assert this is precisely his identifying Christ not with the Body but with the Head. The Head does not grow, yet it is from the fullness of perfection already present in him that there comes the vital energy responsible for the Body's growth (vv. 12-16). This distinction between Christ as Head and his Church as Body had never before been made so strongly.

Nevertheless, the intense realism of the Pauline concept of Body of Christ is in no way lessened. He can still affirm without hesitation that the universal Church is identified with the physical Body of Christ in heaven.[55] This he can do because the ontological distinction which he now sees in no way excludes a 'mystical' identification at one and the same time. The physical Body of Christ pours out its life on Christians and these become his Body in the sense that the mystically present cause is attributed to the effect. The Church quite literally is Christ's Body because she is composed of all Christians who in their material personality are united to the risen Body-Person of Christ and receive through him the new life of the Spirit. It would be vain, says Pierre Benoit, even false, to force Paul's terminology here to mean exclusively either Christ's physical Body and Spirit, or his Body the Church, which is his Spirit communicated to men. In Ephesians Paul means both together, indissolubly united: the individual Body of Christ grown to include all Christians united to him in their own bodies, with the fullness of the Spirit flowing from the Head down through all the members.[56]

From this very cursory summary of a modern exegetical trend, we may conclude that up to 1927 Teilhard's thought is much closer to the earlier and less precise meaning which Paul gave to 'Body of Christ'. His emphasis falls always upon the simple fact of the Christian's physical union with the Body-Person of Christ, and he remains unconcerned in this early period with the Church's own distinctive collective unity precisely as 'Church'. This is not to say that the phenomenon of the Church is to have no interest for him. On the contrary, as we shall see in chapter five, it occupies a central place in his Christology as the point of contact, already in time, between the world in evolution and mankind's destiny at the Parousia. But in this context it is not to Paul's concept 'Body of Christ' that Teilhard links the Church, but to 'phylum of love', 'axis of progress', and 'Christified part of the world', concepts drawn from his own particular system of thought. Moreover, whereas the concept 'Body of Christ' is always linked in Paul's mind to Christ's redemptive death and Resurrection and only implicitly to the Incarnation, the same concept in Teilhard is almost synonymous with the Incarnation and hence closer to the Greek Fathers, whose theology developed at length the Incarnation's role in God's plan of salvation.[57] It is because of this difference in emphasis that Teilhard finds it quite easy to reach the cosmos directly through 'Body of Christ' without mention of the Church at all. For the same reason it is not Christ's relationship to his Church which he associates with the Eucharist, but rather, as we have seen, Christ's relationship to the cosmos. This fact now puts us in a position to ask our second question regarding Teilhard's appeal to St. Paul. To what extent can Paul be said to extend the physical relationship between Christ and mankind to the whole of creation, including therefore all that is material?

The literature dealing directly with an answer to this second question is relatively limited. The three so-called 'cosmic texts' of St. Paul (Romans 8:19-23, Colossians 1:15-20, and Ephesians 1:9-10, 22-3) have usually not been approached by exegetes with the precise aim of determining Christ's relationship to the material world. Speaking of the passage in Colossians, Henri Bouillard has remarked that in his opinion neither theology nor exegesis has as yet given any satisfactory explanation of what Paul means when he places Christ in relationship to the whole of the cosmos.[58] Consequently what we shall attempt here is merely to indicate a direction now being taken by a number of authors currently aware of the problem. We may begin with the earliest of the texts to be considered, Romans 8:19-23. The context is a presentation of the motives for hope possessed by the Christian in the face of suffering and death. Paul has just said that if we suffer with Christ we shall share his glory and that this glory with Christ will more than make up for the sorrows of this life. He then continues:

For creation is waiting with eager longing for the revelation of the sons of God: if it has been condemned to frustration, —not through its own fault but because of him who so condemned it,—it also has hope of being set free in its turn from the bondage of decay and of entering into the freedom of the glory of the children of God. We know indeed that the whole of creation has been groaning until now in an agony of birth. More than that, we ourselves who already possess in the Spirit a foretaste of the future, groan also in our hearts, waiting for the redemption of our bodies.

What is important for us here is first of all Paul's insistence that it is the *whole* of creation, man therefore included, which is the object of redemption, and secondly that it is precisely through the bodies of men that redemption extends to the rest of creation. The use of the Greek word *ktisis* to designate all things created is quite common both in the Septuagint and the New Testament, and is so used by Paul himself in Romans 1:25. Following this interpretation, the relationship between 'creation' and 'sons of God' would be that of the whole to the part, the hope of mankind already being included in the hope of creation. In verse 23, therefore, Paul would be moving from the general to the particular, and asserting in his own way what all biblical authors maintained, that man is the summit of creation and that somehow his own salvation affects the whole of the universe. This is further substantiated by the Greek word *phthora* in verse 21, which means 'physical decay' and which not only emphasizes the material solidarity of man and nature in the first Adam's sin, but also implies an ontological effect upon the whole of creation from the second Adam's work of redemption. Hence the significance of the word 'glory', which in this eschatological context denotes the active and visible presence of God himself, already communicated to the humanity of Christ through the Resurrection and Ascension, and destined to be communicated to humanity as a whole at the general resurrection of the body. This 'glory' of God will then radiate from the Body of Christ and the bodies of men to the universe in its entirety, 'so that God may be all in all.'[59]

This restoration of the entire universe in Christ, barely hinted at in the above passage from Romans, became a few years later a dominant theme of Colossians and Ephesians, both written while Paul was captive in Rome. The occasion for the first letter was a threat to the Church of Colossae, which began to be troubled by dangerous speculations on the heavenly powers, basically Jewish in origin but highly coloured by Hellenistic philosophy. So much importance was being attributed to these 'powers' in their control of the universe and the course of events that the supremacy of Christ would seem to be compromised. The reaction of Paul was instantaneous, almost belligerent. His letter to Colossae asserts with vigour the supremacy of Christ as *Kyrios*, Lord and Master, over the whole universe. In the famous two-strophed hymn of Colossians 1:15-20 Paul goes back to the pre-existence of Christ with the Father, in whose image he is the source as well as the instrument and final end of creation. The Incarnation, crowned by the triumph of the Resurrection, is seen as placing the human nature of Christ at the head not only of the whole human race but also of the entire created universe, the latter indirectly concerned in the salvation of man as it had been in his fall.

He is the image of the unseen God, born before every creation.
In him all things were created.
Heavenly and earthly, seen and unseen,
Thrones, dominions, princedoms and powers—
All things were created through him and for him.
He takes precedence over all and in him all things subsist.

He is also Head of his Body the Church;
For he is the beginning, first-born from among the dead,
That he might come to stand first in everything.
It was God's good pleasure to make reside in him all the Plentitude
And to win back all things through him and for him,
  on earth and in heaven,
Making peace with them through his blood shed on the cross.

For many exegetes today the 'Plenitude' of Christ in this extra-ordinary text, his Pleroma, represents in Paul's mind the extension of Christ's work of redemption to the whole cosmos, the whole of creation. The term itself was quite common in the Stoic vocabulary of the time, and designated God's penetration and envelopment of the material world. In Colossians and Ephesians Paul strips it of its stoic pantheism and gives it a content familiar to the Old Testament, that of the cosmos filled with the creative presence of God. The 'fullness' which resides in Christ, therefore, is 'the plenitude of being', including both the fullness of divinity and the fullness of the universe. Christ is God, and through his work of redemption he unites to himself not only redeemed humanity, for which Paul reserves the term 'Body', but also the whole of the cosmos which is humanity's dwelling place.[60]

In the above text, moreover, as well as in the corresponding passage in Ephesians to be seen in a moment, the multiplication of prepositional phrases ('through him, in him, for him') and the repetition of 'all things', emphasize again that the dependence of the universe on Christ is universal and absolute. Joseph Huby, in his commentary on Colossians, has accurately summarized this all-inclusiveness of Christ's Lordship: 'In him all has been created as in a supreme Centre of unity, harmony and cohesion, which gives to the world its sense, its value and therefore its reality. Or, to use another metaphor, he is the focus, the "meeting-point" as Lightfoot puts it, where all the fibres and generative energies of the universe are organized and gathered together. Were someone to see the whole of the universe, past, present and future, in a single instantaneous glimpse, he would see all beings ontologically suspended from Christ and completely unintelligible apart from him. [61] These very pointed remarks bring us now to our third text, Ephesians 1:9-10, 22-3:

> It was [God's] loving design, centred in Christ, to re-establish all things in him when the fullness of time should come, all that is in heaven, all that is on earth, summed up in him. . . . [God] has put all things under his feet and made him the indisputable Head of the Church which is his Body, the Plenitude of him who is everywhere and in all things complete.

In this brief passage some commentators see a remarkable development in Paul's thought. There is at the very start a description of God's plan of salvation as a 're-establishment', a 'summing up' of all things in Christ, which is unusual and striking because the root meaning of the Greek word *anakephalaioomai* is 'to *head* up'. This is the word responsible for the 'recapitulation' theory of Greek theology as well as for the oft-quoted Latin translation *instaurare omnia in Christo*. It is quite possible from the context that Paul's intention here is to situate squarely within a cosmic framework his Body-of-Christ theme, and at the same time to present the relationship between Christ and the cosmos as an extension of the physical and sacramental relationship between Christ and the members of his Church. Not only is Christ Lord of the universe, he is also its 'Head'. This hypothesis seems to be confirmed by the verses that follow, in which the Church, as the risen Body of Christ, becomes extended as it were, swelled in Paul's mind and equated with the dimensions of the Pleroma, 'the Plenitude of him who is everywhere and in all things complete.' Moreover, the 'fullness of time' in which this Plenitude is to be realized refers most probably to *both* comings of Christ, his Incarnation and work of Redemption in time and his Parousia at the end of time. Thus, in Ephesians 3:19 the Plenitude is seen to be ultimately the Plenitude of God, into which the love of Christ will eventually bring both cosmos and Church in the final and definitive achievement of cosmic as well as salvation history.[62]

At this point it should be recalled that the purpose of our brief study of St. Paul has been to enquire not into the development of Teilhard's Christology but into its starting point. The interpretations we have followed are in no sense universally accepted,[63] but they are representative of a direction well established today in both Catholic and Protestant exegesis.[64] It seems to be certain that Paul saw some type of physical relationship between Christ and the members of his Body-Person. To what extent he also believed that through man this relationship was extended to the whole of creation is still an open question. Yet in the context in which they were made, it is extremely difficult to give his affirmations of Christ's Lordship over the Pleroma a meaning which is juridical and purely extrinsic. The source of the whole difficulty here is, of course, that Paul's message is a message of salvation. He interests himself in the world of nature and man's relationships to that world only in so far as these have religious meaning. He has no desire to elaborate a cosmology as such, and hence no intention whatsoever of explaining *how* Christ is Lord of the cosmos. For Teilhard, on the other hand, a cosmology is at the heart of his whole system, and his appeals to St. Paul are made with the precise purpose of explaining this 'how' and of using the Apostle's thought as a point of departure for his own vision of the world. 'All the same,' he once protested to a close friend, 'I have the right to speak like St. Paul!'[65] What is being emphasized here is simply the fact that, as far as the texts of St. Paul are concerned, the way he speaks is legitimate.

Teilhard's understanding of Christ as physical Centre is put forward, therefore, as a plausible explanation of what Paul's thought can mean when confronted with modern man's knowledge of the universe in which he lives. Fundamental to this whole effort is the elemental concept of a world in which all things participate in a single physical and organic unity, a unity embracing the natural and the supernatural, the spiritual as well as the material. 'Let us return to Paul,' said Teilhard in a 1930 lecture. 'Let us remember that the supernatural nourishes itself on everything, and let us accept fully those magnificent perspectives according to which the Christ of St. Paul appears to us as he in whom all has been created and he in whom the whole world finds its stability, with all its height and depth, its grandeur and greatness, with all that is material and all that is spiritual.' This in turn means seeing everything 'from the point of view of the organization of the Pleroma (which is the only true point of view from which the world can be understood).'[66] The Body-Person of Christ thus becomes the Pole of unity towards which all converges, the Milieu within which this convergence takes place, and the physical Centre holding in existence all the radii of creation.

It would not be too much to say, in conclusion, that this physical influence of Christ over the whole of cosmic reality provides a master key to the many-chambered edifice of Teilhard's Christology. Essentially such an influence is an extension and further explicitation, within a different system of thought, of traditional teaching concerning the Body of Christ as physical instrumental cause of grace. If all grace is the grace of Christ, of which his Body is physical instrumental cause, then it follows that all grace has its effect upon men (and indirectly upon the material world) through the physical mediation of Christ's Body-Person. St. Thomas, interestingly enough, while clearly teaching such physical instrumental causality,[67] tended to shy away from the above conclusion, apparently because he felt unable to explain how Christ could actually come into physical contact with all men in every time and place. The Body of Christ, he said, by reason of its union with the Godhead, possesses a spiritual power which operates not through physical but through 'spiritual contact'.[68]

Yet such a distinction hardly solves the difficulty. From the fact that contact with Christ must be spiritual, it does not follow that physical contact is rendered unnecessary, for it is precisely with a Body-Person that such spiritual contact is made. St. Thomas himself implied as much when he said in another context that all grace is somehow conferred in virtue of the Holy Eucharist,[69] though unlike Teilhard he never seems to have connected the Eucharist with Christ's physical omnipresence. One theologian has suggested that in the case of Christ spiritual contact should rather be considered as a *mode* of physical contact, and he cites as an example of this the encounter in the Gospels between Christ and the woman with the hæmorrhage. Her spiritual contact with Christ consisted in an intensification of her physical contact in and through an act of supernatural faith.[70]

What St. Thomas lacked in dealing with this question was modern scientific data on the physical interdependence of every element in the universe. Such an interdependence is always in the forefront of Teilhard's mind,[71] though he himself was equipped neither as a philosopher nor as a theologian to handle satisfactorily the metaphysical implications of this fact. Indeed, Maurice Blondel is one of the few philosophers and Karl Rahner one of the few theologians to have dealt with the subject at all. Blondel wrote a whole philosophical treatise in which he tried to explain how Christ is the substantial 'bond' linking together the universe and giving life to all creation.[72] He complained a number of times of the extreme deficiency of the notions of body and matter current in the early part of the century. Not only did he believe that all men depended upon each other, but that there is even in one sense interpenetration. 'We are literally made of one another without ceasing to be individual personalities. . . . The problem of the Incarnation appears to me (perhaps even antecedently to every other philosophical question) as the touchstone of a true cosmology, of an integral metaphysics. . . . I share the ideas and the sentiments of Father Teilhard de Chardin in the face of the Christological problem. Before the broader horizons created by science we cannot, without betraying Catholicism, remain satisfied with a feeble and limited Christology, in which Christ appears almost as an accident of history, isolated like a stranger amid the crushing and hostile immensity of the universe.'[73]

Fifty years after Blondel, Karl Rahner has broached the same problem in a number of different theological contexts. Writing on the meaning of death, he says that 'the soul as united to the body must also have some relationship to that "whole" of which the body is part, i.e. to that wholeness which constitutes the unity of the material universe. The unity of the world is certainly not to be conceived as a mere summarizing abstraction, resulting from the process of human thought; nor does it reside merely in the mutual extrinsic actions and reactions of individual things upon each other. No metaphysics (we have in mind the scholastic metaphysics of prime matter and of the analogous·concept of individual material beings) could accept such a superficial view. Yet it is impossible, within the framework of such concepts, to penetrate the problem of this real ontological unity of the universe ... that basic oneness of the world, so difficult to grasp, yet so very real, by which all things in the world are related and communicate anteriorly to any mutual influence upon each other.'74 He exhibits the same preoccupation in discussing the unity between creation and redemption: 'Man cannot fulfil his spiritual or indeed his supernatural life without embodying this fulfilment in material reality; without a turning towards the world, an infusing of the spiritual into the material. Hence the world is really a unity, one thing. The actual interdependence of one thing upon everything else corresponds to the original creative will of God, and objectifies itself in the fundamental mutual relationship based on the essence of individual things themselves.'75 Finally there is a passage from one of Rahner's essays on Christology which will provide an appropriate ending to this present chapter:

> The Incarnation of the Logos (however much we must insist on the fact that it is itself an historical, unique event in an essentially historical world) appears *ontologically* (not merely 'morally' and *a posteriori*) as the unambiguous goal of the movement of creation as a whole, in relation to which everything prior is merely a preparation of scenery. It appears as oriented from the very first to this point in which God achieves once and for all both the greatest proximity to and distance from what is other than he (while at the same time giving it being). . . . Here we must remember that the world is a unity

in which everything is linked together with everything else. When anyone grasps a portion of the world for his own life's history, at one and the same time he takes upon himself the world as a whole for his personal environment. Thus it would not be extravagant, as long as it is done with prudence, to conceive the evolution of the world as an orientation *towards* Christ, and to represent the various stages of this ascending movement as culminating in him as their apex. The only danger to be avoided is the suggestion that such evolution is an ascent which the world accomplishes by forces which are wholly its own. If what St. Paul says in Col. 1:15 is true and not softened by some moralistic interpretation, if furthermore the world as a whole, including therefore its physical reality, is actually in process of reaching in and through Christ that final state in which God is all in all, then the line of thought we are developing here cannot be entirely false.[76]

CHAPTER FOUR

THE REDEMPTION AND THE MYSTERY OF EVIL

CHRIST'S DEATH AND RESURRECTION AS A VICTORY OVER AMBIGUITY IN PROGRESS

The effort of Teilhard de Chardin to assuage modern man's anxiety by elaborating a guarantee of evolution's success is ultimately founded, as we have seen, upon the physical relationship between Christ, mankind, and the material world. It is this relationship, originating in the data of revelation concerning the Incarnation and the Eucharist, which is the point of departure for Teilhard's assertion that creation is not simply a cosmogenesis, but is more accurately a Christogenesis. To this fundamental concept of Christ as physical Centre of evolution he now tries to relate the data of revelation concerning Christ's redemptive death and Resurrection. More concretely this means coming to terms with the existence of evil in this world of which Christ is physical Centre. There is not only the enigma of suffering and death, but there is the deeper mystery of moral evil, and this for Teilhard means especially that capacity of man to endanger the whole movement of evolution by a refusal of Omega. 'In no way does it follow from the position taken up here,' he writes at the end of *The Phenomenon of Man*, 'that the success of hominization is necessary, inevitable and certain.' There is indeed 'the possibility of seeing with certainty certain precise directions of the future,' but only, he adds with emphasis, '*if all goes well*.' For 'however persistent and imperious the cosmic energy of evolution may be in its activity, it finds itself intrinsically influenced in its effects by two uncertainties . . . chance at the bottom and freedom at the top.'[1]

Christian revelation, moreover, gives to the whole problem of evil a totally new dimension. For Christian faith not only reveals an Incarnation; it reveals also that the work of Christ in this present order is a redemption, a deliverance from evil and above all from sin. Consequently if the *total* mystery of Christ is to be rethought in terms of *genèse* (and this is what Teilhard is attempting) then a relationship must be established between Christ's role as Omega of evolution and his role as Redeemer. In a 1942 essay Teilhard states quite clearly what he wishes this relationship to be:

> In the dogma of redemption Christian thinking and piety have up to now chiefly emphasized (evidently for historical reasons) the idea of reparation and atonement. Christ has been regarded chiefly as a Lamb burdened with the sins of the world, and the world itself chiefly as a fallen mass. Yet from the very start this dogma has also included another aspect, a positive one, that of reconstruction or re-creation. A new heaven and a new earth: even for an Augustine this was the prized result of the Sacrifice of the Cross.
>
> Is it not conceivable . . . that these two aspects of Christ's power, one positive, the other negative, should reverse their respective importance in the outlook and piety of the faithful, guided as they are by the Spirit of God? Certainly in our own time, under pressure of events and modern discoveries, the material world and all connected realities are becoming objects of growing interest to followers of the Gospel. This explains a certain 'humanistic' renewal in religion which, without ignoring in any way the dark side of creation, prefers nonetheless to emphasize that side which is luminous and clear. What we are in fact witnessing and taking part in today is an irresistible growth in Christian optimism. . . .
>
> More or less consciously we are all waiting and searching for a sudden expansion of religion. Ought this not to come from a renewal of Christology in which the notion of reparation would be preserved in its integrity and yet recede *in ordine naturae* to second place in the Incarnate Word's work of salvation? *Primario* to lead creation to its fulfilment in union with God, and for this purpose *secundario* to conquer the forces of evil,

regression and dispersion. No longer first to expiate and in addition to restore, but first to create (or to create still more perfectly) and for this purpose to fight against and to atone for evil. . . . In other words Christ the Redeemer, without in the least losing the marks of his Passion, would ultimately be seen in the fullness of his power as Christ the Evolver.[2]

In the following pages we shall deal at length with this approach to the mystery of redemption. Before we start, however, we should note the manner in which Teilhard links this approach to his more general approach to the problem of evil as a whole. This problem is dealt with in two stages. First he tries to explain the place of physical suffering and death in a world in evolution. Into this explanation he then incorporates the positive aspect of redemption which he has stressed above. There then follows a second stage, which is an attempt to deal with moral evil and the abuse of human freedom, and here Teilhard will face the negative aspect of redemption which, as he has just said, he wishes to preserve in its integrity but in a place of secondary importance. As we shall see, however, reparation for sin does not in fact have such a secondary place in his Christology; in spite of his good intentions he can find for it no place at all. What is more significant still, his lack of success in this regard eventually results in an impasse in his whole evolutionary system, an impasse which Teilhard himself apparently never saw, and which in the end constitutes what surely must be called the supreme irony of his life's work. With this rather general orientation we may now proceed to examine in turn each of the two stages of Teilhard's dialectic.

I

There is a double purpose to the first stage of Teilhard's thought on the mystery of evil. He first wants to remove the scandal of suffering and death in so far as they constitute for man a purely intellectual problem. He then wants to treat them in their total reality as human problems and to assign to them a definite positive value for human life and work. He accomplishes his first purpose by situating the existence of physical evil squarely within his own phenomenological analysis of evolution. 'You might think that a world moving towards a greater centration of consciousness should experience nothing but joy. Just the opposite I say. It is precisely a world such as this which ought most naturally and necessarily to experience suffering. Nothing is more blissful than the attainment of union; neither is anything more painful than its pursuit.'[3] From an evolutionary perspective three forms of evil present themselves as a structural part of cosmic development: the evil of growth, the evil of disorder and failure, and the ultimate evil of death. If these three forms are once seen in the context of *genèse*, then 'earth, this microscopic planet on which we are crushed together, no longer looks like a stupid prison where we are all likely to die of suffocation.'[4]

There is, first of all, the inevitability of pain arising from human growth. All progress in the direction of higher consciousness must express itself in terms of work and effort. Under the veil of security and apparent harmony which envelops the advance of man in the noosphere, there is in reality a universe in which the human struggle towards unity is fraught with hardship. For the movement of life is upward, and man, precisely because he can reflect upon this movement, is able to experience both the difficulty of the ascent and the natural inclination to halt. There is indeed a joy in growth which distracts us from the pain, but the pain is always there. 'Arrangement and centration: a twofold and interconnected operation which, like the ascent of a mountain or the conquest of space, can only be accomplished objectively if it is rigorously paid for—for reasons and at charges which, if only we knew them, would enable us to penetrate the secret of the world around us.'[5]

The mind is not unduly troubled by this evil arising from human growth. It immediately tends to rebel, however, when confronted in nature with the evil of disorder and failure. Teilhard wished to show that this too is inevitable, that a world in evolution and a world without disorder are contradictory concepts. If God has chosen that his creation should reach its fulfilment in and through a cosmogenesis, then frustration in all its forms is a necessary consequence. The problem resides not in the Creator but in the structure of created being, and is 'relentlessly imposed by the play of large numbers at the heart of a multitude undergoing organization.'[6] This last statement, from an appendix added to *The Phenomenon of Man* in late 1948, is developed at greater length in a passage from another essay written earlier that same year:

Within the old concept of a cosmos supposed to have come in finished form from the hand of the Creator, it was understandably difficult to reconcile a partially bad world with the existence of a God who was both good and all powerful. But . . . in a universe undergoing cosmogenesis . . . God can go about his work of creation in only one way: by arranging and slowly unifying (through his attractive influence and his use of the tentative interplay of large numbers) an immense multitude of elements, at first infinitely numerous, extremely simple and scarcely conscious, then gradually more singular, more complex and finally gifted with reflection.

Now what is the inevitable counterpart of any success obtained by following a process of this type if not the necessity of a certain amount of waste? Disharmony or physical decomposition among the pre-living, suffering among the living, sin in the domain of freedom: there is no order under formation which does not at every stage imply disorder. There is nothing, I repeat, in this ontological (or more exactly, ontogenetic) condition of participated being which lessens the dignity or limits the omnipotence of the Creator. Neither is there anything savouring of what could be called Manichaeanism. Pure unorganized multiplicity is not bad in itself; but because it is multiple, i.e. essentially subject in its arrangement to the play of chance, it is absolutely impossible for it to progress towards unity without producing evil in its wake through statistical necessity. *Necessarium est ut adveniant scandala.*[7]

For the present let us suspend judgment on the inclusion of sin in this statistical process and limit our attention to the process itself.

Fifteen years earlier Teilhard had expressed himself more concretely on the same subject. In a bunch of flowers, he wrote, it would be surprising to find sickly blossoms because they have all been picked one by one and assembled with art. On a tree, however, which has to fight the internal hazards of growth and the external hazards of climate and time, broken branches and bruised blossoms are all in the right place. They reflect the difficulties undergone by the trunk in process of growth. Similarly, in a universe where every creature formed a self-contained whole, willed for its own sake and theoretically transposable at will, we should find great difficulty in justifying to our intellect the presence of individuals painfully cut short in their hopes and possibilities. On the other hand, if the world represents a conquest still under way, if at our birth we are in fact thrown into the thick of a battle, then we can well understand that, for the success of the total effort, pain is inevitable. 'Looked upon experimentally at our own level, the world is an immense groping, an immense search, an immense attack; it can only progress at the cost of many failures and much pain. The sufferers, whatever the reason for their suffering, are the reflection of this austere yet noble condition. They do not constitute elements which are useless or diminished. They are simply the parts which pay for the progress and triumph of the whole. They are soldiers who have fallen on the field of honour.'[8]

The test, however, of such an intellectual justification of suffering is whether or not it can remove that ultimate scandal to the human mind, the existence of death. Not all the branches of a tree are broken nor all the blossoms bruised, but in the end they all must die. 'If by chance we escape, to a greater or lesser extent, the critical forms of these assaults from without, which appear deep within us and irresistibly destroy the strength, light and love by which we live, there still remains that slow, essential deterioration which we cannot escape: old age little by little robbing us of ourselves and pushing us on towards the end. . . . In death, as in an ocean, all our slow or swift diminishments flow out and merge. Death is the sum and consummation of all our diminishments: it is *evil itself*—pure physical evil in so far as it results organically from that multiplicity of matter in which we are immersed, but moral evil too, in so far as this disordered multiplicity, the source of all strife and all corruption, is propagated either in society or in ourselves by the wrong use of our freedom.'[9]

Again let us pass over for the moment the reference to death as moral evil and focus our attention upon Teilhard's treatment of its physical aspect. 'As long as our constructions rest with all their weight upon the earth,' he once wrote, 'they will vanish with the earth. The radical defect of all forms of belief in progress, as they are expressed in positivist credos, is that they do not definitely eliminate death. What is the use of detecting a focus of any sort in the van of evolution if that focus can and must one day disintegrate?'[10] Hence the importance at this point of his 'fundamental option', which as we have seen constitutes the whole second stratum of his thought. This is his 'psychological act of faith', his postulate on the level of reason of a divine personal Omega, whose existence here and now is alone able to guarantee evolution's ultimate success. This supreme personal Centre is in turn the real object of 'man's desire for survival', a desire which for Teilhard is the mainspring of all human activity.[11] As we saw in chapter one, he was convinced that man cannot in his heart accept ultimate death. Such acceptance would render unintelligible the whole upward movement of consciousness, and place man himself in an absurd universe in which all meaningful progress in the noosphere would necessarily come to a halt.[12]

In an evolutionary process, therefore, in which all persons are destined in and through Omega to reach perfection precisely as persons, death must in some mysterious way contribute to the growth of personality. Teilhard explains this by the specific effect of death upon the operation of radial energy in the noosphere. Radial energy, it will be remembered, is that which tends to draw an element forward towards greater complexity (and therefore greater consciousness), while tangential energy tends simply to link an element to other elements on the same level of organization. True evolutionary progress resides in radial energy, which in man has become psychosocial, urging him forward to ever higher forms of interpersonal communion. In the material world, however, radial energy is not independent, but operates 'only in virtue of the tangential energies of arrangement and thus under certain conditions of spatial juxtaposition.'[13] The significance of human death is precisely the cessation of this dependence of radial upon tangential energy. 'Once formed, a reflective centre can no longer change except by entering deeper into itself [i.e. by growth in its power of reflective consciousness]. To outward appearance, admittedly, man becomes corrupted just like any other animal. But here and there we find an inverse function of the phenomenon. By death, in the animal, the radial is reabsorbed in the tangential, while in man it escapes and is liberated from it. We are thus freed from entropy by a reversal to Omega. Here indeed is a hominization of death itself!'[14] Teilhard explains himself further as follows:

Starting therefore with the grains of thought which form the true and indestructible atoms of its stuff, the universe—a universe well-defined in its outcome—goes on building itself over our heads in the inverse direction of matter which vanishes. The universe is a collector and conserver not of mechanical energy, as we supposed, but of persons. All around us, one by one, like a continual invisible emanation, 'souls' break away, carrying upwards their incommunicable charge of consciousness. One by one, yet not in isolation. For in the case of each, because of the very nature of Omega, there can be only one possible point of final emergence—that point at which, under the synthesizing action of union which personalizes, the noosphere (coiling up its elements round themselves at the same time as it coils up round itself) will reach collectively its point of convergence—at the 'end of the world'.[15]

Thus, in Teilhard's system, the function of death is to act as a metamorphosis between two different stages of personality. Death for man must be considered as one of those 'critical points' in evolution, a profound transformation in nature by which something quite new is produced. 'In every domain, when anything exceeds a certain measurement, it suddenly changes its aspect, condition or nature.'[16] Man's death shows that radial energy's development must undergo discontinuity at the personal level just as it does at all other levels. Having reached a certain limit of centration, the human person is confronted with a threshold, the 'death barrier', which he must cross before he can enter into the sphere of a Centre of a higher order. Death thus becomes a second threshold of reflection, comparable in its effect upon the individual to the crossing of that first threshold of reflection, the hominization of the species. Essentially it is not so much a separation of matter and spirit as the occasion for a new relationship between them. 'What is waiting for us, then, is the pain of being carried away into the prodigious mass of humanity,—or what is even greater, the pain of escaping, either by a slow or quick bodily decay, from that whole limited framework of experience within which we were born.'[17] This understanding of death as a metamorphosis is the reason that Teilhard could write from the trenches of the first world war: 'I feel there is something to be said for a healthy joy in death, for its harmony with life, for the intimate connection (at the same time as separation) between the world of the dead and that of the living as well as for their mutual union within the same cosmos.' And to a close friend he wrote in 1920: 'Strictly speaking, there are no separated souls; there are only souls which change their "sphere" in a world where everything is related to everything else.'[18]

It should be noted again that up to this point Teilhard's purpose has been simply to remove the intellectual scandal of suffering and death. He has been trying to show that in the context of cosmogenesis they no longer appear to be absurd when confronted with God's goodness and power. Yet physical evil is not a mere intellectual problem; it touches the heart of man, causes anguish and despair, and has power to empty life of all hope and joy. 'It is one thing rationally to explain the compossibility of God and evil, and quite another thing to bear up under suffering of body and mind.'[19] Teilhard is speaking here from experience. 'He was indeed an optimist,' writes a fellow Jesuit and close friend, 'in attributing to the universe a sense of direction in spite of the existence of evil and in spite of appearances; but in daily life, in what concerned him personally, he was far from being an optimist. He bore with patience, it is true, trials that might have proved too much for the strongest of us, but how often in intimate conversation have I found him depressed and with almost no heart to carry on. . . . He was at times prostrated by fits of weeping and appeared to be on the verge of despair. But, supported by his strong will and abandoning himself to Christ, who was greater than all and the whole purpose of his existence, he hid his suffering and took up his work once more, if not in joy at least in the hope that his own personal vocation ought thereby to be fulfilled.'[20]

Suffering, therefore, while ceasing to be an intellectual problem, remains for Teilhard the deepest of mysteries. The pages of *The Divine Milieu* are filled with the most poignant lines on the 'passivities and diminishment' in human life, and we have already noted in chapter one Teilhard's personal anxiety in this regard. There is 'the crazy indifference and the heartbreaking muteness of a natural environment in which the greater part of individual endeavour seems wasted or lost, where the blow and the cry seem stifled on the spot, without awakening any echo.' But more painful yet are the passivities which are internal, for these 'form the blackest residue and the most despairingly useless years of our life. Some were waiting to pounce on us as soon as we awoke; natural failings, physical defects, intellectual and moral limitations, as a result of which the field of our activities, of our enjoyment, of our vision, has been ruthlessly limited since birth. Others were lying in wait for us later on and appeared as suddenly and brutally as an accident, or as stealthily as an illness. . . . Sometimes it is the cells of the body that rebel or become diseased; at other times the very elements of our personality seem to be in conflict or to run amok. And then we impotently stand by and watch collapse, rebellion and inner tyranny, and no friendly influence can come to our help.'[21] It is all very well for an intellectual analysis to show that physical evil is inevitable in an evolving universe—

. . . but for our heart to yield without revolt to this hard law of creation, is there not besides a psychological need to find some positive value that can transfigure this painful waste in the process that shapes us, and eventually make it worth accepting? Unquestionably. And it is here that Christianity plays an irreplaceable role with its astonishing revelation that suffering, provided it be rightly accepted, can be transformed into an expression of love and a principle of action. Suffering is still to be treated at first as an adversary and fought against right to the end; yet at the same time we must accept it in so far as it can uproot our egoism and centre us more completely on God. Yes, dark and repulsive though it is, suffering has been revealed to us as a supremely active principle for the humanization and divinization of the universe. Here is the ultimate meaning of that prodigious spiritual energy born of the Cross. . . . A growth of spirit arising from a deficiency of matter. A possible Christification of suffering. This is indeed the miracle which has been constantly renewed for the last two thousand years.[22]

The above passage is significant not only because it highlights Teilhard's second purpose in his treatment of physical evil, but also because it makes clear that such a purpose is to be attained only through faith in Christian revelation. 'Faith' in this context means 'not simply the intellectual adherence to Christian dogma . . . [but] the practical conviction that the universe, between the hands of the Creator, still continues to be the clay from which he shapes innumerable possibilities according to his will.'[23] Consequently once more there is to be a simultaneous use of two sources of knowledge, the data of one leading to a fuller understanding of the data of the other. More specifically, Teilhard will use biblical data concerning Christ's death and Resurrection to show with certitude that in God's plan for mankind deficiency of matter is indeed meant to be the occasion for growth in spirit. This conclusion is then used to throw further light upon the positive aspect of Christ's work of redemption and thereby to relate that work more closely to a universe undergoing genèse. Let us see how Teilhard accomplishes this twofold effort.

There is first the certitude which comes from revelation that the true meaning of suffering and death is the passage to new life in and through Christ. 'We shall find the Christian faith absolutely explicit in what it affirms and practices. Christ has conquered death not only by suppressing its evil effects but by reversing its sting. Through the power of the Resurrection nothing any longer kills inevitably, but everything is capable of becoming the blessed touch of the divine hands, the blessed influence of the will of God upon our lives. . . . *Diligentibus Deum omnia convertuntur in bonum.*' This power of Christ to give life shows itself in a special way when, 'as a result of his omnipotence impinging on our faith, events which show themselves experimentally in our lives as pure loss become an immediate factor in the union we dream of establishing with him.' Most of all is this the case with that 'final stripping by death which accompanies our recasting *in Christo Jesu.*' Just as he submitted to death, so we must 'undergo an eclipse, which seems to annihilate us before being reborn in Christ. . . . It is Jesus who forewarns us: . . . the same pain which kills and putrifies matter is necessary for a person's growth in life and spirit.'[24] From the Christian point of view, says Teilhard, 'the "collection" of spirit displayed during the "coiling" of the universe takes place in two stages: a) first by slow "evaporation" (the death of individuals); and then, simultaneously, b) by man's incorporation into a collective organism (the "Mystical Body") whose maturation will not be completed until the end of time by the Parousia.'[25]

The great victory of the Creator and Redeemer, in the Christian vision, is to have transformed what is itself a universal power of diminishment and extinction into an essentially life-giving factor. God must in some way or other make room for himself, hollowing us out and emptying us, if he is finally to penetrate into us. And in order to assimilate us into him, he must break the molecules of our being so as to recast and remodel us. The function of death is to bring about this opening up of our inmost selves which God desires. It will force us to undergo the disunion he is waiting for. It will put us into the state organically needed if the divine fire is to descend upon us. And in that way its fatal power to decompose and dissolve will be harnessed to the most sublime operations of life. What was by nature empty and void, a return to bits and pieces, can, in every human existence, become fullness and unity in God.[26]

This last text from *The Divine Milieu* leads us one step further in understanding how there can be growth in spirit from a deficiency of matter, namely through transformation. 'It is astonishing that so few minds should succeed . . . in grasping the notion of transformation. Sometimes the thing transformed seems to them to be the old thing unchanged; at other times they see in it only the entirely new. In the first case it is spirit which eludes them; in the second case it is matter.' For the true meaning of transformation we must look to the Cross. Christ's crucifixion and death 'signifies to our thirst for happiness that the term of creation is not to be sought in the temporal zones of our visible world, but that the effort required of our fidelity must be consummated beyond a total transformation of ourselves and everything around us.' We have no way of knowing, for example, 'under what guise our natural faculties will pass over into the final act of the vision of God.'[27] The reason is that 'spirit is apparently unable to free itself except by a rupture, an escape, which is of a *totally different order* from that slow process by which matter succeeded in elaborating the human brain.' In formal logic the notion of fullness excludes that of emptiness, but in real life this is not so at all. There are some fullnesses which continue and even become more perfect when they are emptied. Cavities essential to an organism, for example, usually appear at their primary stage in the shape of bulky wholes that eventually hollow themselves out. So it is with man. He is led by the very logic of his development to be changed into something greater than himself. For the fruit to break open it must first be ripe and mature. By death we transfer to Christ the ultimate centre of our existence, and thereby undergo a radical sacrifice of egoism, 'a sort of breaking-up and recasting of our whole being, the condition for recreation and integration into the Pleroma.' Hence we must 'cherish, along with the fulfilments of our life, everything that diminishes us, that is to say, all the passive purifications which Christ has planned for us in order to transform into himself those elements of our personality which we seek to develop for him.'[28]

What is continually being lost sight of, however, is that this growth in spirit is not that of something entirely new. It takes place precisely in and through a transformation of *matter*. 'The material totality of the world . . . contains a certain quantity of spiritual power, the progressive sublimation of which *in Christo Jesu* is, for the Creator, the fundamental operation taking place.' The task of Christ, living in his faithful, is patiently to sort out from matter these heavenly energies and to unite them to his own Body. Just as a current causes a ship to deviate from its set course, so this influence of Christ, gradually extracting a 'chosen' substance, is responsible for 'the general "drift" of matter towards spirit. This movement must have its term. One day the whole divinizable substance of matter will have passed into the souls of men; all the chosen dynamisms will have been recovered. . . . Who can fail to perceive the great symbolic gesture of baptism in this general history of matter? Christ immerses himself in the waters of the Jordan, symbol of the forces of the earth. These he sanctifies. And, in the words of St. Gregory of Nyssa, he emerges streaming with water and elevating along with himself the whole world.' Hence Teilhard is able to pray: 'By virtue of your suffering Incarnation, disclose to us the spiritual power of matter, and then teach us how to harness it jealously for you.'[29]

This emphasis on Christ's power to elevate the 'chosen' part of the world will enable us to understand more easily why Teilhard insists so strongly upon a positive meaning for redemption and consequently upon its relationship to a universe undergoing *genèse*. The French word *élu*, 'chosen', is in fact frequently used in the context of a purification of matter under the salvific influence of Christ. 'The Incarnation will be complete only when that portion of chosen substance contained in every object—spiritualized first in our souls and a second time along with our souls in Jesus—shall have rejoined the final Centre of its completion.' The 'attraction or repulsion exercised upon souls by the Cross' is 'a sorting of the good seed from the bad, the separation of the chosen elements.'[30] This is why Teilhard's love of the world is not directed to everything created. He speaks of 'the need which the treasures of the world have to be purified', and insists that 'the true earth for me is that portion of the universe which is chosen, which is still spread out everywhere, but which is in process of . . . finding in Christ its true measure and substance.'[31] Hence, what the Christian must develop is an ability to 'distinguish that portion of chosen being which is subject to Christ's drawing power.' The Body of Christ thus appears as 'a loving, active principle of purification and detachment', and this is especially true of the Eucharistic Body of Christ, as Teilhard points out again and again, for the Eucharist is the presence throughout time of the total mystery of redemption, 'the natural continuation of the redeeming and unitive action of Christ.'[32]

It is perfectly true that the Cross means going beyond the frontiers of the sensible world and even, in a sense, breaking with it completely. The final stages of the ascent to which it calls us compel us to cross a threshold, a critical point, where we lose touch with the zone of sensible realities. . . . But this agonizing breaking away from experiential zones, symbolized by the Cross, is only (and this should be strongly emphasized) the sublimation of that law common to all life. . . . The royal road of the Cross is in fact precisely the road of human endeavour, in so far as this has been supernaturally straightened and extended. . . .

Jesus on the Cross is both symbol and reality of the immense labour of the centuries which little by little raises up created spirit to restore it to the depths of the divine Milieu. He represents and, in a true sense, he is creation, as it re-ascends the slopes of being, supported by the hand of God, sometimes clinging to things for support, sometimes tearing itself from them in order to transcend them, and always compensating by physical suffering for setbacks caused by its moral failures.[33]

The positive meaning of redemption is, therefore, the support given by Christ's suffering, death and Resurrection to the upward movement of man in the noosphere. Christ gives this support because 'in him there was not merely a man but Man, total Man,'[34] and hence he achieves in his own Body-Person the purpose of the whole evolutionary process, namely the spiritual union of humanity with God in and through a purification of matter. For those who are united to Christ through faith, physical evil has once and for all been placed in the service of spiritual growth. 'The world is above all a work of creation continued in Christ. . . . Christ saves the world in the sense that without Christ . . . man's effort would be without hope in a final outcome, and this would mean his losing the taste for life and abandoning altogether his task on earth.' Consequently Teilhard is against any understanding of redemption which conveys 'the impression that the kingdom of God can only be established in gloom, by thwarting and going against the energies and aspirations of man. . . . The Cross is not something inhuman but superhuman. . . . It has been placed on the crest of the road that leads to the highest peaks of creation. . . . The Christian's task is not to swoon in its shadow but to climb in its light.'[35]

This 'task of the Christian' climbing upwards in the light of the Cross is given a final clarification by the positive function which Teilhard assigns to Christian resignation. His concern here is modern man's bitter reproach to the Gospel for fostering passivity in the face of evil, an accusation 'infinitely more effective at this moment in preventing the conversion of the world than all the objections drawn from science or philosophy.' Christian submission to the will of God is in fact the very opposite of capitulation. Far from 'weakening and softening the fine steel of the human will, brandished against all the powers of darkness and diminishment', such submission is precisely a resolute resistance to evil in order to reach through faith that 'chosen point' where God is to be found. For God is not present simply anywhere at all in our passivities, but solely at that point of equilibrium between our tenacious endeavour to grow and the external opposition which finally overwhelms us. Only at this 'chosen point' does our capacity to submit to God's will reach its maximum, for at that moment our submission necessarily coincides with the optimum of our fidelity to the human task. There is thus to be found in Christian resignation a truly human value, a positive aspect corresponding in the individual's life to that positive aspect of Christ's total work of redemption.[36]

Our study of Teilhard's thought on the mystery of evil now puts us in a better position to understand the relationship he wishes to establish between this positive aspect of redemption and his overall effort to rethink the mystery of Christ in terms of *genèse*. Once more, as in his previous speculation concerning the Body of Christ, there is an interplay of two sources of knowledge. Human reason had led Teilhard to postulate a transcendent personal Centre for the evolutionary process, and his Christian faith had then led him to identify this Centre with Jesus of Nazareth. This identification, examined in the light of revelation concerning the Incarnation and the Eucharist, showed Christ to be Centre of the universe in and through the physical omnipresence of his Body-Person. It is this fundamental concept of Christ as physical Centre which has now guided Teilhard's whole approach to the mystery of redemption. For if through his Incarnation Christ has become a physical Centre for humanity, then his work of salvation must necessarily mean accepting the full weight of that cosmic development of which man is the culmination and principal aim. This weight Jesus bore in his Body, not only during his Passion but also in the victory of his Resurrection; he bears it now in his glorified Body and will go on doing so until his Parousia at the end of time. Mankind is able to continue its ascent towards personal communion with God only because Christ has broken the 'death barrier', and by so doing has transformed physical evil into an instrument for the purification of matter and the growth of spirit. Christ is therefore Redeemer precisely *as* Omega. His work of redemption is, in the present supernatural order, the ultimate reason why there *is* such a thing as evolution in Teilhard's sense of the word.

Projected against a universe where the struggle with evil is the condition *sine qua non* of existence, the Cross assumes new importance and fresh beauty, and is capable of captivating us all the more. Unquestionably Jesus is still he who bears the sins of the world; in its own mysterious way suffering makes reparation for moral evil. But above all Jesus is he who overcomes structurally, in himself and in behalf of us all, that resistance to spiritual ascent which is inherent in matter. He is the One who bears the weight which is inevitably part of all created reality. He is both symbol of progress and at the same time its heroic achievement. The full and ultimate meaning of redemption is no longer seen to be reparation alone, but rather further passage and conquest.[37]

We may conclude this first stage of Teilhard's thought by noting its similarity as well as its marked contrast to the thought of Duns Scotus. The emphasis of Scotus falls always upon the central place of Christ in God's work of creation. In his theology the primary motive of the Incarnation is not to counteract the effects of sin in the world, either original or personal, but to unite all reality, material and spiritual, natural and supernatural, divine and human, in the Person of the Incarnate Word, God's masterwork, the goal and crowning achievement of his goodness, power and love.[38] This is surely the thought of Teilhard. In his system, however, it is to be found in the context of cosmogenesis, and it is this context which forces him to shift the point at issue from the primary motive of the Incarnation to the primary motive of the redemption. That is to say, in the present evolutionary structure of things willed by God, the Incarnation cannot be considered an end in itself, in the same way it might have been in a static universe. Its primary motive, and consequently the primary motive of creation itself, can be nothing else than a *work* of Christ, and this we know from revelation to be his work of salvation. Christ must therefore be the goal of creation in so far as he is its Saviour. The whole question is whether salvation is to be conceived primarily as a reparation for sin or primarily as an elevating of created reality and a leading it to its fulfilment in union with God. Or, to use Teilhard's terminology, whether Christ the Redeemer is to be considered primarily as Christ the Evolver.[39]

It is important to underline both this similarity and this contrast between the two thinkers. The similarity must be emphasised because of the irreproachable orthodoxy of Scotus' teaching on the secondary place of reparation for sin in the divine plan for the God-Man. But the contrast must likewise be stressed, since Teilhard reacted strongly against an abstract theology that could discuss the human nature of Christ as if it were in itself independent of suffering and death. In this he is closer to St. Thomas than to Scotus, who saw between the Incarnation and redemption a mere extrinsic association.[40] In Teilhard's writings the human nature of Christ never appears as an abstract entity, but always as an integral part of an evolutionary process in which physical evil is to a large extent inevitable. The Incarnation, therefore, is already redemptive in a true sense of the word, since it involves a 'kenosis into matter' which can only mean a participation in that suffering and death which is the lot of all men.[41] This outlook is well summarized by Teilhard himself in a sentence written towards the end of his life: 'My constant preoccupation has been to have radiate from a transcendent and personal Christ the "redemptive" qualities of the pain engendered by evolution.'[42]

II

In dealing with the mystery of redemption Teilhard's chief concern is, as we have seen, to stress its positive aspect. Christ's conquest of physical evil is man's guarantee that in spite of suffering and death both individual and species can now reach their ultimate development in personal union with God. Yet any such guarantee immediately raises the more fundamental question of whether individual and species *will* reach such a successful spiritual outcome. Hence follows the second stage of Teilhard's thought on the mystery of evil, which concerns man's capacity to abuse his freedom, his moral culpability, and the reparation made by Christ for the sins of the world. For Christ not only bore the painful weight of human progress; he also bore the weight of man's refusal to love, and in Teilhard's system refusal to love is the sole obstacle capable of blocking the upward movement of spirit. It is at this point, however, that we encounter a strange and unexpected impasse in the system itself. For logically there should be a strong emphasis on the negative aspect of redemption. At the very minimum there should be sufficient emphasis to indicate that it occupies that place of secondary importance which Teilhard assigns to it in his Christology. But there is no emphasis at all. To appreciate the significance of this fact we shall consider first Teilhard's line of approach to moral evil in general, and then we shall enquire into the cause of that mental block which prevented him from seeing any relationship whatsoever between the success of evolution and the reparation made by Christ for the sins of the world.

The line of approach which Teilhard takes to moral evil in general is best understood by beginning with the role played by freedom and love in his system of thought. It is of the very essence of this system that in and through man evolution has not only become conscious of itself but also free to dispose of itself,—it can give itself or refuse itself. 'We hold it [evolution] in our hands, responsible to its future for its past.' If our efforts flag, then 'the whole of evolution will come to a halt,—*because we are evolution.*' Tangential energy must continue its inevitable technical progress, but the forces of radial energy are subject to no such inevitability. For in man these are now free and psychosocial, urging him forward towards ever higher forms of interpersonal communion. Whether or not, therefore, radial energy continues to advance towards higher consciousness depends entirely upon the free decisions of men, and 'each individual can repudiate the task of ascending higher towards union.'[43] This will not happen, according to Teilhard, but only because of the existence of Omega, 'loving and lovable at this very moment', whose influence is alone able to conquer the forces of repulsion and hatred, and so motivate sufficiently large numbers of men towards growth in spirit.

Sufficiently large numbers, but not necessarily all. The future of the noosphere hinges for Teilhard upon the growth of amorization, i.e. the free circulation of love energy over the surface of the earth, for love is the highest form of that radial energy upon which true evolutionary progress depends. While it is not out of the question that 'some sort of unanimity will reign over the entire mass of the noosphere,' and that 'hatred and internecine struggles will have disappeared in the ever warmer radiance of Omega, . . . there is another possibility.'[44] This other possibility is that a whole segment of humanity will reject Omega. Teilhard never loses sight of the fact that 'the right outcome' of evolution is one thing, while that of the individual quite another. Ultimate victory for humanity through union with Omega does not mean personal victory for each human being. The progress of radial energy could well become a stumbling block for many, since such progress means a growth of consciousness and consequently a growth of tension in the free decisions of men. 'Essentially progress is a *force* and the most dangerous of forces. . . . Progress is directed towards fostering in the human will reflective action and fully human choice.'[45] It is precisely because he sees clearly that the growth of evolution means the growth of personal responsibility that Teilhard can envision a partial failure for the whole human enterprise.

Obeying a law from which nothing in the past has yet been exempt, evil may go on growing alongside good, and in the end may also attain its paroxysm in some specifically new form. . . . Refusal or acceptance of Omega? A conflict may spring up. In that case the noosphere, in the course of and by virtue of the process which draws it together, would, once it has reached its point of unification, split into two zones each attracted to an opposite pole of adoration. . . . Universal love would give life to and finally detach only a fraction of the noosphere in order to bring it to fulfilment,—the part which decided to 'cross the threshold', to go outside itself and into the Other. . . . [There would be] an internal schism of consciousness, ever increasingly divided on two opposite ideals of evolution, and a positive attraction by the Centre of centres upon the hearts of those who turn towards it. . . .

A split [would take place] in the noosphere, divided on the form to be given to its unity; and simultaneously, endowing the event with its whole significance and value, a liberation of that percentage of the universe which, across time, space and evil, will have succeeded in laboriously synthesizing itself to the very end. There is not to be indefinite progress, which is an hypothesis contrary to the convergent nature of noogenesis, but an ecstasy transcending the dimensions and the framework of the visible universe. Ecstasy in concord or discord; but in either case by excess of interior tension: the only biological outcome proper to or conceivable for the phenomenon of man.[46]

The evil spoken of in the above passage is clearly moral evil, and its essence for Teilhard consists in the free rejection of Omega. More accurately moral evil is a refusal to *love* Omega, a refusal of that 'fundamental energy of life' which is 'the very bloodstream of spiritual evolution', and which alone can unite men together and bring them to their final end. Love in Teilhard's mind is thus the key to the whole moral order; it is 'that psycho-moral energy' which 'physically builds up the universe'.[47] Its deliberate rejection, therefore, is a true injury to one's own person as well as to humanity as a whole, a turning away from ultimate 'happiness of growth, happiness of love and happiness of adoration'.[48] The object of such love and adoration is, of course, Omega. 'In a universe acknowledged to be in a state of spiritual transformation, the general and supreme law of morality is that *sin consists in a limitation of this energy* [of love], unless by doing so one obtains its further increase.'[49]

It is love, moreover, which establishes a connection in Teilhard's thought between moral evil, suffering and death. Ultimately there can be growth in spirit from deficiency of matter only through love. 'There is growth in spirit from matter in the exact measure that love begins to spread itself out everywhere.'[50] On the other hand, without love suffering and death remain untransfigured and tend to degenerate into freely chosen instruments of that disunion within and between persons which for Teilhard is synonymous with moral evil. This explains why he can say that death, which is physical evil in its purest form, becomes 'moral evil too, in so far as disordered multiplicity, the source of all strife and all corruption, is propagated either in society or in ourselves by the wrong use of our freedom.' Creation reascends the slopes of being, 'always compensating, by physical suffering, for the setbacks caused by its moral failures,' and 'suffering in its own mysterious way makes reparation for moral evil.'[51]

It will be noticed that Teilhard is not dealing here with subjective guilt in the individual conscience, but with objective moral evil in so far as it affects humanity's progress towards Omega. This is constantly his outlook and is forced upon him by the whole inner orientation of his thought. Consequently while he conceives moral evil to be on a different plane from physical evil, since it originates in the free will of man, it is easy to see why he likewise conceives the two forms of evil to be part of one and the same evolutionary process. 'There is only one type of evil, disunion. We call it "moral" when it affects the free zones of the soul. But even then it remains essentially physical, just as the good, whose function is to unite, is also essentially physical.'[52] If we remember that the word 'physical' in Teilhard refers to whatever has existence in this concrete order of things, it immediately becomes evident that he can include objective moral evil in the structural make-up of the universe, without necessarily compromising thereby either its tragedy or its perversity. The emphasis is simply shifted from the drama taking place within the individual soul to the drama taking place in the cosmos. 'It would therefore be a complete misunderstanding of the vision here proposed,' he says at the end of The Phenomenon of Man, 'to see it as a sort of human idyll instead of as the cosmic drama which I have in reality wished to describe.'[53]

Hence Teilhard can say that moral evil, like suffering and death, is statistically necessary in a humanity undergoing genèse. 'Disharmony or physical decomposition among the preliving, suffering among the living, sin in the domain of freedom: there is no order under formation which does not at every stage imply disorder. There is nothing, I repeat, in this ontological (or more exactly, ontogenic) condition of participated being which lessens the dignity or limits the omnipotence of the Creator. Neither is there anything savouring of what could be called Manichaeanism.'[54] Notice the reason here for insisting upon the inevitability of moral evil: to locate its source in human freedom, and not in the Creator or in some Manichaean principle of evil independent of God. Teilhard makes this point several times. 'In virtue of his very perfections God cannot ordain that the elements of a world in the course of growth—or at least of a fallen world in process of rising again—

should avoid shocks and diminishments, even moral ones. . . . His perfections cannot run counter to the nature of things, and a world assumed to be progressing towards perfection, or "rising after a fall", is of its nature still partially disorganized.'[55]

There is nothing new, it should be noted, in this mode of conceiving moral evil as both necessary and culpable. The Council of Trent emphasized man's slavery to sin in spite of his freedom, and in its exposition appealed several times to the thought of St. Paul. St. Thomas also taught that without grace it was impossible for man to avoid serious sin for any length of time.[56] 'Statistical necessity,' says Teilhard, 'does not imply obligation, does not suppress liberty. It is statistically necessary that in any large number of letters there will regularly be mistakes: stamps forgotten, addresses incompleted, etc. Yet each sender is free not to make mistakes.' In *The Phenomenon of Man* he notes that 'every organism is always and inevitably reducible into its component parts. But it by no means follows that the sum of its parts is the same as the whole. . . . That what is "free" in man can be broken down into determinisms, is no proof that the world is not based on freedom—as indeed I maintain that it is.' At the end of the same work he is emphasizing again that 'statistically, at every degree of evolution, we find evil always and everywhere, implacably forming and reforming itself in us and around us. *Necessarium est ut scandala eveniant.* This is relentlessly imposed by the play of large numbers at the heart of a multitude undergoing organization.'[57]

Passages such as the above are responsible for the criticism that Teilhard reduces moral evil to a multiplicity which is quantitative.[58] This is to forget that 'multiplicity' for him is an analogous concept. It is synonymous with disunion and evil, and just as these cease to be purely material on the level of spirit, so multiplicity ceases to be quantitative and becomes personal, that is to say, it becomes a multiplicity which can be reduced to unity only through freedom and love. There remains nevertheless the same intimate connection between the two levels of multiplicity which exists between the two levels of evil, and this explains why Teilhard can speak about both in the same breath. When, however, he is not speaking of the evolutionary process as a whole but of the spiritual development of man alone, as he does in *The Divine Milieu*, he can be quite categorical on the lack of correspondence between the person and mere quantitative multiplicity: 'No, it is not the rigid determinism of matter and large numbers, but the subtle combinations of spirit that give the universe its consistency.' It should be noted, moreover, that for Teilhard 'the true evolution of the world takes place in the souls of men and in their mutual union. Its inmost agents are not mechanistic but psychological and moral.'[59] Nor should it be forgotten that many of the Greek Fathers and even St. Augustine looked upon sin as a splintering of man, a sinking deeper into 'multiplicity'.[60]

At this point we should underline the fact that, however strongly Teilhard maintained that the existence of malice on the level of freedom is part of the same evolutionary pattern responsible for suffering and death, he never says nor did he for a moment believe that this was the *total* explanation. On the contrary, he explicitly notes that there is a dimension to man's rejection of love which constantly keeps eluding all rational explanation. This he describes on the phenomenological level as that 'mysterious surface of growing repulsion which more often than not opposes human molecules to each other,' and it is such opposition which leads him to doubt 'that the tightening of the mass of humanity [over the earth's surface] is sufficient *by itself alone* to increase the psychic temperature [of love].' There is also that disturbing question at the end of *The Phenomenon of Man*: 'Is it really certain that the quantity and malice of evil spread *hic et nunc* throughout the world does not betray a certain *excess*, inexplicable to our reason, unless to the normal effect of evolution there is added the extraordinary effect of some catastrophe or primordial deviation?' Years before, in *The Divine Milieu*, he had already answered this question, but his answer had come from Christian revelation: 'Above all, by revealing an original fall, Christianity provides our intelligence with the reason for a certain disconcerting excess in the overflow of sin and suffering.'[61]

Once more, therefore, Christian faith gives an added depth to

Teilhard's thought, this time to his general approach to moral evil. His attention focuses itself upon two elements which make up the Christian sense of awe before the mystery of salvation, first the mystery of hell and secondly man's total dependence upon the redemptive grace of Christ. In the mystery of hell Teilhard finds a new dimension for what he has seen to be the great danger from radial energy's crossing the threshold of consciousness, namely the power of man to refuse Omega, the 'fostering in the human will of reflective action and fully human choice'.[62] Christian teaching on hell thus confirms the possibility of a partial failure for the whole human enterprise. In 1916, speaking of Christ's warning to beware of the world, Teilhard specifies that this means 'the world which is cultivated for itself, closed upon itself, the world of selfish pleasure, the damned portion of the world which withdraws into self adoration.' Two years later he notes that if a portion of reality refuses submission to Christ, 'this portion can find no other natural Centre apart from Jesus around which to group itself.' It must 'wander away without goal, irresolute and disorganized, towards some mysterious antipodes of spirit. This is the damnation of outer darkness.' Again in 1919 he says that 'in order finally to triumph over the earth, or at least (if it is true that humanity must end in a great spiritual schism) in order fully to reign over that chosen portion which shall have decided to follow him, Jesus is waiting, I believe, for men to reach out, in a natural effort sustained by him, towards that high standard of morality which will bring to each the fullest degree of consciousness, that is to say, which will make them fully human.'[63]

In this last text, it should be noted, there again appears the French word *élu*, 'chosen', which we have already seen in the context of the spiritual purification of matter. Now, however, the context is man's freedom of choice and Christ's role as Judge. Consider, for example, the following text written in 1927:

The history of the kingdom of God is, directly, one of reunion. The total divine Milieu is formed by the incorporation of every chosen spirit in Jesus Christ. But to say 'chosen' is to imply a choice, a selection. We should not understand the universal action of Jesus in a fully Christian manner if he were to be seen merely as a Centre of attraction and beatification. It is precisely because he is the one who unites that he is also the one who chooses, who separates, and who judges. The Gospel speaks of the good seed, sheep, the right hand of the Son of Man, the wedding feast and of the fire that kindles joy. But there are also weeds, goats, the left hand of the Judge, the closed door and outer darkness. At the antipodes of the fire that unites in love, there is the fire that destroys in isolation. The total process by which the New Earth gradually comes to birth is an *aggregation* and simultaneously a *segregation*. . . .

The powers of evil in the universe are not simply an attraction, a deviation, a minus sign, an annihilating return to multiplicity. In the course of the spiritual evolution of the world, certain conscious elements or monads deliberately detach themselves from the mass drawn forward by your attraction. Evil has, as it were, become incarnate in them, 'substantialized' in them. I am surrounded now by dark presences, evil beings, malign things, intermingled with your luminous presence. And that separated whole constitutes a definitive and immortal waste from the genesis of the world. There is not simply *lower* darkness but *outer* darkness. That is what the Gospel tells us. . . . I shall accept the existence of hell on your word, *as a structural part of the universe*. . . . The fires of hell and the fires of heaven are not two different forces but contrary manifestations of the same energy.[64]

The above passage, taken from the dense and terrible pages on hell in *The Divine Milieu*, is echoed in more sober terms in 1944. Is it indeed true, asks Teilhard, that Christ's work of salvation will not be accepted by all men? Christianity gives us no answer to this question. What it does is to remind us that some loss is possible, and that, if such be the case, the condemned would be separated for ever, cast out to the antipodes of God. 'From this point of view, the existence of hell is simply a negative way of affirming that, from physical and organic necessity, man is incapable of finding happiness and fulfilment except by fidelity to the movement which carries him onward towards the ultimate limit of his development. Ultimate life (i.e. a fullness of consciousness embracing at once all reality) or ultimate death (i.e. an infinite splintering of consciousness upon itself): that is the alternative which the existence and meaning of hell places before us.'[65]

Notice the emphasis here on 'fidelity to the movement' which carries man forward. Such fidelity is in fact a fidelity to the movement of grace, for in Teilhard's mind the radial energy of evolution is moving towards no natural end. In the present supernatural order the physical Centre of cosmogenesis is the Body-Person of Christ, and cosmic development in its totality is oriented towards the union of humanity with Christ-Omega in the final Pleroma.[66] This is the reason for Teilhard's frequent references to the divine initiative in both the life of the individual and that of the species. 'The triumph [of progress] will come from God, under the form of his providence, at his own appointed time, and in excess of our expectations. The worker who puts his confidence in God knows that neither endeavour nor aspiration is lost if it is done in grace; they reach their goal because they pass through the living Centre of every useful activity.' . . . 'Christ is the principle of unity who saves a culpable creation in process of returning to dust. By the force of his attraction, by the light of his moral teaching, by the "cement" of his very being, Jesus comes to re-establish at the heart of the world the harmony of human effort and the convergence of human beings.'[67]

In 1927, at the start of *The Divine Milieu*, Teilhard's approach to grace takes a slightly different form from that of the early texts we have just quoted. 'Not only as a theoretically admitted entity, but rather as a living reality, the notion of grace impregnates the whole atmosphere of my book. . . . What is most divine in God is that, in an absolute sense, we are nothing apart from him. The least admixture of what may be called Pelagianism would suffice to ruin immediately the beauties of the divine Milieu in the eyes of the "seer".' Later in the same work he points out that 'his grace anticipates our action, and is therefore always on the alert to stimulate our first look and our first prayer. In the end the initiative, the awakening, always come from him.' Christian faith means 'the practical conviction that the universe, between the hands of the Creator, still continues to be the clay from which he shapes innumerable possibilities according to his will.' Yet the responsibility of human freedom is never far from Teilhard's mind: 'It is *we* who save ourselves or lose ourselves', and this holds true especially for 'every soul that is lost in spite of the call of grace.'[68]

The emphasis upon the divine initiative which we have seen so far has had a predominantly individual accent, though it is always found in an evolutionary context. With the passage of years this accent begins to shift to the human race as a whole. In 1940 Teilhard is speaking of 'God as Providence, directing the universe with loving, watchful care.' In 1946 he writes: 'It is the "Christic" vision of the world which is ready to provide human effort with two elements without which our action would not be able to push to an end its forward march: 1) valorization and 2) amorization. First, a divine guarantee that, in spite of every type of death, the fruit of our labour is irreversible and cannot be lost. Secondly, the attraction of a Goal which, because it is by nature super-personal, is capable of unleashing in the depths of our souls the energies of love, in comparison with which all other forms of spiritual energy pale and fade into nothingness.'[69] Two years later there is a similar insistence that 'for the Christian believer . . . the final success of hominization (and thus cosmic coiling) is positively guaranteed by the power of restoring to life which belongs to God incarnate in his creation.' Again that same year he says: 'For a Christian . . . the final biological success of man on earth is not a simple probability but a certitude, for Christ (and in him, virtually, the world) is already risen.'[70] Finally in 1950 he states that for the believer 'the vital tension of the world is no longer simply maintained by psychological artifice or by rational discovery of a goal or its corresponding ideal, but, as an effect of "grace" and "revelation", is directly infused in the depths of our being through love, which is this tension's highest, most immediate and ultimate form.'[71]

Up to this point we have been following the line of approach which Teilhard takes to moral evil in general. We focused attention first upon the role played by freedom and love in his system, and we then considered those two mysteries which demonstrate most clearly man's capacity for self-destruction, namely the existence of hell and man's need of redemptive grace. Hell is a terrible thing indeed as seen through the eyes of Teilhard. Nor does he hesitate to say quite explicitly, in *The Divine Milieu*, that original sin increases the risks of freedom in a fallen world, complicates the natural phenomenon of death, and is the ultimate reason that matter represents a perpetual impulse towards failure.[72] Teilhard thus presents evolution to us as a movement endangered from within by a weakness inherent in man, its crowning achievement, namely the fragility of human love and human freedom. Unless man's love can be strengthened and his freedom supported by some power outside the evolutionary process, the ultimate success of cosmogenesis must forever remain doubtful and insecure. Consequently at this point we should expect a very strong affirmation of the negative aspect of redemption, namely the reparation made by Christ for the sins of the world. For sin alone is capable of destroying forever man's power to love, thus killing him spiritually and wiping out all hope of true progress towards Christ-Omega. Within the logic of Teilhard's own system it is precisely sin which presents the greatest threat to man's future, for there can be no victory for evolution unless there is first victory over sin.

Yet no such affirmation is anywhere to be found. Nowhere in all his writings does Teilhard ever connect reparation for sin with evolution's success. On the contrary, his approach to the negative aspect of redemption, namely Christ's bearing the sins of the world, tends to be rigidly impersonal, that is to say, he never speaks of its essential character as a bearing of the weight of man's refusal to love. Such an omission is all the more surprising because it is in stark contrast to the personalism and spiritual tension which is the flower of his own distinctive approach to evolution. Thus we have statements like the following, made in 1952: 'If we translate and transpose "bearing the sins of the guilty world" into terms of cosmogenesis, it becomes exactly the same as "bearing the weight of a world in the course of evolution".'[73] There is an even more

extraordinary text from 1933: 'It can be said that the moderniza-
tion of Christology would consist simply in substituting for the
word "sin" in theological and liturgical formulations, the word
"progress".'[74] By 'progress' Teilhard means of course, as he himself
says in the same essay, 'the battle against evil which is the *sine qua
non* of existence', sc. man's progress through physical suffering and
death towards growth in spirit and union with Christ. Nevertheless,
in the light of what he has said regarding the mystery of hell and
the risk of fully human choice, such observations have the odd
effect of forcing upon the reader a new pair of lenses, by which the
symmetry and logical movement of his thought are suddenly
thrown out of focus. This sensation of something being out of
focus comes through even in very early texts, such as this one
written in 1916:

> Following the 'classical' view, suffering is above all a punish-
> ment, an expiation; it is efficacious as sacrifice; it originates
> from sin and makes reparation for sin. Suffering is good as a
> means to self-mastery, self-conquest, self-liberation. In contrast,
> following the ideas and tendencies of a truly cosmic outlook,
> suffering is above all the consequence and price of a labour of
> development. It is efficacious as effort. Physical and moral
> evil originate from a process of becoming: everything which
> evolves experiences suffering and moral failure. . . . The Cross
> is the symbol of the pain and toil of evolution rather than the
> symbol of expiation.[75]

These texts are typical of Teilhard's strange tendency to depersonalize sin when speaking of Christ's work of redemption. He
consistently disassociates the concept of reparation from that of
love. The net result is not simply to consign reparation to a place
of secondary importance, which Teilhard frequently states as his
purpose and which is in itself a legitimate theological position.
Rather what results is that, in spite of his protests to the contrary,
the negative aspect of redemption disappears altogether and the
positive aspect alone remains. Because it is never connected with
man's refusal to love, reparation for sin tends to become absorbed
and identified with the union of all creation in Christ by reason of

the Incarnation. Redemption comes to mean *solely* that Christ, through his suffering, death and Resurrection, overcomes in himself (and therefore in humanity as a whole) that resistance to spiritual ascent which is inherent in matter.[76] What Teilhard apparently never sees when dealing with redemption is that the one essential condition for spiritual ascent, the one certain guarantee of evolution's success, can only be Christ's conquest of that mysterious capacity in man for disunion and hatred on the personal level. Now this is an anomaly of the first order, an utterly illogical omission for a mind which in its own analysis of evolution saw spiritual tension as the key to the universe. The question we are faced with, therefore, is how to explain this mental block by which sin comes to be reduced to the level of the obvious and the ordinary.

The answer here proposed is that Teilhard failed to link reparation for sin with refusal to love (and therefore with evolution's success) because he was dominated by the fear that any emphasis at all on reparation would immediately obscure, if not entirely do away with, the cosmic character of Christ's work of salvation. Why should he fear this? Because in his mind reparation was inextricably connected with an approach to the *origin* of sin which was taught to him early in the century and which did in fact obscure for him the cosmic character of salvation. Every text cited a moment ago, in which sin appears to be something less than a personal rejection of love, has as its context the relationship between original sin and redemption. This is the great danger which strides his train of thought like a colossus, blocking his view and forcing him in the end to be both illogical and superficial. Contrary to what one might at first suppose, scientific reservations on the subject of monogenism (or origin of all men from a single couple) had relatively little influence on Teilhard's approach to the problem, although once his attitude crystallized, such reservations undoubtedly added support.[77] It is not to reconcile scientific and religious data that he treats original sin, but primarily to safeguard the connection between Christ's work of redemption and man's role in the universe as carrier of creation's upward movement. Christ's death and Resurrection are for Teilhard the ultimate guarantee of this movement's success, and the approach to original sin with which he was familiar seemed to him to call this guarantee into question, first in Christian theology and secondly in the Christian life.

Teilhard was afraid, first of all, that this approach was too narrow, and for this reason tended to obscure the cosmic character of redemption in Christian theology. A number of texts will serve to underline this overriding preoccupation. 'In order for Christ to be truly universal,' he wrote in 1920, 'it is necessary that redemption and therefore the fall be extended to the whole of the universe. Henceforth original sin must assume the cosmic proportions that tradition has always ascribed to it.' That same year he insists that 'the fundamental dogma [of original sin] is the *universality* of corruption caused by the first sin of man. The *whole* universe, so the faithful believe, has been changed by this disobedience of Adam; and it is precisely for this reason that redemption likewise extends itself to the entire universe and that Christ has become Centre of the new creation. . . . There is a Christ *in quo omnia constant*. Every other belief is secondary and subordinate to this fundamental article of faith. Christ is everything or he is nothing.' Four years later there is the same concern: 'To safeguard the Christian view of Christ the Redeemer, it is clearly necessary that we keep original sin as large as the world, otherwise Christ will have saved only part of the world and not be the Centre of everything.'[78] In 1947 he makes this point again but at greater length. Notice how his statement of the problem reflects his own understanding of Christ as physical Centre as well as St. Paul's preoccupation in Romans 8:19-23, both of which we treated in the previous chapter.

Christ must be kept as large as creation and remain its Head. No matter how large we discover the world to be, the figure of Jesus, risen from the dead, must embrace it in its entirety. Since St. John and St. Paul, that is the fundamental rule for theology. Now is anyone sufficiently aware that this first principle has an immediate corollary in regard to the nature of the 'first Adam'? No one questions the fact that the radius of Christ's sovereign power is by definition the radius of his redemption. But what happens from the point of view of Christology if, within our modern perspectives of historical cosmogenesis, we continue to think of original sin on the same small scale, i.e. as an accident which took place towards the end of the Tertiary era in some small corner of the earth? Obviously Christ's power would not, *directly, organically* and *formally*, reach or project beyond a thin little spindle of the universe around us. Juridically and by designation Christ could still, by reason of his divine dignity, be declared Master of other parts of the cosmos. But in the full sense of St. Paul he would cease to be he *in quo omnia constant*. Hence it follows that we must . . . reflect upon the phenomenon of the fall in order to see how it may be conceived or imagined, not as an isolated event, but as a general condition affecting the whole of history.[79]

Teilhard's second fear was that the understanding of original sin current early in the century was too negative, and so tended to obscure the cosmic character of redemption in the Christian life. Such negative emphasis seemed to him the chief reason for the lack of Christian interest in purely human aspirations, as well as for a certain mistrust of progress and a withdrawal from responsibility in purely temporal affairs. For Teilhard this was the great scandal to non-Christians and the principal cause of modern unbelief. Thus he writes in 1933: 'Original sin (under its present form) opposes at every point the expansion of our religion on the natural level. It cuts the wings of our hope. Every time we are about to launch out into the open spaces of optimistic conquest, it inexorably pulls us back into the oppressive gloom of reparation and expiation.' The very strong influence upon his own spiritual life from the cult of the Heart of Christ did not prevent him from noting, in regard to Pius XI's 1932 Encyclical on reparation: 'There are sentences which strike at the most legitimate hopes of modern man at least as much as did the Syllabus of Errors. We are never going to convert the world with such an outlook.' In 1947 he speaks again of 'the *historical* presentation of the fall, which paralyzes under our very eyes the much needed creation of a Christian *Weltanschauung* that is fully human and humanizing.' Six years later there is a further insistence: 'Christianity is not going to recover its power of contagion until it rejects the last traces of Manichaeanism and Platonism, and begins to think of original sin no longer in terms of a fall but of progress. This means that Christians must cease looking upon cosmogenesis as something tainted, outside of God's plan, and representing in its totality a haphazard pasting together with which they need not concern themselves.'[80]

It should be emphasized, before we proceed further, that the above texts are an accurate statement of a theological and psychological problem which was far more acute a half century ago than it is today. Teilhard was reacting strongly against an approach to original sin which tended to consider it as a purely negative reality, a unity in itself, isolated, as it were, from the total Christian message concerning sin and salvation. Such a theology of the fall rarely gave first place to Christ the Redeemer, whereas in point of fact God's permission of original sin is almost unintelligible if separated from the idea of a humanity already destined through his love and mercy to become the Body of his Incarnate Son—'created in Christ Jesus', to use the expression of St. Paul.[81] St. Thomas himself went so far as to say that even before the fall, Adam had an implicit faith in Christ the Redeemer, since without Christ no salvation was possible in this present order.[82] Today theologians are more disposed to see as the central privilege of Paradise this supernatural vocation of man to build a humanity united to the Body of Christ, and consequently to consider sanctifying grace and the infused virtues of Adam as the supernatural means to achieve this destiny. Modern exegesis, moreover, has made it clear that the scriptural account of Paradise intended to convey neither geographic, biological nor psychological information, and this has resulted in detaching the dogma of original sin from that biblical framework which is so repugnant to an evolutionary view of the world. Hence the avoidance today of speaking of a world coming finished from the hands of the Creator, and of history after the fall as a gigantic effort of humanity to return to a primitive state of natural perfection.[83] There is likewise much less emphasis upon the natural perfections of the first couple or their mastery over their material surroundings. Many theologians even feel that death, in so far as it constitutes a purely biological end to all life on earth, should no longer be considered the result of original sin. What comes from original sin, they insist, is rather that darkness of human death by which man undergoes a painful and agonizing rupture instead of a simple transformation into glory.[84]

Nevertheless, it is quite clear that this delicate question needs much more study. In spite of the important exegetical and speculative work of recent years, there are serious problems still to be solved, and ultimately such a solution must come from the Church herself, who alone can give an authentic interpretation of revelation. If today theologians and exegetes no longer see in original sin the sole explanation of physical evil, they do tend to emphasize more and more its relationship to each man's experience of his own personal sin. This means that attention has come to be focused upon the meaning of the dogma for the adult rather than for the newly born infant, which is surely the point of view of the Old Testament and of St. Paul. Such a line of enquiry seeks to place original sin against the larger background of man's consciousness of individual and collective responsibility, and hence to consider the fall of Adam less as an isolated and static event and much more as a power of sin that grows with the growth of humanity itself. In this sense it would approach that transhistoric reality which Teilhard wished it to be. Original sin would thus be the primitive transgression of a primitive man, who was nevertheless sufficiently developed wilfully to reject God's grace in a serious moral matter. Descendants of Adam not only inherit this sin; they also ratify it on their own superior level of culture, with a more mature awareness of themselves and a more complete mastery over the world in which they live. Something to this effect actually crossed Teilhard's mind once, though he does not seem to have followed the thought very far.[85] The culpability of Adam could thus be compared to a snowball whose weight has been growing with the passage of time, each generation making its own that original revolt by resisting the movements of grace. In this way the personal and collective sins of men ceaselessly proclaim and ratify that first disobedience at the dawn of the human race.[86]

Unfortunately Teilhard knew nothing of these developments. Even in their most innocuous form they would have been rigidly excluded from seminary teaching before the first world war. Unable as a consequence to see how original sin was to be related to the universal and cosmic character of redemption, Teilhard decided that the weakness of this teaching must reside in its emphasis upon the historical and personal character of original sin. This decision at once placed him in an impasse from which the only escape seemed to be a formulation, the general lines of which may be summarized as follows. The doctrine of original sin 'expresses, translates and personifies, in an instantaneous and localized action, the perennial and universal law of deficiency which governs humanity in virtue of its being *in fieri*.' From this point of departure 'redemption is immediately seen to be universal because it provides the remedy for a state of things (the presence everywhere of disorder) which is bound up with the most elemental condition of the universe in process of creation.' The theological necessity of baptism is explained 'by the genetic solidarity of all men in the bosom of a single humanity (impregnated with sin by statistical necessity) where the bonds uniting individuals have greater reality and greater depth than any link that is purely hereditary and "linear".' Teilhard admits, moreover, that 'the evil inherent in the world by reason of its mode of creation could be regarded as being particularly individualized on earth the moment that responsible human beings appeared who could say"I". This would be original sin in the *strict* theological sense of the word.' Thus, 'as far as appearances go, there is no trace at all of original sin, since its visible sanction becomes identified with evolution: expiation coincides with the pain of toil.' In this way 'the double notion of "statistical evil" and "evolutionary redemption" rectifies and completes the idea of sin as a catastrophe and expiation as an act of reparation.'[87]

The above solution is, then, an effort to universalize original sin by identifying it first with the physical imperfection of the world at the moment of creation, and then with the inevitable presence of physical evil in the ensuing process of evolutionary change. In this sense it must be considered the 'cosmic fundament' of moral evil and not its 'historical actuation', which would occur only with the advent of fully responsible human action.[88] The most obvious thing about such a solution is that it ignores completely the essential kernel of the mystery as it has been formulated since the Council of Trent, namely that 'original sin comes from a sin committed in actual historical fact, by an individual Adam, and that it has been handed down to, and is consequently present in, all of us by reason of our descent from him.'[89] What is not so obvious, perhaps, is that Teilhard's treatment of this subject is extremely tentative and consistently proposed with the greatest hesitation, almost always for the consideration of professional theologians. His 1924 essay, for example, was prompted by a request from a professor at the Jesuit theological faculty at Enghien in Belgium. 'On this delicate question,' he wrote in 1942, 'I expressly declare once more that I am in no sense trying to anticipate or even to influence the decisions of the Church. But it appears to me essential to insist that theologians give [this problem] their serious attention.' His lengthy essay of 1947 was simply 'offered to theologians for their criticism', and a 1954 letter tells another theologian: 'But please, take what I am going to tell you as the candid opinion of a searcher—not of a teacher. I am not infallible.'[90] On the other hand, when he was not writing for theologians but for a much larger audience, as in *The Divine Milieu*, his references to original sin were extremely prudent and could hardly be more orthodox.[91] In itself, therefore, Teilhard's own particular solution to the problem is of decidedly minor importance. It represents an honest attempt at much needed reform which, for lack of theological judgment, inevitably miscarried.

However, as soon as these opinions on original sin, in themselves of little theological value, are placed within the context of Teilhard's total system, their significance becomes immense. For they seem to have caused a mental block which prevented him from seeing any relationship whatsoever between the success of evolution and the reparation made by Christ for the sins of the world. And it is this mental block which certainly constitutes the supreme irony of Teilhard's thought. For his life's work, as we have seen, was dedicated to elaborating a series of guarantees for evolution's success, the ultimate guarantee being the death and Resurrection of Christ-Omega. Here was final assurance, on the level of Christian faith, that in the case of the human species there is to be not merely survival after death, but an actual growth in spirit in and through the deficiency of matter. Yet the approach to original sin with which he was familiar, narrow and negative as it was, seemed to him to obscure completely this whole cosmic aspect of redemption. This led him to search for a reason, and the sole reason he could find for this threat was that, at its origin, sin was presented as something historical and personal. The result was not simply an effort to do away with the personal element in original sin, but to de-emphasize this same element in *all* sin and therefore in reparation for sin. The inevitable consequence was that the concept of love was separated from that of reparation, and reparation in turn separated from any influence upon evolution.[92]

Thus in Teilhard's treatment of the negative aspect of redemption we do not find that spiritual tension between human freedom and the divine initiative which is the key to his whole analysis of evolution. The statistical aspect of sin, perfectly true as far as it goes, tended to become the *only* aspect, and this gradually made it quite impossible for him to see that Christ's bearing the sins of the world meant in reality his bearing the weight of man's refusal to love. Yet it is love, the highest expression of man's freedom, which is in Teilhard's mind the nerve centre of that ambiguity in progress, the conquest of which was the driving motive of his life. Hence the immense irony in his inability to see that what he envisioned as a danger was in fact the only source of hope. The ultimate guarantee of evolution's success has to be Christ's victory over sin, for without such a victory the relationship between Christ and the universe, that is to say, the whole positive aspect of redemption, can neither be safeguarded nor even correctly understood. There can be no growth in spirit from deficiency of matter except in so far as the love of Christ fosters love among men. And for this to take place there must first be a healing of that 'disconcerting excess' in man's rejection of love, the sole source of which is the reparation made by Christ for the sins of the world.

We may bring this chapter to a close by making three observations regarding Teilhard's treatment of the mystery of evil. Perhaps what is most obvious is that 'evil . . . inevitably seeps out through every nook and cranny, through every joint and sinew of the system in which I have taken my stand.'[93] It is a 'fatal mistake', he wrote, 'to be obtuse to evil and absorbed in one's own part, to underestimate evil's power, i.e. the dangers of failure for earthly evolution.'[94] Secondly, it is not too much to say that Teilhard's approach to the cosmic aspect of redemption constitutes a major step forward towards a fuller understanding of the relationship between the Person of Christ and the natural evolutionary process. The Incarnate Word is he who conquers that ambiguity inherent in a world where human progress must take place in the midst of suffering and death. Teilhard affirms in the strongest terms that all hope for man's future must ultimately be supernatural. The natural hope which he possessed in abundance is always to be found within his supernatural hope in Christ, whose death and Resurrection were for him the sole guarantee that God's designs for his universe must inexorably succeed in spite of all opposition. It is Christ alone who can bring the natural movement of radial energy to its final supernatural goal, which is the union of humanity with himself for all eternity. During the first world war he wrote that 'no idea better expresses to our minds the redemptive function of the Word than that of the unification of all flesh in one single Spirit.' Much later in life he predicted: 'Whatever may be the future progress of Christian thought, one can assert confidently that it will be in the direction of a closer organic unity between the energies of death and the energies of life at the heart of a changing universe, which is to say in the end, between evolution and redemption.' And shortly before he died he said once more that Christianity 'is the only religion capable (because of the twofold power of its Cross and Resurrection understood in their fullness at last) of becoming the moving force of evolution.'[95]

Finally, there is Teilhard's strange tendency to depersonalize sin when speaking of reparation. His attitude here is both illogical and superficial, since he thereby divorces reparation from the function of love in his own system and tends to consider sin itself simply as a regrettable but inevitable invasion of physical evil into the realm of freedom. Chief responsibility for this attitude must certainly be borne by the theological problems caused by the representation of original sin current at the time. Nevertheless, we may well ask whether the ultimate reason for such an attitude was not Teilhard's own over-sensitivity to evil. Is it not possible that he himself felt the terror of man's rejection of love too deeply to consider it objectively? Could not his optimistic unconcern for sin have been a reaction against a natural disposition towards extreme pessimism? During a period of deep discouragement he once wrote to a close friend: 'Spiritual forces have a much greater power and mystery than the forces of matter.'[96] Did he perhaps unconsciously try to depersonalize sin in his theology of redemption because what he knew of it from revelation had already become too personal for him? The pages on hell in *The Divine Milieu* might lead one to believe so. There is also the following extraordinary text which allows us a rare glimpse of Teilhard's deepest feelings. Its appeal to Christian faith makes a fitting conclusion to his thought on the mystery of evil.

After what I have just said of my conviction that a term exists for cosmic evolution which is divine and personal, one could imagine that I look forward in future years to a life that is luminous and serene. . . . Nothing could be further from the truth. Though I am certain, more and more certain, that I must continue to live as if Christ were waiting for me at the goal of the universe, I experience no special assurance at all that he is there. To believe is not to see. As much as anyone, I think, I walk in the darkness of faith.

The darkness of faith . . . To justify this obscurity, so strangely incompatible with the divine sun, scholars explain that the Lord deliberately hides himself in order to test our love. One has to be hopelessly lost in intellectual games, or never to have encountered either in oneself or others the sufferings of doubt, not to see what is detestable in such an answer. O my God, your creatures stand before you, lost and in anguish, appealing for help. To have them rush to you, it would be enough to show them a single ray of your light, the fringe of your cloak,—and you would not do this for them?

In my opinion, the obscurity of faith is simply a special instance of the problem of evil. I see only one possible way to avoid being seriously scandalized by it, and that is to recognize that if God allows us to suffer, to sin, to doubt, it is because he is *unable*, now and at a single stroke, to heal us and to show himself. And if he is unable, the sole reason is that we are still *incapable*, at this present stage of the universe, of receiving higher organization and thus more light. . . .

No, God does not hide himself to make us search for him, of that I am sure,—much less to let us suffer in order to increase our merits. On the contrary, bent down over his creation which moves upwards to him, he works with all his power to give us happiness and light. Like a mother he watches over his newly born child. But our eyes are unable to see him yet. Is not precisely the whole course of centuries needed in order for our gaze to accustom itself to the light?

Our doubts, just as our sufferings, are the price and condition for the perfection of the universe. Under these conditions I consent to walk right to the end along a road of which I am more and more certain, towards an horizon more and more shrouded in mist.[97]

CHAPTER FIVE

THE CHURCH AND THE PAROUSIA

CREATION AS A CHRISTOGENESIS TOWARDS THE FINAL PLENITUDE OF CHRIST

Up to now we have considered two separate stages in Teilhard's effort to elaborate through Christian revelation a guarantee of evolution's success. He began, as we have seen, with the physical omnipresence of Christ's Body-Person as known through the mysteries of the Incarnation and the Eucharist. This he saw to be a confirmation, on the level of revelation, of his initial identification of Jesus of Nazareth with Omega, the transcendent personal Centre which, on the level of reason, he had postulated for evolution. He then proceeded to analyze Christ's work of redemption in order to show that in his role of Redeemer Christ acts precisely as Omega: through his death and Resurrection he conquers that ambiguity in progress caused by suffering, death and especially sin, although the latter's full significance within his own system was apparently lost on him. Hence his central assertion up to now has been the biblical truth that the ultimate salvation of man through union with the humanity of Christ is also the ultimate salvation of the cosmos. The humanity of Christ embraces not only the human race but also the cosmos in so far as this is united to man, that is to say, in so far as evolution produces man, and in so far as man freely fosters that personal unity in the noosphere which is the key to evolutionary progress. It is thus in and through man that the redemptive mission of Christ is directed to a 'chosen' part of the world. Begun in the noosphere before it was the complete envelope it is today, the work of redemption continues throughout time to bring God's creation to that end which the Word destined it to achieve from all eternity.

In this present chapter we pass to a third stage of Teilhard's theological enquiry in which he attempts to analyze, within the context of evolution, this continuation of Christ's work of redemption from the time of the Resurrection until the time of the Parousia. For Teilhard the Resurrection is that 'tremendous cosmic event' which inaugurates the actual exercise by Christ of his function as physical Centre by which, in the words of St. Paul, he 'fills all things'. The use of this text from Ephesians 4:10 in the context of the Resurrection recalls at once Paul's use of the word Pleroma (the Greek word for 'fills' here is *plērōsē*) which, as we have seen in chapter three, means most probably the plenitude of being, both fullness of divinity and fullness of the universe, the whole of the cosmos filled with the creative presence of God. 'In a universe seen to be in a state of convergence, you have taken, by the prerogative of your Resurrection, the leading position of universal Centre in whom everything is gathered together.'[1] It is this perspective which enables Teilhard to see such a close relationship between redemption and the act of creation. Creation as an action of the past is far less important for him than creation as an action of the present and the future. Indeed, he felt quite strongly about this subject of continuous creation.[2] The biblical theme of God exercising his creative power in and through his Word is thus extended in Teilhard's mind so as to include Christ's relationship in the cosmos now and until the end of time, and he even attempts to grasp the interior unity of this continuous creative act in a metaphysical theory which he calls 'creative union'.

More immediately, however, what Teilhard wishes to establish is a relationship between creation, redemption, and the action of the Christian in the world. This explains why he now turns his full attention to the mystery of the Church, in an effort to analyze its function in time in regard to both the natural evolutionary process and the supernatural consummation of mankind. He was in fact constantly preoccupied with the union of all men in Christ, even when he did not refer this explicitly to the Church. 'The unique affair of the world is the physical incorporation of the faithful in Christ who is possessed by God.' This early assertion from 1916 is echoed ten years later: 'Across the immensity of time and the disconcerting multiplicity of individuals, one single operation is taking place: the annexation to Christ of those whom he has chosen. One single thing is being formed: the Mystical Body of Christ.' Later still he says that 'the universe represents the laborious and personalizing unification in God of countless souls, distinct from God but dependent upon him, by their incorporation into Christ, God Incarnate, through the building up of that collective unity, both human and Christian, which is the Church.' Towards the end of his life he speaks of Christ's 'growth through the Church', of his 'power to fill the whole universe . . . by reason of the Resurrection' and 'to assimilate organically and integrate into the unity of a single Body the totality of the human race'.[3]

In this third stage of his Christology, therefore, Teilhard seeks to relate the mystery of Christ's work of redemption to the mystery of God's continuous creation in time. This he does from two distinctly different points of view. First it is Christian action in the world which is the object of his analysis; secondly it is the eternal creative action of God. From the first point of view it is the role of the Church on earth which occupies his attention; from the second it is God's eternal plan to direct the evolutionary process towards the Parousia at the end of time. From each of these points of view, moreover, Teilhard seeks to explain how there can be such a thing as Christogenesis, and how in the end we can legitimately speak of the two movements of Christogenesis and cosmogenesis as ultimately one and the same. To see how he accomplishes this, we shall now follow the gradual elaboration, from this double point of view, of his concept of creation as a temporal Christogenesis moving towards the final Plenitude of Christ.

I

To understand Teilhard's concept of Christogenesis we must begin with his analysis of Christian activity and its role in the evolutionary process. The problem is broached for the first time in an essay written in 1916. 'When our action is animated by grace,' says

Teilhard, 'it builds up a true Body, that of Christ, who wished to be completed through each one of us.' But it must be remembered that this Body of Christ is a *physical* reality, which through the Incarnation has been inserted into a humanity and into a universe undergoing evolutionary change. Hence the incompleteness of the Body of Christ in regard to humanity is a *physical* incompleteness and it is this which enables us to see and love in Christ both 'he who is', and 'he who is in process of becoming'. Christ has 'not yet drawn to himself the last folds of his garment of flesh and love made up of those who believe in him.' A Christian's contribution to man's progress, therefore, 'is not simply a question of promoting a human work, but of bringing Christ to completion in some way.' Because 'the cosmos is centred upon Jesus, it should be clear that in one way or another collaboration in the future of the cosmos is an essential and primary part of Christian responsibility. Nature grows towards fulfilment and the Body of Christ reaches its complete development in one and the same movement.'[4] Teilhard then attempts his first tentative formulation of what he considers to be a valid Christian outlook on the world:

The whole of the Church's dogmatic and sacramental economy teaches us to respect matter and to value it. Christ had to assume and wanted to assume real flesh. He sanctifies human flesh by special contact and he prepares its physical resurrection. For the Christian, therefore, matter has a role to play in the cosmos, an inferior role but one which is nevertheless primordial and essential for union. Because it has been assimilated into the Body of Christ, something from matter is destined to pass into the foundations and walls of the heavenly Jerusalem.

What is to be the source of this privileged matter, chosen for service in the New Earth? Should we simply look upon it as a by-product of grace washing up upon the perishable outer covering of sanctified souls? Perhaps. But is it not more natural that the purified substance of a resurrected organism should give part of its perfections to the sum total of all efforts made in evolutionary progress? Without being able to prove it at all, a cosmic outlook cherishes such a hope, because it brings with it the joy of feeling that in the most earthly of our works there is something which will never die.[5]

In the ten years following this early essay, Teilhard returns a number of times to this distinctive outlook on the world. He is concerned first of all with the Christian's subjective attitude. 'Who will be the Christian,' he asks, 'to make every drop of sap from the world flow into his own movement towards the divine Trinity? It will be he who has understood that to be fully a child of God, to accomplish fully his holy will, one must show oneself more diligent in earthly work than any servant of Mammon.' For some this will mean a life of contemplation, in which the Christian component of the evolutionary process appears, so to speak, in its 'pure state'. Yet even though the motive of such separation from the world is to help it all the more, such a Christian vocation is the exception and not the rule. For the majority, even those vowed to practice the evangelical counsels, the sacred task of advancing life on earth will constitute one of the most immediate and efficacious factors in their sanctity. For such a task is meant to be a free co-operation in the unifying and creative action of God, and as such must spring from faith and a right intention. 'If we have faith, the irresistible forces of life and matter really become for us the organizing action of Christ assimilating us to himself,' and 'our total human effort, the more it is done with a good intention, collaborates towards the fullness of the Incarnation.' It is this 'combined power of faith and intention' which 'reveals to the Christian a zone at the heart of the universe in which *quidquid patimur, Christum patimur; quidquid agimus, Christus agitur.*'[6]

Besides this concern for the Christian's subjective attitude, there is also concern in these early years for that objective relationship which 'in some way' must exist between human progress on earth and the gradual completion of Christ. These two movements are not to be confused; but neither are they to be separated, for their destiny is to form one continuous organic growth in which the supernatural is continually being formed by God through a new creation of the natural. 'Not only by fidelity to obedience, but also by the work being done, we are building up towards the fullness of

Christ and preparing the more or less proximate matter to be transformed into his Plenitude.' Through the total efforts of those united to him, 'Christ is completing himself little by little through the ages. . . . Without biological evolution which produced the brain, there would be no sanctified souls; similarly, without the evolution of collective thought which alone can realize on earth the fullness of human consciousness, could there be a consummated Christ? In other words, without the constant striving of every human cell to unite with all the others, would the Parousia be physically possible?'[7]

In point of fact the Christian holds the key to this natural movement of evolution, since Christian charity represents a supernatural force for union between men which is far stronger than anything in evolution itself. Charity's own proper movement is towards the Pleroma, but through the Christian it becomes incarnated into history, and is thus able indirectly to affect the natural process of growth and direct it towards a superior form of supernatural union with Christ. Hence Teilhard can say that 'the whole movement of material growth in the universe is ultimately directed towards spirit, and the whole movement of spiritual growth is ultimately directed towards Christ.' There is to be 'some natural human unity that will act as a preparation and foundation of that higher unity *in Christo Jesu*.'[8]

All the various elements of this Christian outlook on the world, elaborated gradually over this ten-year period, are in 1927 gathered together for the first time in the pages of *The Divine Milieu*. 'In our universe,' writes Teilhard, 'where all spirit moves towards God Our Lord, everything that is sensible exists in its turn for spirit.' Consequently in loving and saving each soul, 'God loves and partly saves the whole world since each soul sums up the world in a way which is singular and incommunicable.' Hence it follows that growth of the soul is inseparable from growth of the universe into which it is born, and all effort towards individual spiritualization must slowly bring to matter that which will eventually make of it the heavenly Jerusalem and the new earth. 'We may imagine perhaps that creation was finished long ago. This is not true. It continues more gloriously than ever . . . and we serve to complete it, even with the humblest work of our hands. . . . In each of our works we labour, in a very minute but real way, to build the Pleroma. . . . In action I adhere to the creative power of God; I coincide with it; I become not only its instrument but its living extension.' Indeed, 'by virtue of creation and still more of the Incarnation, nothing here below is profane for those who . . . can distinguish that portion of chosen being which is subject to Christ's drawing power.'[9]

But such adherence to the creative power of God does not take place automatically. Because the present supernatural order means that God's continuous act of creation is ultimately directed towards the Pleroma, our participation in it will necessarily depend upon our union with Christ through faith, a right intention, and most of all through love. 'God is infinitely attainable in the *totality* of our action,' but only 'if we are Christians.' It is first of all through faith that our purely human effort undergoes a metamorphosis, as 'the tremendous power of the divine attraction is focused upon our frail desires and microscopic intents, . . . the special effect of which . . . is to make man's effort holy.'[10] Secondly, this sanctification of human endeavour depends upon 'the initial and fundamental role of one's intention, which is indeed . . . the golden key which unlocks our interior world to the presence of God.' A Christian living in the world must be as convinced as any hermit of the worthlessness of all success envisaged as a benefit either to himself or to others without reference to God. 'It is God and God alone whom he pursues through the reality of created things. His interest lies truly in things, but in absolute dependence upon God's presence in them.'[11] Thirdly, and most important of all, it is Christian love which enables 'the divine Milieu, which will ultimately be one in the Pleroma, [to] start becoming one during the earthly phase of our existence.' Love is in fact the key to man's participation in the creative action of God:

> To what power is it reserved to burst asunder the envelopes in which our individual microcosms tend jealously to isolate themselves and to vegetate? To what force is it given to merge

and exalt our partial rays into the principal radiance of Christ? To charity, the source and consequence of every spiritual relationship. Christian charity, preached with such solemnity by the Gospel, is nothing else than the more or less conscious cohesion of souls engendered by their communal convergence *in Christo Jesu*. It is impossible to love Christ without loving others (in the measure that these others are moving towards Christ); and it is impossible to love others (in a spirit of broad human communion) without in one and the same movement coming closer to Christ. Automatically, therefore, by a sort of living determinism, the individual divine milieux (in so far as they form themselves), tend to fuse one with another, and to find in this mutual association a boundless increase of fervour.... The only subject ultimately capable of spiritual transfiguration is the totality of men forming together a single body and a single soul in charity.[12]

The 'increase of fervour' spoken of in the above passage is an early allusion to what Teilhard will begin during the next decade to call 'amorization' or 'an increase in the psychic temperature of the noosphere', concepts which we have already dealt with in chapter two. During these years between *The Divine Milieu* and *The Phenomenon of Man*, years marked by a growing interest in the relationship between love energy and the planetary maturation of mankind,[13] Teilhard gradually gains deeper insight into the role which Christian charity is destined to play in the natural evolutionary process. 'Up until now,' he writes in 1933, 'love of one's neighbour has meant doing him no harm and binding up his wounds. From now on, without losing any of its compassion, charity will complete its work in lives dedicated to human progress.... Indeed, such a Christianity is still the true Gospel, for it represents the same force applied to lifting up humanity beyond the material in a love which is universal.' Three years later there is the same emphasis: 'Charity no longer demands that we merely bind up wounds; it urges us to build a better world here on earth and to be in the first ranks of every campaign for the full development of mankind.'[14]

Now it is this gradual *rapprochement* between charity, as the driving force in the Christian movement towards the Pleroma, and love energy, as the ultimate key to unity in the noosphere, which results at the end of this ten-year gestation period in a new and totally original concept of the Church. To appreciate this concept at its full value it will be helpful if we first take a glance at what Teilhard has had to say about the Church before the year 1937.

The earliest references to the Church appear in 1916 and 1919. They are significant because they contain the germ cell of what will eventually be Teilhard's master idea, namely the Church's mysterious capacity to reconcile within her own unity movements and tendencies which are in themselves divergent. 'You understand as well as I,' he writes in a 1916 letter, 'how complex these questions are [concerning human effort and Christian detachment], and how they have to be treated in union with the spirit and the living tradition of the Church.' Three years later he returns to the same point: 'I am absolutely certain that there is infinitely more truth in the complex attitude of the Church, based on experience, than in all our simplified philosophical solutions. The experience of the saints is the true "real" imposed upon us and made concrete before our eyes. It is this which must guide our very attempt to systematize, since ultimately it must outstrip them all. As for our speculations, they will remain sterile for ourselves as well as for others unless in our lives we conform to them, and turn them into an example for other men to follow.'[15]

In 1926 Teilhard begins to use the word 'axis' in connection with the Church and to link it more closely to the evolutionary process. 'I believe I see more and more that there is no axis of salvation for the world outside the Christian axis.' This statement is expanded a year later. The light of Christ's omnipresence 'radiates from an historical source and is transmitted along a solidly defined axis of tradition. . . . At the heart of the divine Milieu, as the Church reveals it, things are transfigured, but from within. They bathe inwardly in light, but in this incandescence they retain—this is not strong enough, they magnify—all their most characteristic traits.' Two years later, in 1929, Teilhard says once more, 'Never have I been more sincerely convinced that there is no possible *issue* for the noosphere outside the Christian axis.'[16]

This brief backward glance at Teilhard's early references to the Church will serve as background for the concept which he is now about to propose, namely that this Christian 'axis' is in reality a 'phylum of love' inserted by God into the evolutionary process. The concept appears first in a brief phenomenological analysis dating from 1937, the purpose of which was to determine a parameter for measuring the relationship between religion and evolution. Before Christianity, says Teilhard, the religious instinct of man was already moving towards the conclusion that, because God is a Spirit, he can be reached only through spirit. But it was only with Christianity that this movement reached its term in the definitive conviction that God is love and can ultimately be reached only through love. This was indeed a psychological revolution and the true secret of Christianity's expansion. Unless this essential nature of the Christian phenomenon is recognized, the historian of religion will have no norm to judge the success of the Gospel, but will lose his way amid the countless upheavals of Church history and in fruitless efforts to determine what proportion of the world has been or must still be 'converted'. No, the historian of religion must be like the naturalist, who makes up his mind that the true parameter of evolution is the rise of consciousness, and is henceforth able to follow the true direction of life's movement amid a countless multiplication of species. As soon as the historian of religion decides to measure the movement of Christianity not only by numerical expansion, but by the qualitative evolution of an act of love, he will immediately find himself tracing the curve of a true progress.[17]

Let me not be misunderstood here. The growth of man's collective consciousness does not mean that there have not already been in the world ... men far more gifted individually than many of our contemporaries. No more do I deny that in a Paul, an Augustine or a Teresa of Jesus, divine love found a certain potential for spiritual growth which we might have difficulty finding in any Christian living today. Rather what I mean is that, precisely because of the spiritual genius of saints like Paul, Augustine and Teresa, the theory and practice of total love have never ceased since the time of Christ to become more precise and to be transmitted in ever wider circles. The result is that, after a spiritual experience of two thousand years, our capacity for union with the personal Centre of the universe has grown as much in the richness of its power to express itself as has our capacity for union with the natural spheres of the world after two thousand years of science. Christianity, I would venture to say, is nothing else than a 'phylum' of love within the world of nature.[18]

This concept of the Church as a 'phylum of love' will be better understood if we pause a moment to consider the importance of phyla for Teilhard. Reduced to its simplest terms a 'phylum' is a zoological group or branch, a living 'bundle', one of the natural unities of life. 'What serves not only to define the phylum, but also to classify it without ambiguity . . . is its power and specific law of autonomous development. It is no metaphor to say that it behaves like a living thing, though it does so in its own way: it grows and it expands.' Moreover, there is in every phylum 'a profound inclination towards socialization. . . . Since definitive groupings of organized and differentiated individuals or aggregates (ants, bees, men . . .) are relatively rare in nature, we might be tempted to think of them as something exceptional in evolution. But this impression soon gives way to the opposite conviction that they exemplify one of the most essential laws of organized matter. . . . Whatever the fundamental reason may be, the fact is there: once the elements of a phylum have attained their definitive form . . . they tend to come together and form societies just as surely as the atoms of a solid body tend to crystallize.'[19] In the *Phenomenon of Man* Teilhard goes to some length to describe the gradual growth of a phylum:

In virtue of analogies which correspond . . . to a deep bond of nature, the development of a phylum is strangely parallel to the successive stages undergone by an invention made by men. . . . Roughly the idea first takes the shape of a theory or a provisional mechanism. Then follows a period of rapid modifications. The rough model is continually touched up and adjusted until it is practically completed. On the attainment of this stage, the new creation enters its phase of expansion and equilibrium. Qualitatively there is no further change apart from minor details; it has reached its ceiling. Quantitatively, however, it spreads out and reaches full stability. This is the story of every modern invention, from the bicycle to the airplane, from photography to the cinema and radio.

In exactly the same way does the naturalist see the curve of growth followed by the branches of life. At the outset the phylum corresponds to the 'discovery' by groping of a new type of organism, both viable and advantageous. But this new type will not attain its most economical or efficient form all at once. For a certain period of time it devotes all its strength, so to speak, to groping about upon itself. . . . At last perfection comes within sight, and . . . the new invention, having reached the limit of its potentialities, enters into its phase of conquest. Stronger now than its less perfected neighbours, the newly born group spreads out and at the same time consolidates. It multiplies but without further diversification. It has now reached the maximum both of its growth and of its stability.[20]

As we have already seen in chapter two, the whole orientation of evolution for Teilhard is towards the formation of the human phylum, which in its turn carries the movement of life across the first threshold of reflection and into the noosphere. What he now wishes to say is that, on the phenomenological level, the Church also acts as a phylum, or more precisely, that it acts as a phylum of love growing within the human phylum and moving in the same direction. When such an assertion is transposed to the level of Christian revelation, the Church immediately appears as the true source of love energy and therefore the true carrier of human life (and thus of the whole evolutionary process) in its upward movement towards Christ-Omega and the second threshold of reflection. Let us see how Teilhard develops this idea, again making use, as always, of two sources of knowledge.

Following the first mention in 1937 of the Church as a phylum, the idea is taken up again during the writing of *The Phenomenon of Man* between 1938 and 1940. 'It is a phenomenon of capital importance,' writes Teilhard, 'that on an appreciable region of the earth there has appeared and grown a zone of thought in which a genuine universal love has not only been conceived and preached, but has also been shown to be psychologically possible and operative in practice. It is all the more capital in as much as, far from decreasing, the movement seems to wish to gain still greater speed and intensity.' It may well be asked, therefore, 'is not the Christian faith destined, is it not preparing, to save and even to take the place of evolution?' Rooted in the past, yet ceaselessly developing in the present, Christianity exhibits all the characteristics of a phylum. Seen as part of an evolutionary process interpreted as an ascent of consciousness, this phylum shows itself to be progressing in the direction presumed to be that of the leading shoot of biogenesis, namely towards a synthesis based on love. Consequently it must be through Christianity that the principal axis of evolution now passes, since in its visible structure it constitutes the unique current of energy in the noosphere in which faith and hope reach their fulfilment in love.[21]

Up to now the idea of 'Church-phylum' has been dealt with on the level of phenomena. In 1944 Teilhard approaches it for the first time on the level of revelation. 'From the point of view . . . of Catholic dogma,' he says, 'there is at the basis of the Christian outlook a faith in the reality of the Church phylum, in which and around which Christ continues to develop his total personality in the world.' To say that the Church is infallible is simply to recognize that it possesses what any living phylum possesses, namely the capacity to find its way through innumerable gropings towards maturity and fulfilment. Moreover, it is in perfect conformity with the great law of 'cephalization' which dominates the whole of biological evolution, to localize this phyletic infallibility either in the Councils or in the Pope, in so far as they formulate the thought of the Church. Outside Catholicism there are undoubtedly very many who know and love Christ and who are therefore just as united to him as Catholics, perhaps more so. But these 'are not grouped together in the "cephalized" unity of a *body* which reacts in a living way, as an organized whole, to the combined energies of Christ and humanity. They drink the sap of the tree as it flows from the trunk, but they neither penetrate beneath the bark to the tree's life source, nor do they participate in its inner growth. . . . To be a Christian in the fullest and deepest sense one has to be a Catholic.'[22]

It would not be out of place, before proceeding further, to insist upon a point which is sometimes overlooked and which in the above passage is abundantly clear: the 'Church-phylum' for Teilhard is always the Catholic Church. 'It is around Christianity (considered in its "phyletic" or Catholic form) that the principal axis of hominization coils itself ever tighter.' From Rome in 1948 he writes: 'At St. Peter's I really experienced how awe-inspiring is the Christian phenomenon: I mean this undisturbed assurance, unique in the world, of being in direct contact with a personal Centre of the universe.' . . . 'It is here in Rome that we find the Christic pole of the earth; through Rome, I mean, runs the ascending axis of hominization.'[23] In 1950 the same conviction is recorded several times: 'Only in the Roman "trunk" taken in its entirety, do I see the biological support sufficiently vast and differentiated to carry out the enduring transformation of humanity which we await.' This 'Catholic phylum' is 'the very centre of the privileged zone where the upward cosmic movement of "complexity-consciousness" is united with the downward personal movement of attraction with its power to personalize.' In a 'neutral' lecture on the influence of religion that same year he adds: 'Were I to speak here as a Catholic, I should have to add that the Church, not from arrogance but from structural necessity and under pain of denying her own identity, simply cannot avoid considering herself to be the axis upon which the awaited movement of convergence and gathering-together can and must take place.'[24] Significantly enough, this belief in the central importance of the Catholic Church is asserted most strongly during those years when very severe strictures were being imposed upon him by his religious superiors as well as by other authorities in Rome.[25] And he asserts it once more shortly before he died: 'No religious faith, either now or at any moment in history, has ever released a greater warmth, a more intense dynamism for unification, than Christianity is doing at the present time, the more it is Catholic.'[26]

This conception of the Church as a phylum of love marks a turning point in Teilhard's theological thought. Elaborated between 1937 and 1947, it serves to tie together into a single image all the various lines of his previous analysis of Christian activity and is directly responsible during these same years for his effort to explain how there can be such a thing as Christogenesis. This will become clear in the following pages. Moreover, we shall now see the full force and relevance of that block of speculation already dealt with in chapter three, concerning the physical omnipresence of Christ's Body-Person which, up to its final elaboration in 1927, had never been linked explicitly by Teilhard to the mystery of the Church. This concept of Christ as organic Centre is now to be fused with that of the Church as organic phylum, and the fusion is to take place precisely in and through the concept of Christogenesis.

The first time Teilhard uses the word 'genesis' in connection with Christ is in the following brief text from a 1938 essay: 'Between the genesis of humanity in the world and the genesis of Christ in humanity through his Church, there is at present neither independence nor discord, but coherent subordination. The two processes are in their structure inevitably linked together,—the second demanding the first as material which it unites with in order to suranimate.'[27] The word 'Christogenesis' itself makes its appearance the following year, and is related more explicitly to the physical nature of the Incarnation. 'A universe whose structure evolves—as long as one understands the direction of such a movement—could well be, after all, the milieu most favourable for developing a great and homogeneous understanding of the Incarnation. . . . What better than an ascending anthropogenesis to serve as a background and foundation for the descending illuminations of a Christogenesis?' . . . 'If the world is convergent and if Christ occupies its centre, then the Christogenesis of St. Paul and St. John is nothing else and nothing less than the extension, both awaited and unhoped for, of that noogenesis in which we experience the culmination of cosmogenesis. Christ invests himself organically with the very majesty of his creation.'[28] It is 1942 when Teilhard next uses the word, the context again being the physical relationship between Christ and the evolutionary process: 'The natural and supernatural fulfilments of the world envelop each other, the latter incorporating and transforming the former; that is to say, God unites himself in such a way to the axis of the natural evolution of spirit, taken in its entity, that Christogenesis appears as the sublimation of the whole of cosmogenesis.'[29]

A lengthy passage in a 1943 essay incorporates this concept for the first time into an analysis of the role of Christian charity. That whole year Teilhard is again preoccupied with man's psychological need actually to love human progress before he can dedicate himself to it completely. 'Now how are we going to love something like the world or even humanity, realities that are collective, impersonal, even monstrous in certain respects?' This is precisely the problem of all naturalistic humanisms; the enthusiasm and zeal they engender eventually dry up and become cold, joyless and hard. Hence what modern man needs is to find the source of a truly universal love in order to conquer his 'dread of that frightful cosmic machinery in which he finds himself entangled.' This can only come from Christianity, which alone can teach a man 'not merely how to serve (which is not enough) but how to love deeply, in all its manifestations, . . . a universe whose very evolution has been impregnated with love.'[30] Teilhard's explanation of this is the following:

Because everything in the universe is in fact ultimately moving towards Christ-Omega; because cosmogenesis, moving in its totality through anthropogenesis, ultimately shows itself to be a Christogenesis; because of this, I say, it follows that the real is charged with a divine presence in the entirety of its tangible layers. As the mystics knew and felt, everything becomes physically and literally lovable in God; and, conversely, God can be possessed and loved in everything around us. . . . I repeat, if the whole movement of the world is in the service of a Christogenesis (which is another way of saying that Christ is attainable in his fullness only at the end and summit of cosmic evolution), then clearly we can draw near to him and possess him only in and through the effort to bring all to fulfilment and synthesis in him. And this is the reason that life's general ascent towards higher consciousness as well as the whole of human endeavour enter organically and by right into the preoccupations and aspirations of charity. . . .

We have seen that Christ, by reason of his position as Omega of the world, represents a focus towards whom and in whom everything converges. In other words, he appears as One in whom all reality . . . establishes union and contact in the only direction possible: the line of centres. What can this mean except that every action, as soon as it is oriented towards him, takes on, without any change in itself, the psychic character of a centre-to-centre relationship, that is to say, of an act of love. . . . At first the Christian aspired only to be able to love . . . *while* acting. Now he is aware that he can love *in* acting, that is to say, he can unite himself directly to the divine Centre through action itself, no matter what form such action takes. In him all activity is, if I may use the expression, 'amorized'. . . . There are men today . . . among whom the lived conjunction of the two ideas of Incarnation and evolution has led to the creation of a synthesis of the personal and the universal. For the first time in history men have become capable not only of understanding and serving, but of *loving evolution*.[31]

The concept of Christogenesis is given further precision in 1944 when Teilhard links it to the mystery of the Holy Eucharist. Through the Eucharist, he says, 'passes directly the axis of the Incarnation, that is to say, the axis of creation.' In its ultimate operation, the Eucharist 'is but the expression and manifestation of the divine unifying energy applying itself little by little to every spiritual atom of the universe. To unite ourselves to Christ in the Eucharist, therefore, is *ipso facto* inevitably to incorporate ourselves little by little into a Christogenesis which is itself the soul of universal cosmogenesis.'[32] The 'exaltation of the historical Christ to a function in the universe which is physical' ultimately means 'an identification of cosmogenesis with Christogenesis', and the Christian is able 'to look upon the discovery of Christogenesis as an ultimate explanation as well as a final crowning of the cosmogenesis discovered by science.'[33]

The meaning of this 'final crowning' becomes quite clear in 1946 when Teilhard gives what he calls 'an ultimate and final definition of the Omega Point'. Omega is the Person of Christ in his Plenitude at the Parousia, acting as unifying focus for three centres, one inside the other, which reach a point at the top of the cone of time. The outside centre is the natural summit of the humano-cosmic cone; within this is the supernatural summit of the humano-Christic or Church cone; and the innermost centre is the transcendent divine Trinity. With this explanation we are able 'to penetrate more deeply into the nature of the Christian phenomenon. The Church is not simply a teaching body but a living organism: the embryo of a super-life inserted into the heart of the noosphere by the historical appearance of Christ Jesus; not a parasite, adding to and deforming the evolving human cone, but a cone within the human cone, gradually impregnating, spreading over and sustaining the whole rising mass of the world, and causing it to converge concentrically upon the same summit.'[34] Consequently, 'in the genesis of humanity's social organism, the Church is not an epi- or a paraphenomenon but forms the axis itself, the nucleus around which men are destined to gather together.'[35]

Up to now Teilhard's development of the concept of a Christogenesis has been due chiefly to his analysis of the Church's role as a phylum of love within the evolutionary process. Between 1947 and his death in 1955 he completes this analysis of the Church and Christian activity with his theme of the 'Upward' and the 'Forward', and thereby indicates how we can speak of the two movements of cosmogenesis and Christogenesis as ultimately one and the same. We have already seen that as early as 1942 and 1943 Teilhard had touched briefly upon the need for a synthesis of those two currents of psychic energy, represented by Christian charity and human progress.[36] In 1944 he again referred in passing to the same subject, and in 1947 he speaks for the first time of these psychic currents as 'two types of faith', one in the transcendent action of a personal God, the other in the immanent perfectibility of a world in evolution.[37] Later that year these tentative formulations come to maturity, and beginning in 1948 Teilhard's thought ripens into his final mode of expressing man's participation in the creative activity of God, as well as his final understanding, from the point of view of Christian activity, of the relationship between the Church, the evolutionary process and the coming of the Parousia.

He begins with what he calls 'the problem and the synthesis of two faiths', and he coins the two nouns *l'En-Haut* and *l'En-Avant* in an effort both to express the problem and to resolve it.[38] The real drama in the present religious conflict, he says, is the apparent impossibility of reconciling two types of faith, a Christian faith in God whose movement is vertical, and a 'natural' faith in the primacy of man whose movement is horizontal. Teilhard calls one faith the 'Upward', the other the 'Forward'. In regard to the Christian, it would seem at first that his faith should immunize him against any strong desire to promote human progress, while materialists on the other hand would seem to regard a transcendent absolute as a threat to their confidence in man's future on earth. And yet, if Christ is truly the physical Centre for cosmogenesis, then these two psychic energies towards the Upward and the Forward must in reality be moving in the same direction. For Teilhard's supposition is that just as the first coming of Christ demanded that men have already reached a certain anatomical and social development, so his second coming at the end of time would seem to demand that the human species as a whole have already reached its full natural development in order to be capable of receiving from Christ its supernatural consummation. 'The point of human maturation' would thus be 'a condition (not indeed sufficient and determinative but necessary)' for 'the point of the Parousia of Christ.'[39]

Hence the task of Christian activity in the world today should be an effort to synthesize these two energies and direct their combined power towards the true progress of radial energy in the noosphere.

The direction of Christian faith has to be 'rectified' slightly or 'explicitated' towards the Forward; that of modern man's faith in himself rectified slightly towards the Upward. In this way 'the Christian Upward combines with the human Forward, not by becoming immersed in it but by "supernaturalizing" it.' Such a juncture 'is in no sense a half-measure, a compromise between heaven and earth, but rather a resultant force combining [both energies] and re-enforcing one by the other. . . . Salvation (which would be the outcome) is at the same time Upward and Forward,— in a Christ who is both Saviour and Mover not only of individual men but of anthropogenesis in its entirety.'[40]

It should be noted that this Christian effort to unite the Upward and the Forward is not simply curative but creative, for it helps to activate the Church's role in human progress, which is to infuse into the evolutionary process the full power of Christian charity. This charity of Christ is alone capable of raising the psychic temperature of the noosphere high enough to bring about the eventual planetary maturation of mankind. 'The charity of the Gospel is coming to be seen as ultimately a love of cosmogenesis "Christified" down to its roots.' From this point of view, 'noospheric maturation (since it is linked to a concentrated form of "charity") can not be completed without the animating action of the Church growing at the heart of humanity. Which is another way of saying that . . . earthly progress will reach its point of liberation in "the lightning of the Parousia" only if it has been Christified from the inside.' Consequently 'what is now going on at the heart of the social phenomenon is a sort of ultra-socialization, by which the "Church" slowly takes shape by bringing together through her influence all the spiritual energies of the noosphere in their most noble form and giving them life;—the Church, that Christified part of the world aware of itself as such;—the Church, principal focus of inter-human relationships through the intensity of its charity;—the Church, central axis of universal convergence, the very spot where the universe and the Omega Point come rushing together.'[41]

Ultimately, therefore, it is the Christic energy of charity, present in the world through the Church and the individual Christian, which leads Teilhard to insist that the evolutionary process must be described as 'a Christogenesis in which the Upward and the Forward become reconciled.' Since Christ is Prime Mover of evolution, 'he *ipso facto* acquires and develops in the fullest sense a real omnipresence of transformation. Under his influence and attraction, every energy, every event of our lives is suranimated. In the last analysis cosmogenesis, discovered along its principal axis to be biogenesis and then noogenesis, culminates in Christogenesis, the object of every Christian's veneration.'[42] This omnipresence of Christ was preoccupying Teilhard three days before he died in 1955, and in an effort to bring together the various elements in Christogenesis he made the following entry in his diary:[43]

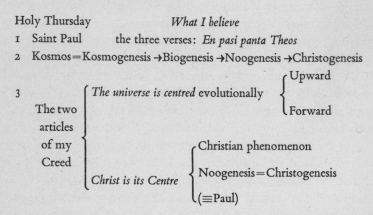

Holy Thursday   *What I believe*

1   Saint Paul   the three verses: *En pasi panta Theos*

2   Kosmos=Kosmogenesis →Biogenesis →Noogenesis →Christogenesis

3   *The universe is centred* evolutionally   { Upward, Forward }

The two articles of my Creed   *Christ is its Centre*   { Christian phenomenon, Noogenesis=Christogenesis, (≡Paul) }

The theme of the Upward and the Forward was of major concern for Teilhard towards the end of his life,[44] and with this last affirmation just before his death we come to the end of one whole segment of his thought. His aim throughout has been to relate Christ's work of redemption to that of God's continuous act of creation. His point of view has been that of Christian action in the world and the chief object of his attention has been the mystery of the Church. We may briefly summarize his thought as follows. He has said, first of all, that Christian activity in the world, in so far as it is motivated by charity, is a participation in the creative power of God and hence a divine instrument for building up 'in some way' the supernatural

Plenitude of Christ. This conclusion on the level of revelation then merged with Teilhard's rational analysis of the role of love energy to give him the idea that the source of this energy's presence in the world was indeed an organic body, a phylum inserted by God into evolution precisely in order to guarantee that the human phylum reach the fullness of its natural and supernatural development. Christian activity is therefore related to evolution not simply because it is motivated subjectively by charity, but much more so because it takes place within an objective, corporate and highly organized phylum, whose whole *raison d'être* is to act as the source of love energy in the world.[45] The Church's destiny, therefore, is to be the true carrier of human evolution towards Christ-Omega between the Resurrection and the Parousia; and it is this fact which is gradually responsible for Teilhard's referring to the evolutionary process not so much as a cosmogenesis but rather as a Christogenesis.[46]

From this first point of view, therefore, Christogenesis designates the growth of the Church phylum within the human phylum, a growth which sustains the whole movement of cosmogenesis, providing it with a nucleus around which men are destined to gather, and causing it to converge concentrically upon Christ-Omega. Teilhard's earlier concept of Christ as organic Centre is thus fused with that of the Church as organic phylum, for it now becomes clear that Christ is physical Centre for mankind and the material world precisely because he is physical Centre for the Church. The result is a new mode of expressing the Christian's participation in the creative activity of God, namely as an effort to bring about in the evolutionary process itself that juncture between the Upward and the Forward, between the energy of charity and the energy of progress, which has already been achieved in the Body-Person of Christ himself. In this way Christian activity serves as both microcosm and catalyst for the movement of the cosmos towards the Parousia. The gradual building up of the Pleroma is thus seen to be the unique purpose of true human progress (i.e. the movement of radial energy towards higher consciousness) and, conversely, no earthly enterprise may rightfully be called progress in the true sense unless it contributes in some way to the gradual growth of the total Body of Christ.

II

From the point of view we have just considered, namely that of Christian action in the world, Teilhard's analysis of the Church as a phylum of love is what is primarily responsible for his speaking of the evolutionary process as a Christogenesis. From this point of view too, the mystery of God's continuous creation is intimately linked with Christ's work of redemption and is not simply the unfolding of a pre-existent plan. The outcome is indeed to be the Plenitude of Christ, but this Plenitude is conditioned by the extent to which men freely choose to be transfigured by Christian charity and thereby participate in God's creative power. For Teilhard such participation is the necessary but insufficient condition for the coming of the Parousia, and the world will end only when men have, through charity, freely pushed the movement of radial energy to its point of planetary maturation.

It is important to underline this first outlook of Teilhard, because it differs considerably from the second point of view we are now about to consider. The object of Teilhard's analysis from his second vantage point is not Christian action in the world, but the eternal creative action of God; not the Church's task in the evolutionary process, but God's design from all eternity to direct this process towards the Parousia. Christogenesis is to be seen now not in so far as it is an accomplishment of man's freedom, but in so far as it is a work of divine omnipotence and love, and the key concept of 'organic phylum' is to be replaced by that of 'Pleromization'. 'It is characteristic of the ordinary economy of Christian life,' wrote Teilhard in 1940, 'that certain elements of revelation which have long lain dormant should suddenly receive a powerful development according to the needs and demands of a new age. It seems to me that in our time this is the role reserved to the great concept of the Christian Pleroma, which is such an integral part of dogma, . . . the mysterious synthesis of the created and the Uncreated—the complete fulfilment (at once qualitative and quantitative) of the universe in God.'[47] The slow maturation of the universe into this 'mysterious synthesis' at the Parousia Teilhard calls 'Pleromization', and its analysis constitutes the final phase of his effort to rethink the mystery of Christ in terms of *genèse*.

For purposes of clarity we may divide his treatment into two main parts. There is first a metaphysical theory which Teilhard calls 'creative union', the starting point of which is a strong affirmation of Christ's election at the beginning of time to be Head of all creation. The theory itself then attempts to explain the three mysteries of creation, Incarnation and redemption in terms of a single evolutionary movement towards the final Plenitude of Christ. The second part of Teilhard's approach to Pleromization is a tentative speculation concerning the planetary maturation of mankind. In his system this will take place at the moment of the Parousia, for it is then that Christ will bring Christogenesis to an end and unite all of mankind in the fullness of his Body-Person. We shall now examine in greater detail these two parts of his analysis.

The starting point of Teilhard's theory of 'creative union' is the data of revelation concerning Christ's relationship to the whole of creation from the very beginning of time. Here Teilhard puts special emphasis on Colossians 1:15-17, a text which we have discussed already in chapter three. Early essays are filled with allusions to these verses as well as to Ephesians 2:10 and I Corinthians 8:6. 'By him all things have been created, sanctified, vivified. That is the constant and common teaching of St. John and St. Paul.' . . .'He is Alpha and Omega, beginning and end, foundation-stone and keystone, the fullness which fills all else. He who consummates and stabilizes all things.' . . .'The prodigious extent of time before the first Christmas was not void of him but penetrated throughout by his powerful influence.' . . .'[God] willed his Christ, and in order to have his Christ he had to create a world of the spirit, men in particular, in which Christ would germinate; and to have man, he had to launch the enormous movement of organic life. . . ; and for the latter to spring up the whole tumult of the cosmos was

169

necessary.' . . . 'Everything takes place as if God were ontologically engaged [in the cosmos] even before his Incarnation.'[48]

This insistence of Teilhard upon Christ's role in creation calls attention to an aspect of St. Paul's thought which, as we have already noted, is receiving considerable attention today.[49] Paul seems clearly to affirm a pre-existence for Christ, and apparently it is always the concrete, historical God-Man of whom he is thinking, never the Word independent of his humanity. How this is to be explained theologically is a question for which there is as yet no satisfactory answer. Teilhard's own theory is that 'every cosmic particle, even the tiniest electron, is rigorously coextensive with the totality of space and time.' Hence 'the body of a living being, far from limiting it inside the universe, is simply the expression and gauge of its interiority and its "centreity".' But 'in the case of Christ, this coextension of coexistence has become a coextension of domination,' and the reason Christ's Body has such a privileged position in the universe is to be traced to 'the transforming effect of the Resurrection.'[50]

This relationship of Christ to the whole of creation provides the key to an understanding of Teilhard's theory of 'creative union'. To treat this theory as a purely rational analysis, as some have done,[51] is to distort it completely and to create theological difficulties which do not in fact exist. 'The philosophy of creative union . . . is nothing but the development . . . of what the Church teaches us concerning the growth of Christ. It is the philosophy of the universe conceived in function of our knowledge of the Mystical Body.' This 'philosophical extension of faith in the Incarnation', as Teilhard also calls it,[52] is therefore meant to deal with God's continuous act of creation not only on the level of reason but also on that of revelation. It is an attempt to give a metaphysical explanation of evolution's movement by making use of two sources of knowledge, and in strict theological terminology its precise object would not be 'creation' but 'elevation', that is to say, creation in Christ. This is quite clear in the ensemble of Teilhard's writings. 'The world is still being created and it is Christ who brings himself to completion in it.' Because he is 'Plenitude of the universe, all things are created in him since in him all are united. These are the two terminations of creative union.' Christ possesses 'all the capacity for unity which is spread throughout creation.' Outside the 'unifying influence of Christ, nothing in the world has any real existence. From top to bottom things find in Christ their sole principle of stability: *In eo omnia constant.*' The world is 'above all a work of creation continued in Christ.'[53]

Hence, were it not for the data of revelation regarding Christ's presence at the beginning of time and the existence of his Pleroma at the end of time, Teilhard would never have conceived his philosophy of creative union. It is necessary to insist on this point because, in the more important of the two essays which treat the subject in depth, the elaboration of his theory follows immediately after his hyperphysics and his option of a personal Omega, and begins with the following statement: 'I shall [now] try to reconstruct deductively, i.e. *a priori*, the system thus observed, including its extensions in theology and revelation, from certain general principles assumed to be absolute.'[54] Such a statement would indeed seem to announce a purely rational analysis. Yet what gradually becomes evident from the context (and this will appear presently) is that these 'general principles' are actually inspired by Christian revelation, and that the '*a priori*' means not 'antecedent to revelation' but 'antecedent to a phenomenological analysis'. Consequently, although creative union may be placed *logically* prior to Teilhard's theology in so far as it is a metaphysical theory, it is in fact an integral part of his overall theological effort to clarify the concept of Christogenesis.[55]

Teilhard begins his exposition by defining being in terms of a movement indissolubly associated with it, that of union. Thus, in its active sense, being would mean 'to unite oneself or to unite others', while in its passive sense it would mean 'to be united or unified by another'. Teilhard adds immediately that 'others' in the active formula applies even to God, but only in regard to 'Pleromization', not in regard to 'Trinitization'.[56] He then distinguishes four successive 'moments' in his metaphysics of union. The first moment is a recognition of a divine and self-sufficient First Cause, that is to say, an acceptance of the philosophic option of a personal Omega which we have already analyzed in chapter two. The second moment, 'in conformity with "revealed" data,' is a recognition that the existence of this Centre, 'who is both beginning and end,' consists in the act of opposing and uniting himself triunely to himself. However, it is in the third and fourth moments that Teilhard begins to explain how, in and through the Pleroma of Christ, God can be said to 'complete' himself in the act of creation. Here is the complete text:

By the very fact that he unifies himself interiorly, the First Being *ipso facto* causes another type of opposition to arise, not within himself but at his antipodes (and here we have our third moment). At the pole of being there is self-subsistent Unity, and all around at the periphery, as a necessary consequence, there is multiplicity: *pure* multiplicity, be it understood, a 'creatable void' which is simply nothing,—yet which, because of its passive potency for arrangement (i.e. for union), constitutes a possibility, an appeal for being. Now everything takes place as if God had not been able to resist this appeal, for at such depths our intelligence can no longer distinguish at all between supreme necessity and supreme freedom [except by recognizing the presence of the Free in the infallible sign of an accompanying love].[57]

In classical philosophy or theology, creation or participation (which constitutes our fourth moment) always tends to be presented as an almost arbitrary gesture on the part of the First Cause, executed by a causality analogous to 'efficient' and according to a mechanism that is completely indeterminate: truly an 'act of God' in the pejorative sense. In a metaphysics of union, on the contrary,—although the self-sufficiency and self-determination of the Absolute Being remain inviolate (since pure, antipodal multiplicity is, I insist, nothing but pure passivity and potentiality)—in such a metaphysics, I say, the creative act takes on a very well defined significance and structure. [It is now seen to be] 'Pleromization' (as St. Paul might have said), that is to say, the giving of reality to participated being through arrangement and totalization. Pleromization is thus the fruit of God's reflection, not upon himself but outside himself; it appears somehow as a sort of replica or symmetry of Trinitization. Somehow its actuation fills a void and it finds its place in the scheme of things. At the same time we can give it expression by using the very terms which served us to define being. To create means to unite.[58]

These 'four moments' of creative union call for some comment, first because of Teilhard's statement on the relationship of God to matter, and secondly because of his statement on the gratuity of creation. We shall omit discussion of a third question which has been frequently raised in this context, sc. whether Teilhard actually held a multiplicity which was positive and which in some sense existed prior to creation. He himself went to some pains to reject such a notion, not only in the passage we have just quoted but in numerous other essays, and Henri de Lubac has already gathered these texts together and treated the problem with both precision and depth.[59] Consequently we shall limit ourselves to the first two questions, since they have far more direct relevance to Teilhard's concept of Christogenesis.

In regard to the relationship of God to the material world, Teilhard begins by saying that creation is a reflection, an image, of the life of the Blessed Trinity. This is what imposes upon it that metaphysical structure by which it must necessarily move from multiplicity to unity, and more precisely towards an ultimate unity with God. This is the sense of Teilhard's statement in 1942 that 'evolution is not "creative" . . . but is the expression of creation in space and time.'[60] Thus far there is no difficulty for traditional Christian teaching; St. Thomas made practically the same statements, although obviously not in Teilhard's evolutionary framework.[61] Nor is there any serious difficulty from the fact that Teilhard states elsewhere that, since evolution is our only experience of creation and since to create means to unite, it could well be that this is the only way God could go about uniting the world to himself. This opinion, Teilhard says, is merely probable.[62] Nor does he ever incorporate it into his theory of creative union, since his primary concern here is always with the world which God did in fact create.

However, the assertion that the world's movement towards unity 'completes' God in some way is unusual and needs to be clarified. Again it must be kept in mind that Teilhard is referring always to the building up of the Body of Christ in the present supernatural order. In 1924, after outlining creative union as a theory which sees everything taking place in the present evolutionary order as if the One were being formed by successive unifications with the many, he adds immediately: 'These formulas are to be weighed carefully so as not to be misunderstood. They do not mean that the One is formed from the many. . . . [but] that the One appears to us only after [our knowledge of] the many, through his supremacy over the many, since his formal and essential action is to unite.' Shortly afterwards, in *The Divine Milieu*, he speaks of 'the mysterious Pleroma, in which the substantial One and the created many fuse without confusion into a totality which, without adding anything essential to God, will nevertheless be a sort of triumph and generalization of being.'[63] Consider also the following statement from 1932:

> The idea we are trying to form today of multiplicity, its structure and function, is closely linked up with the Christian vision of the final consummation of the universe. On the other hand, because of the Incarnation, God can no longer do without the many among whom he has immersed himself— at least from now on in the present order. On the other hand, that reality which is to be found *in Christo Jesu*, namely 'God plus the many', seems both in Christian practice and Pauline spirituality to represent a perfection which, however wholly extrinsic to God it may be, involves a real completion in the symmetry of the universal Being.[64]

From these texts it is clear that what Teilhard is doing is nothing more nor less than simply asserting in an evolutionary context the paradox which is already contained in St. Paul: the Pleroma of Christ cannot constitute an intrinsic completion of God himself, but it will nonetheless in some sense be a real completion. But why go to such lengths to insist on the second half of the paradox? The answer is that Teilhard wants to do away once and for all with the idea that God's continuous act of creation is one of *absolute* gratuity. It is important to note here the operative word. For Teilhard has no intention whatsoever of denying the sovereign freedom of God the Creator. What he means is that, from all eternity, creation in God's mind is creation in Christ, and that consequently it cannot be considered an 'arbitrary act'. The world is not something 'radically contingent', a mere 'superfluous accessory' which, in the present supernatural order, God can somehow do without. Mankind is not a matter of indifference to God; its evolutionary development is meant to move towards and in some way contribute to the final Pleroma of Christ. By his own sovereignly free decision, therefore, God is no longer 'absolutely' and 'radically' self-sufficient.

Hence Teilhard is able to say (in the text a few pages back dealing with the 'four moments' of creation) that, granted we accept creation as the beginning and continuation of Pleromization, 'everything takes place *as if* God had not been able to resist this appeal [for being].' The italics have been added here because the two words throw light on what follows immediately: '. . . for at such depths our intelligence can no longer distinguish at all between supreme necessity and supreme freedom, except by recognizing the presence of the Free in the infallible sign of an accompanying love.' It is therefore God's love which constitutes his sovereign freedom and which is at one and the same time responsible for his dependence upon men. In our Christian activity, says Teilhard in *The Divine Milieu*, 'let us test every barrier, try every path, plumb every depth. *Nihil intentatum.* . . . It is the will of God, who has willed that he should have need of it.'[65] If the universe is not pure contingency in the present supernatural order, this is due uniquely to the divine initiative, by which all has been created in Christ, centred upon Christ, and destined to remain united to Christ for all eternity.

Teilhard felt very strongly about this need of man under which God has freely placed himself out of the abundance of his love. If the whole movement of the cosmos were merely a divine game, he writes in 1945, then 'why the supreme interest attached to the completion of the mysterious Pleroma in the most positive texts of Scripture? God is completely self-sufficient, and yet the universe brings to him something vitally necessary.' In this same context of revelation he writes a few years later: 'If creation can involve an unlimited number of phases, it cannot in return be carried out more than once in the "life of God", if I may venture to say so, a little like Trinitization. Indeed, once the reduction of multiplicity has begun, there remains no form of opposing void, either interior or exterior, to be "pleromized". Every possibility for union we can think of, whether active or passive, is exhausted, and "being", having reached this level, is completely saturated.' Nor is there any doubt of the reason behind so strong a statement: ' "Participated being", which means each one of us, is beginning to ask itself whether the radically contingent condition to which theologians reduce it really justifies the effort it has to make to evolve. . . . If man is presented with the so-called revelation of his radical inutility, how is he going to avoid distaste for action? . . . In point of fact, what gives life to Christianity is not the sense of the created world's contingency, but the sense of the mutual completion of God and the world.'[66]

What Teilhard is denying, therefore, is not the abstract idea of God's freedom in creation, but the concrete idea that he is personally independent of this present world whose destiny from all eternity was to be created in Christ. Nor does he wish by this to compromise in any way the added gratuity of the present supernatural order. On the contrary, as we have seen in chapters two and three, he takes pains to assert it clearly and without ambiguity as an integral part of his Christology.[67] Consequently it should come as no great surprise to find him insisting upon the following conclusion to the 'four moments' of creative union: 'Thus it is that a series of ideas, long regarded as independent, come gradually more and more to link themselves together organically before our eyes. Up to a certain point there is no God [i.e. considered in his Pleroma] without creative union, no creation without [God's] incarnate immersion into it, no Incarnation without redemptive compensation. In a metaphysics of union the three fundamental "mysteries" of Christianity are seen to be but three aspects of a single mystery of mysteries, that of Pleromization, or the reduction of multiplicity to unity.'[68]

Note that the emphasis here is upon the unity of these three mysteries in the divine plan for the human race. What is being questioned is not their gratuity but their separability in the present supernatural order. 'Creation, Incarnation, redemption each mark a higher degree in the gratuity of the divine operation, but are they not also three acts which are indissolubly united in the appearance of participated being?' In this sense the ultimate mystery of God's dealings with man is to be found 'not precisely in the mechanism of creation or of the Incarnation or redemption, but in "Pleromization", by which I mean the mysterious relationship of "repletion" (if not completion) which links the First Being with participated being.'[69] We have therefore 'one single process, which is Christogenesis, considered either in its moving principle (creation), or in its unifying mechanism (Incarnation), or in its uplifting struggle (redemption).'[70]

'Creative union', 'Pleromization', 'Christogenesis', are therefore synonymous terms to describe the exercise of Christ's power as organic Centre of the universe, a continuous influence which is both creative, unitive and redemptive, and which culminates in his Plenitude at the Parousia. 'Because all the lines of the world converge and knit themselves together in him, it is he who physically and literally gives his own stability to the whole structure of matter and spirit. It is consequently in him as "Head of creation" that the fundamental cosmic process of cephalization, in its universal extent and supernatural depth, and yet in harmony with all the past, culminates and draws to its close.'[71] The world in evolution thus cannot be explained except by Christ; yet by the same token one might also say that in Teilhard's system the full meaning of Christ in his Plenitude cannot be explained except by evolution. This is what is meant by the question: 'Christ indeed saves evolution, but should we not add immediately that he is at the same time saved by evolution?' The word 'save' here is poorly chosen but Teilhard's intention is clear, as it is also in the following formulation: 'Just as Christ makes evolution possible by giving meaning to the world, evolution makes Christ possible by disclosing a summit for the world. . . . The total Christ can be consummated only at the end of the world's evolution.'[72]

This theory of creative union, which we have just outlined along with its important conclusion, involves two minor problems which we shall treat briefly now before proceeding to the larger question of the coming of the Parousia and the end of the world. The first of these concerns a number of expressions coined by Teilhard as synonyms for the 'total Christ'. Two of them we have encountered already: 'the cosmic Christ' and 'the universal Christ'. A third is 'the Christic', a noun which refers to the state of humanity's union with Christ rather than to the Person who unites, in the same way as Teilhard speaks in his hyperphysics of 'the human' instead of 'man' when he is referring to the state of thought in the noosphere rather than the person who thinks.[73] These three expressions cause no great difficulty; three others, however, have connotations which tend to confuse rather than clarify, and Teilhard would have been well advised to drop them altogether: 'the universal Element', 'the Soul of the world', and 'the Super-Christ'.[74] All of these are synonyms and refer to the Body-Person of Christ in so far as he is here and now being 'completed', that is to say, in so far as he physically unites mankind to himself through his creative and redemptive power. As we have seen in chapter three, Teilhard himself is well aware of one problem raised by expressions like these, and this is why he goes out of his way to insist that in using them he is always speaking of Jesus of Nazareth.

But there is another expression, used in the same general sense as those above, which is more easily open to a total and dangerous misunderstanding, especially if taken out of context. This is the casual reference Teilhard makes twice to a 'third nature' for Christ. Here are the two texts in question, the first from 1948, the second from 1955. 'Between the Word on the one hand and Jesus the Man on the other, a sort of Christic "third nature" comes into being, if I dare use the term. One can see the idea everywhere in the writings of St. Paul, that of the total Christ who totalizes, in whom the individual human element born of Mary is transformed by the

178

Resurrection into the state not simply of a cosmic Element (or Milieu or Compass) but of an ultimate psychic Centre for the gathering together of the universe.' . . . 'In the total Christ (and on this point Christian tradition is unanimous) there is not just Man and God; there is also he who in his "theandric" being gathers together the whole of creation: *in quo omnia constant*. Up to now, and in spite of the dominant place given to it in St. Paul's vision of the world, this third aspect or function of Christ (or even this third "nature", taken in its true sense, not a human or divine nature but a "cosmic" nature) has not yet attracted much explicit attention among theologians and faithful.'[75]

What Teilhard wants to do here is to compare the union between Christ and humanity with the union between Christ's human and divine nature. Such a comparison is legitimate up to a point, but in no sense whatsoever can the first union be called a third 'nature'. Teilhard himself was obviously aware that something was wrong with the word, since the French phrase 'taken in its true sense' means that the expression being used is poor but the idea is correct. His whole Christology, moreover, is based upon the fact that Christ is physical Centre of the universe precisely in and through his human nature. To introduce a 'third nature' for Christ in any real sense of that word is therefore not only untenable in the light of revelation, but also completely superfluous to his own system.[76] Quite clearly from the context, however, the expression means neither more nor less than the Pleroma spoken of by St. Paul. Its use here is rather careless, but its purpose is simply to emphasize once more the organic character of this final Plenitude of Christ.

The second problem raised by the theory of creative union is that of the place of pantheism in Teilhard's thought. He himself admits that his natural tendency towards pantheism was very strong.[77] But he insists over and over again that the pantheism which he embraces is that expressed in I Corinthians 15:28, 'so that God may be all in all,' a text which he always interprets in the context of the Pleroma of Christ.[78] Hence he often prefers the term 'pan-Christism', which highlights the fact that union with God is obtained not by identification (God becoming all) but by the differentiating action of Christian love, 'God finally becoming *all in all* within an atmosphere of pure charity.' Christ 'aggregates to himself the total psychism of the earth by a continual act of communion and sublimation. . . . This is indeed a superior form of "pantheism" without trace of the poison of intermixture or annihilation: the expectation of perfect unity within which each element will reach its own consummation at the same time as the universe.'[79] In *The Divine Milieu* there is an even clearer distinction between pantheism of identification and Christian pantheism of union:

> Pantheism seduces us by its vistas of perfect universal union. But ultimately, if it were true, it would give us only fusion and unconsciousness; for at the end of the evolution it claims to reveal, the elements of the world vanish in the God they create or by which they are absorbed. Our God, on the contrary, pushes to its furthest possible limit the differentiation among the creatures he concentres in himself. At the peak of their adherence to him, those who are chosen discover in him the consummation of their individual fulfilment. Only Christianity therefore saves along with the rights of thought, the essential aspiration of all mysticism: *to be united* (that is, to become the other) *while remaining oneself.* More attractive than any world-Gods, whose eternal seduction it embraces, transcends and pacifies—*In omnibus omnia Deus* (*En pasi panta Theos*)—our divine Milieu is at the antipodes of false pantheism. The Christian can plunge himself into it whole-heartedly without the risk of finding himself one day a monist.[80]

It is love, therefore, which is the key to a correct understanding of 'pan-Christism', since it underlines the fact that the creative union of Pleromization is a union which differentiates more and more the individuals united to Christ. We have already seen in chapter two that in Teilhard's own system the ultimate unity of the universe can be brought about only by union between persons, and he himself never tires of repeating the expression 'union differentiates'.[81] What he continually criticizes in the pantheism

of Eastern religions is the fact that it gives no value to the development of the human person precisely as person. Eastern religions
seek to reduce multiplicity to unity by doing away with it altogether,
and where such an identity exists there can be no place at all for the
tension of love. Only the 'Route of the West', as Teilhard calls it,
gives primacy in things spiritual to the person, and thereby makes
the maximum distinction between elements coincide with their
maximum union.[82]

Up to the present our study of Christogenesis under its aspect of
Pleromization has brought us from the starting point of Teilhard's
theory of creative union on through a summary of the theory itself,
which as we have seen, seeks to unite into a single movement
towards the Pleroma of Christ the three mysteries of creation,
Incarnation and redemption. We may now go on to the final part
of Teilhard's analysis of the eternal creative action of God, which
concerns the consummation of Christogenesis at the moment of the
Parousia. We have already noted earlier in this chapter Teilhard's
conviction that the coming of the Parousia is conditioned by the
planetary maturation of mankind. This condition is physically
necessary but not sufficient, as Teilhard points out again and again,
and by this distinction he means that the Parousia, while remaining
a gratuitous intervention of God, is not an arbitrary event but is
connected somehow with man's co-operation in bringing the
evolutionary movement to its term of growth.[83] What must now
be emphasized is that this term of growth in Teilhard's system is not
a *state* which humanity reaches *before* the Parousia, but a critical
point coinciding *with* the Parousia. In other words, for Teilhard the
'human point of planetary maturation' takes place not *within*
history but at its *end*.

Here again there can be occasional ambiguity because the same
event is spoken of on different levels of thought. On the level of
phenomena, as we have seen in chapter two,[84] the law of complexity
consciousness indicates that radial energy is gradually moving
towards a certain collective act of reflection for mankind, and that
to reach this supreme consciousness the human race may well have
to pass another 'critical point', a second threshold of reflection

analogous to that of hominization. On this phenomenological level, Teilhard is naturally led to speak of this final 'super-human' condition of man as if it were 'ultra-human', that is to say, produced within time by the natural evolutionary process. From revelation, however, Teilhard knows that the critical point *par excellence* for the human race is to be the Parousia of Christ, and that this will take place at the end of human history as we know it. The 'super-human' condition of mankind which follows will not in fact be 'ultra-human' at all, but 'trans-human', that is to say, a union of the human species with the Body-Person of Christ which is the work of God alone and of which the movement of evolution is in no sense a cause but merely the necessary preparatory condition. In other words, just as Teilhard's concept of a personal Omega was influenced by the knowledge he had through faith of the Person of Christ, so also his extrapolation from phenomena of a second threshold of reflection for the human race was strongly influenced by his knowledge of the Parousia and Pleroma of Christ. 'The task of the world consists not in engendering in itself some supreme reality, but in bringing itself to fulfilment through union with a pre-existent Being.'[85]

Let us repeat, therefore, what was said a moment ago: for Teilhard the temporal success of the world, the collective consummation of humanity on earth, is not an infra-temporal millennium but a very precise moment at the end of time, that moment when the psychic temperature of the noosphere, in conformity with the law of complexity-consciousness, reaches its maximum of tension. This critical point of collective maturation will be a point of paroxysm and ecstasy, by which mankind will emerge into a state of consciousness ' beyond the time-space matrix of the universe', and it 'coincides concretely with the point called the Parousia of Christ. . . . It is in this supreme event, when, as faith tells us, history is to be welded to the Transcendent, that the mystery of the Incarnation culminates and asserts itself in the realism of a physical interpretation of the universe.'[86]

Hence there follows the importance in Teilhard's system of what he calls 'the hominization of death', namely the notion of transformation and rebirth, already treated in some detail in the previous chapter. Here however the application is not to the individual but to the species as a whole. 'The end of a "reflective" species: not disintegration and death but a new break-through, a new rebirth (this time beyond time and space) . . . an escape on the physical level through an excess of consciousness.' At this supreme point of reflection the species as a whole will be forced 'to abandon its organo-planetary support in order to centre itself outside itself in the transcendent Centre of its growing concentration. . . . The end of the world: an overthrow of equilibrium, fulfilling spirit at last and detaching it from its material matrix in order to make it rest henceforth with all its weight upon God-Omega. The end of the world: critical point at one and the same time of emergence and emersion, of maturation and escape.'[87]

It is this insistence upon the fact that the human person can reach full development only by an escape from the 'time-space matrix' which places Teilhard's thought at the antipodes of Marxism. He himself spoke of Marxism's 'depersonalizing action' and 'messianism', which 'still attributes ultimate stability to the material infrastructure of things.'[88] Against all such 'pitiable millenarianisms' he maintained that, even though true spiritual progress must mean improving man's economic condition in the world, 'still it is not a question of *well-being* but a thirst for *more-being*, which of psychological necessity is alone able to save the thinking earth from the *taedium vitae*.' There is not to be 'an indefinite progress, which is an hypothesis contradicted by the convergent nature of noogenesis, but an ecstasy transcending the dimensions and framework of the visible universe.'[89] To confuse an expectation of 'more-being' with that of mere 'well-being' is to do away completely with any hope of an *issue* from the world and thereby imprison man in an absurd universe where, as we saw in chapter one, death would be the ultimate end of everything. This contrast between a pagan and a Christian love of the world is thrown into sharp relief in the following passage from *The Divine Milieu*:

With his faith in the heavenly value of human endeavour, . . .
by his respect for the spiritual powers still latent in matter, the

Christian may often bear a striking resemblance to those who worship the earth. But here again, as in the case of pantheism, the resemblance is only external, such as is often found in opposite things.

The pagan loves the earth in order to enjoy it and confine himself within it; the Christian in order to make it purer and to draw from the world itself the strength to escape from it.

The pagan seeks to embrace whatever is perceptible to the senses in order to extract therefrom the last drop of delight; he clings to the world. The Christian multiplies his contacts with the world solely in order to harness the energies which he will take, or to submit to those which will take him, home to heaven. Before all else he clings to God.

The pagan believes that man is divinized by being closed in upon himself; that the final gesture of human evolution, for individual as well as for species, is to become established within oneself. The Christian sees his divinization solely in the fact that his achievement is assimilated by an 'Other'; in his eyes the highest point of life is death, but a death which culminates in union.[90]

For Teilhard, therefore, the coming of the Parousia as well as the end of the world are events which are to take place primarily on the spiritual and personal level. They are to constitute a point of ultra-reflection and maximum interior tension which, as we saw in chapter four, will also be mankind's point of maximum freedom. Although the human race as a whole is destined to reach a state of 'more-being', this is not necessarily true for the whole of the human race. If there is indeed to be a split in mankind, then 'universal love would give life to and finally detach only a fraction of the noosphere in order to bring it to fulfilment,—the part which decided to "cross the threshold", to go outside of itself and into the Other.'[91] Consequently what will take place is 'a psychic rather than a siderial reversal, resembling death possibly, but which will in fact be liberation beyond the plane of matter and history, an ecstasy in God.' For 'once there is a reversal of spirit, a change in its zone, that is quite sufficient to alter the whole shape of the world.'[92]

Ultimately then, the end of the world is to come not through some cataclysm in nature but through the paroxysm of human freedom.

Nevertheless, there is still to be an 'end' for the material world as we know it, a 'reversal' corresponding to that reversal on the level of spirit to be undergone by the human race. 'The world's fulfilment is to be brought about only by a death, a "night", a reversal, an excentration.' This is to be compared, Teilhard says, to a 'universal transubstantiation', which, as we saw in chapter three, takes place through the Eucharist 'in a secondary and generalized but true sense'. The material world is to be united to 'your Body in its total extension, that is to say . . . the world changed, through your power and my faith, into the magnificent and living crucible where everything will disappear to be reborn.' . . .'In order to be divinized the world has to be stripped of its visible form, in each of us as well as in its totality.' The earth is to undergo 'a total recasting *in Christo Jesu*, in which it must appear to founder completely.' There is to be a sort of ' "positive" annihilation, an annihilation which is subordinate to growth, . . . requiring . . . that individuals and world be matured and ready for the final threshold of reversal and excentration.'[93]

Teilhard's approach in the above explanation is remarkable in that it manages to incorporate two different New Testament traditions regarding the coming of the Parousia and the end of the world. The author of II Peter 3:7-12, probably because of a strong Stoic influence, tends to conceive the end of the world as a rupture and total destruction. St. Paul on the other hand tends to speak of transformation rather than of rupture: the Parousia is to bring not total annihilation but renewal, a deliverance of the whole of creation and its rebirth in Christ. We have already analysed in chapter three Paul's affirmations in Romans 8:19-23, as well as the texts regarding the Pleroma of Christ in Colossians and Ephesians. What Teilhard does, therefore, is to give a plausible explanation within his own evolutionary system of how these two traditions complement each other in describing from different points of view the same crisis, the same gathering together of mankind, the same spiritual consummation of the universe.[94] A passage from a 1924 essay tries to capture these three themes in their fundamental unity, and in doing so provides an excellent summary of the ultimate phase of Christogenesis as Teilhard conceives it:

The Parousia will undoubtedly take place when creation has reached the paroxysm of its capacity for union. The unique action of assimilation and synthesis which has been going on since the beginning of time will be revealed at last, and the universal Christ will appear like a flash of lightning amid the clouds of a world which has gradually become sanctified. . . . The monads will rush to their irrevocable destiny, . . . some, whose matter has been spiritualized, to the limitless fulfilment of eternal communion; others, whose spirit has become materialized, to the conscious agony of eternal decomposition.

At that moment, St. Paul tells us (I Cor. 15:23ff.), when Christ shall have emptied of themselves all the powers of creation (casting aside any factor of dissociation and suranimating any force of unity), he will bring to completion the unification of the universe by giving himself up to the divine embrace in his full grown Body, its capacity for union at last completely fulfilled.

Thus will be constituted the organic complex: God and the world, the Pleroma. We cannot say this mysterious reality is greater than God alone, since God has no need of the world, but neither can we think of it as absolutely unessential without rendering creation incomprehensible, the Passion of Christ absurd, and our human effort meaningless.

Et tunc erit finis.

Like an immense wave, Being shall have dominated the agitation of beings. In the midst of a becalmed Ocean whose every drop of water shall be conscious of remaining itself, the extraordinary adventure of the world shall reach its term. The dream of every mystic shall have found its full and legitimate satisfaction. *Erit in omnibus omnia Deus.*[95]

The purpose of this chapter, it will be recalled, has been to follow Teilhard's effort to clarify his key concept of Christogenesis by relating the mystery of Christ's work of redemption to that of God's continuous creation in time. This has led us through an analysis of Christian action in the world as well as of the Church's role in human development, and then through an attempt to conceive creation and salvation as different aspects of a single divine plan for the universe, moving from nothing to the Plenitude of Christ. Two significant points have emerged from these analyses and they deserve to be stressed once more before we close. The first is that the process by which cosmogenesis becomes Christogenesis is one of gradual transformation and rebirth. It is through a growing spiritualization that the body of humanity becomes united to the Body of Christ. Consequently there is no question whatsoever of trying to give some divine stability to the natural evolutionary process. On the contrary, of itself evolution is characterized by a radical instability. Only in Christ, its physical Centre, does it find a force capable of stabilizing it at all its various stages and of guaranteeing its ultimate success at the end of time. For only the Spirit of Christ 'can bring about the beginnings and fulfilment of the great metamorphosis which sums up all inward perfection and towards which your creation yearns: *Emitte Spiritum Tuum et creabuntur et renovabis faciem terrae.*'[96]

The second point is that Christogenesis, however dependent upon this transcendent action of God, is nonetheless conditioned by the mysterious capacity of man somehow to make his own history. For Teilhard this means that the Parousia depends upon planetary maturation, which in turn depends upon a hyperpersonalization which can be brought about only through love. The building of the earthly city in its highest and most enduring form is thus to be accomplished by the same energy which builds the eternal city, the direction in the one case being towards the Forward and in the other towards the Upward. The Christian's task in the world is precisely to foster a juncture between these two free movements of the human spirit, thereby producing a resultant force with the combined energy of human love and Christian charity. The success of the human enterprise and the coming of the Parousia will depend upon this juncture. Hence Teilhard can say that 'noospheric maturation (since it is linked to a concentrated form of "charity") cannot be completed without the animating action of the Church growing at the heart of humanity.'[97] In the end, therefore, the Plenitude of Christ, like the work of redemption in the individual soul of which it is the final culmination, will be brought about by the omnipotence of God impinging with reverence and respect upon the delicate mechanisms of human freedom and human love.

CHAPTER SIX

INTELLECTUAL SYNTHESIS AND THEOLOGICAL RISK

TEILHARD'S THOUGHT AS A CATALYST TOWARDS DEVELOPMENT IN CHRISTOLOGY

The man whose theological thought we have presented in the previous pages has, within a decade after his death, gained a notoriety and renown which would have altogether amazed him during his life. He has succeeded in disturbing scientists as well as philosophers and theologians, and finds both strong support and violent opposition among Christian and non-Christian alike. He has been called a genius, a harbinger of a new and strong Christianity, and also a dangerous innovator saved from ecclesiastical condemnation by his good faith alone. For some he is a daring thinker of great depth and originality, for others simply a scientist who has wandered from his exacting professional discipline to speak in poetic language of a personal religious experience. Although completely unsympathetic with scholasticism as he understood it, he has been called by a well-known modern scholastic 'one of the boldest and most spiritual of the theological thinkers of our time'.[1]

All of these paradoxical reactions to the thought of Pierre Teilhard de Chardin are in some measure justified. They spring ultimately from the paradox in the man himself and depend in large measure on the extent to which a given individual shares Teilhard's own intellectual and spiritual experience. 'Above all,' he once wrote his Superior General, 'I feel you must resign yourself to taking me as I am, that is, with the congenital quality (or weakness) which ever since my childhood has caused my spiritual life to be completely dominated by a sort of profound "feeling" for the organic realities of the world. At first it was an ill-defined feeling in my mind and heart, but as the years have gone by it has gradually become a precise, compelling sense of the general convergence of the universe upon itself; a convergence which at its summit culminates in and coincides with him *in quo omnia constant*, whom the Society has taught me to love.' Later in the same letter he says that the immediate effect of this interior attitude 'is to rivet me ever more firmly to three convictions which are the very marrow of Christianity. The unique significance of man as the spear-head of life; the position of Catholicism as the central axis in the converging bundle of human activities; and finally the essential function assumed by the risen Christ at the centre and peak of creation to bring all things to their fulfillment.'[2]

In the course of the three preceding chapters we have studied in some detail the various aspects of Teilhard's master idea to rethink the mystery of Christ in terms of *genèse*. There does not seem to be any need at this point to restate these analyses or to summarize again the conclusions we have already drawn from them. What does seem necessary, however, is to look once more at Teilhard's thought in the light of the perennial problem of synthesis and risk in theology. 'In every case,' he said once, 'synthesis implies risk.'[3] This is doubly true in theology, where the original data is that of Christian revelation. In this final chapter, then, it would be well for us to turn our attention to the chief characteristics of the synthesis which Teilhard has attempted, and then to enumerate some of the risks which such a synthesis inevitably forced him to take.

I

'Analysis—that marvellous instrument of scientific research to which we owe all our advances, but which, breaking down synthesis after synthesis, allows all the principles of life to escape one after the other, leaving us confronted with a pile of dismantled machinery and evanescent particles.'[4] The burden of this present study has been that the thought of Teilhard de Chardin is primarily an attempt at synthesis, personal as well as intellectual, and that it begins and ends in a spiritual experience. The nature of this experience we have described in chapter one: a fundamental anxiety to find some *issue* for human life, and the corresponding conviction that the ultimate guarantee of life's movement is the Person of Jesus Christ. This spiritual experience is at the heart of Teilhard's theological speculation and constitutes its first major characteristic. 'In spite of certain appearances of dialectical exactness,' he writes at the start of one of his more important essays, 'the following considerations seek . . . to recount a direct psychological experience, just sufficiently reflected upon to become intelligible and communicable without losing its objective and incontestable value as a lived document.' In his last theological effort shortly before his death he says again that 'the pages which follow are not simply a speculative dissertation setting out the main ideas of some system thought out over a long period and cleverly put together. They are the testimony borne in all objectivity to a certain interior event, a certain spiritual experience.'[5]

Many years earlier, in 1924, he had already spoken of his total system of thought as 'bearing testimony' to what had already taken place in his own life. 'Whether or not I am qualified as a philosopher, one fact will always remain, that an average man of the twentieth century, because he shared normally in the ideas and preoccupations of his time, could find equilibrium for his interior life only in a conception of Christ and the world which was at once scientific and unified; and that he found therein peace and limitless scope for personal expansion.' How many others were going through this same experience? Teilhard had reason to believe that their number was very large. It was thus imperative for him to speak, 'because destiny has placed me at a privileged crossroads of the world, where it has been possible for me, in my double role as priest and man of science, to be aware of two powerful currents, one human and the other divine, both passing through me in the midst of very diverse and stimulating sets of circumstances.'[6] Two years later he witnesses to the same phenomenon in a letter from China:

The day before yesterday, before a mixed audience of Chinese and Americans, a very likeable Harvard professor gave a simple and modest explanation of how he understood the dawn of thought in the animal series. I couldn't help thinking of the abyss that divides the intellectual world I was in and whose language I knew, from the theological world of Rome with whose idiom I am also familiar. At first it was something of a shock to realize that the latter could be, and indeed must be, just as real as the former; and then I told myself that now perhaps I was capable of so using the first language as to make it express correctly what the other contains but puts into words that most people can no longer understand. However far-fetched the notion might appear at first, I realized in the end that, *hic et nunc*, Christ was not irrelevant to the problems that interest Professor Parker; it only needed a few intermediate steps to allow a transition from his positivist psychology to a certain spiritual outlook. This realization cheered me up. Ah, there lie the Indies that draw me more strongly than those of St. Francis Xavier! But what a vast problem has to be solved, no longer one of rites but of ideas, before they can be really converted![7]

Teilhard's belief, therefore, was that the great apostolic work of his life lay precisely in bearing testimony to the unity in his own life between Christianity and the world of science. 'To tear away the mask of atheism from these new currents of thought and expose them as Christian—that is my great hope, and I need not tell you that it urges me on as a vocation.' This statement from a 1916 letter is echoed in 1919: 'Because I am conscious of having a very intense awareness of the aspirations deep at the heart of my age (as others have of the miseries), I feel it my duty to bear this testimony before my brothers in the apostolate, a testimony which is the fruit of a long and certain personal experience.' Several years later there is the same conviction: 'To point out this strong, genuine and total coherence, this will be my whole "apologetic".'[8] The Omega of evolution must be shown to be none other than the Christ of revelation, just as the God of philosophers and wise men was seen in former ages to be none other than the God of Abraham, Isaac and Jacob.

This 'apologetic' is to be directed, Teilhard says, to Christian and non-Christian alike. 'I am slowly putting together the elements of a "divinization" (of the earth) *ad usum Christianorum*,' he wrote a close friend in 1925, 'which will continue the "hominization" written *ad usum gentilium* which I have not yet shown you. Both together will be my apologetic, an apologetic based on evolution yet whose spirit seems to me to be truly and equally Christian.'[9] Teilhard was well aware that modern man's unbelief is based less upon intellectual motives than upon a profound pessimism regarding the sense of existence and especially of man's future on earth. This is why his 'hominization' attempts to show that without belief in a meaning and destiny for life man cannot go on living and acting, and that nature itself obliges him to have confidence in the fidelity of a God-Omega, thereby preparing the way for an acceptance of Christ who can alone guarantee man's future. His 'divinization', on the other hand, tries to point out to the Christian all that is best in the world around him, since 'the great schism which threatens the Church' is the fact that ' "Christian" and "human" no longer tend to coincide.'[10] The Christian is thus awakened to a realization that the whole of his human effort can be Christified in its totality if it is once seen as a meaningful participation in that continuous act of creation by which God builds up the Pleroma of Christ.

This first characteristic of Teilhard's theological speculation, the fact that it is an expression of a personal spiritual experience, is responsible quite naturally for its second, the fact that it is, and was always meant to be, tentative and partial. In spite of their boldness and daring, his writings are consistently presented to readers with a modesty which is sometimes quite surprising. He himself prayed to be kept 'equally humble and bold,' and wrote in 1916: 'My ideas are far from being clear and need to be strongly controlled by those who are very saintly and very human.'[11] One of his early essays was written 'to clarify my doctrine in my own mind and to facilitate the task of criticism and correction for those who have the right to guide me.' A major theological essay, written in 1924, 'in no sense pretends to furnish any definitive explanation of the world. . . . In spite of the clumsiness and approximation of the terms I use, a spiritual tendency has tried to take form in me which others will take note of later on. . . . I repeat: they will find here only a rough draft.' A 1933 essay on Christology and evolution begins: 'The following pages are not really completely new, and above all their form is not definitive.' And that same year he writes to his friend Auguste Valensin: 'The only thing I ask is that I be given advice.'[12]

Statements like the above are even to be found in such a finished work as *The Phenomenon of Man.* 'The views I am attempting to put forward here are, of course, largely tentative and personal.' This, Teilhard insists, is almost inevitable, because what he is trying to do is to grasp reality as a whole. 'While this aura of subjective inter-pretation may remain imperceptible where the field of observation is limited, it is bound to become practically dominant as soon as the field of vision extends to the whole.' Towards the end of his book he admits that 'in this arrangement of values I may have gone astray at many points. It is up to others to try to do better. My only hope is that I have made the reader feel both the reality, difficulty and urgency of the problem and, at the same time, the scale and the form which the solution cannot escape.'[13]

When Teilhard first began to elaborate his theory of creative union in 1917 he said that its 'philosophical importance is obviously very limited'; and when its final draft was finished in 1948 he called it 'precarious and provisional'.[14] We have already seen in chapter four how tentatively he proposed his explanation of original sin. In 1945, again writing on the delicate relationship between Christian-ity and evolution, he states that his aim is simply 'to make an individual contribution to the common labour of the Christian conscience which is expressing, in my own particular case, the *fides quaerens intellectum*; to suggest, and not to affirm or to instruct.' A letter from the same period says that 'the more the years pass, the more I begin to believe that my function shall have been simply to be the one who announces and declares what is to come, like the Baptist, though in a much smaller way.' Yet another letter expresses the same sentiment in 1952: 'I have an awareness (and it is important that I keep it) of being an example rather than a model or pattern for what you yourself have to say. I see quite clearly that my power (or if you prefer, the reason I can have influence) does not at all come from what I have "invented", whatever that may be, but simply from the fact that I have found myself "resonating" in the right way to a certain vibration, a certain human and religious note, which is now in the air everywhere.'[15]

This second characteristic of Teilhard's Christology, its tentative nature, explains a number of things which would be very surprising in a more finished synthesis. With a few rare exceptions, his works form a long series of relatively short, disconnected essays, all treating more or less the same themes, sometimes in the language of prose-poetry which often brings more inspiration than light. Many of his categories of thought, moreover, are derived from the scientific world in which he was immersed. When these categories are superimposed upon a religious experience and then laboriously used to articulate a theological reflection, the result is not simply a hybrid terminology, but a terminology whose content is not always clear even in Teilhard's own mind, and which inevitably leads to misunderstanding as well as misinterpretation in the minds of others. Teilhard himself was well aware of this situation, and he was content to let it stand because he was also well aware of his own inability to remedy it. 'It is infinitely more worthwhile to present, for the time being, a mixture of truth and error, than to mutilate reality by trying prematurely to separate the wheat from the weeds. I have followed this Gospel principle without hesitation, since it is the principle of all research and all scientific progress.'[16]

Teilhard was thus not only willing patiently to search over the years for the expression of his vision, but also prepared to accept the risk of expressing himself badly. Indeed, many of his essays were merely private exercises by which he sought to clarify ideas for himself. These he sometimes passed on to various theologians and friends for purposes of discussion, but a number of them he had no intention of publishing at all. Throughout these writings it is inevitably the same vision searching for its intelligible formulation.

'Under control of the *Ecclesia docens*, it is necessary to organize and develop the *Ecclesia quaerens*.'[17] This early statement was given new expression in 1947 when Teilhard received a letter from his Superior General forbidding him to publish anything whatsoever of a philosophical or theological nature. After stating that he will naturally obey without hesitation, his reply continues: 'Since 1939 (all my incriminating writings are previous to that date, I think) I have, on the advice of authorized theologians who are following my thought, made great progress towards explicitating correctly a point of view which (given my experience of the "gentiles") seems to have a real chance to be of some service to the kingdom of God. Do you not think it would be a shame to reject without examination a fruit which is perhaps just about to ripen? And do you not believe that the best reparation for what has been less good in my past work would be for me to produce at last something whose worth is incontestable?'[18]

Karl Rahner has said recently that in the realm of theology it is legitimate to experiment and to work with hypotheses as long as one remembers that such experimentation may turn out to be barren when tested by the criticism of one's fellow theologians: 'Theology is certainly anything but a mummified structure of thought. It can create openings for adventures of the mind and of the heart, if we have but the courage to embark upon them, and both the courage and humility to retrace our steps as soon as we become aware of having erred.'[19] Teilhard lacked neither courage nor humility, for throughout his life he knew the painful awkwardness and hesitation of all those who grope their way towards the expression of a new insight or a new interior experience. The following poignant lines, written less than a month before he died, are an eloquent testimony to this:

How does it happen that, still intoxicated by my vision, I look all around me and find myself practically alone? How is it that I alone should have *seen*? How is it that I am incapable, if someone asks me, of citing a single author, a single work, where there is to be found clearly expressed that marvellous 'diaphany' which in my eyes has transfigured everything?

And, above all, how can it be that, 'having come down from the mountain,' and notwithstanding the splendour of my vision, I find myself so little better, so little pacified, so incapable of communicating to my own actions, and therefore to others, the marvellous unity in which I feel myself plunged? The universal Christ? The divine Milieu? May I not after all be simply the victim of some mental delusion? That is what I often ask myself.[20]

This candid avowal will enable us now to see in its proper perspective the third characteristic of Teilhard's theological thought: however personal and tentative it is, there is no doubt whatsoever that its ultimate intention is to modify the perspectives of current Christology. What precise form such modification is eventually to take, Teilhard would have been the last to say. But its general area, he insists, is the relationship between Christ and the universe, and its dominating event the modern discovery of cosmic and organic evolution. Indeed, Teilhard's theological significance consists precisely in the fact that he tried as a scientist to come to grips with a religious and theological problem,—'in the hope of making them [theologians] conscious of a situation which they can certainly face better than I, but which I can perhaps, for various reasons, see more clearly than they.'[21] Theology can no longer go on simply asserting the fact that no opposition exists between Christianity and modern scientific developments. Something has to be done to demonstrate concretely how the two can exist in harmony and mutual enrichment.

Significantly enough, wrote Teilhard once, Christology in contrast to Mariology, has made practically no progress at all in recent centuries.[22] One explanation for this is that up to the present it was impossible for theologians either to conceive or to explain the Incarnation other than in terms of a static universe, just as it was impossible for the writers of the New Testament to speak of Christianity in relationship to modern social problems. Now, however, there is an opportunity to rethink the data of revelation concerning the Person of Christ within a totally different physical framework. What is even more important, such rethinking will put theologians in a position to give a truly theological significance to the whole evolutionary process. Theology cannot continue asserting that Christ is Lord of the universe and at the same time abandon an intelligence of that universe to disciplines incapable of explaining its divine meaning. To do so would be to acquiesce in a stagnant theology, unfaithful to itself as well as to its long tradition of renewal and adaptation.[23]

It should be noted that the question here concerns changes in the formulation and expression of dogma, not in dogma itself. 'It is quite natural,' said John XXIII at the start of the Second Vatican Council, 'that innovations of times and of circumstances suggest different forms and attitudes of external transmission and of clothing the doctrine itself. But the living substance is always purity of evangelical and apostolic truth in perfect conformity with the teachings of the Holy Church.'[24] No one was more aware of this than Teilhard. 'Truth, even revealed truth, is preserved only by a continual effort to possess it,' he wrote during the first world war; and in 1942 he insisted that 'theology evolves, not by adding to or substracting from its content, but by a relative emphasis and de-emphasis in its treatment [of revelation], the process leading each time to the "emergence" of a concept or an attitude that is more richly synthetic.'[25] This distinction between a transcendent Christian faith and its theological formulation at any given historical period is what enabled the Fathers to assimilate Greek culture and St. Thomas to assimilate Aristotle, and today theologians are once again giving it very serious consideration.[26]

The threat of Modernism at the turn of the century made the Church extremely vigilant that the data of revelation remain intact under changing formulations. The whole Modernist movement in fact tended to create the impression that between modern thought and traditional Church teaching there could be no compatibility at all. If Teilhard de Chardin has a special mission in the Church, it would seem to be to remove this impression once and for all. Nor is it without significance that, whereas such modern thinkers as Rudolf Bultmann can see only rupture between today's world outlook and the 'mythical' data of the New Testament,

Teilhard keeps insisting that this same world outlook can ultimately be understood only by the light of this data, and that in the last resort only Christian faith can grasp the full meaning of the obscure human searchings present in every scientific achievement.[27] 'Teilhard went further than anyone else,' Cardinal König has said, 'in dedicating himself to the task of finding positive evidence of agreement between science and religion. Would it not be worthwhile for groups to follow up his basic ideas?'[28]

II

Teilhard's attempt to unite the world of theology and the world of science, the data of revelation with that of evolution, has provoked over the past decade some severe criticism.[29] Much of this has been based on misunderstandings, explained in part by the startling originality of Teilhard's thought, in part by the fact that the gradual publication of his works has made this thought available to the public only very slowly and in incomplete form. On the whole, however, such criticism cannot be dismissed as unjustified. Even though in some cases it comes from prejudice against evolution or general opposition to new forms of thought, in many other cases it is based not on hostility at all but on serious scientific, philosophical or theological argument.[30] Teilhard would have been the last to resent such criticism and the first to acknowledge its need if his dream of a *rapprochement* between science and theology is to become a reality. His efforts at theological synthesis clearly involve risks, therefore, and these must be recognized honestly if they are to be avoided or neutralized by those seeking to build on the foundation which he has laid.

The first risk involved in Teilhard's effort at synthesis is what has been called its uncompromising 'evolutionism'. By this is not meant (or *should* not be meant) the fact that he uses evolution as a framework for his Christology. He can no more be criticized for this than can St. Thomas, who transposed into his theological speculation the concepts and categories drawn from the static world of Aristotle. Indeed, the idea of evolution has been supported by far stronger arguments than were ever proposed in favour of a steady-state universe.[31] Nor could anyone accuse Teilhard of materialism who had even the most rudimentary knowledge of his mode of interpreting the scientific data. His overall method, however one may criticize the use he makes of it, is thus in itself basically that of Aristotle and St. Thomas, whose starting point was the physical world known at the time, and whose metaphysics was conceived as an explicitation of the laws of being through reflection upon physical reality. This scholastic tradition was well known to Teilhard and gave him some of the categories most essential to his thought, as we have seen in chapter two, that of person, spirit, Prime Mover, the primacy of being, etc. The language of that tradition he abandoned completely, of course, forging instead a terminology which he took for the most part from the physics and biology of modern man.[32]

It is not out of place to insist on the legitimacy of this method, since not to recognize it is to render quite impossible any fruitful evaluation of what Teilhard has accomplished. St. Thomas himself believed that it was legitimate not only to apply philosophy to dogma but 'physics' as well, in order that a rigorously exact expression be found for the data of revelation.[33] And a number of philosophical notions most essential to scholastic theology, those of 'nature' and 'act and potency', for example, are in their early Aristotelian form certainly linked very closely to biology. Life for Aristotle was the axis of all reality, and even his treatise on the soul could justly be entitled a treatise on life.[34] Teilhard, for his part, believed that any attempt to understand reality without scientific roots must necessarily be ineffectual, since to explain *why* things happen, one has to begin with phenomena, with an explanation of *how* things happen. A metaphysics concerned with 'what could be or could not be, with abstract conditions of existence, all that appears to me invincibly deceptive and fragile.'[35]

But if to speak of Teilhard's 'evolutionism' does not mean a criticism of his point of departure, it does mean to underline the dangers of a mentality which in Teilhard's case tended to dominate his theological speculation. 'In my opinion,' he wrote in 1946, 'a simple incorporation and assimilation by Christian thought of modern evolutionary ideas does away completely with the barrier between reason and faith which has been building up for four centuries. Once the obstacle of "fixism" has been done away with, there is nothing else to prevent Catholics and non-Catholics from moving forward hand in hand along the great highways of discovery.' Or consider a statement from 1933: 'In my opinion the whole internal vitality of Christianity, and consequently its whole power to spread itself abroad, are dependent upon the solution to the following problem. . . . What must our Christology become in order to remain itself in the modern world? . . . It must become reconciled with evolution.'36

There is obviously question here of adaptation and not substitution, since Christology is to 'remain itself'. Nevertheless, to speak of 'the whole internal vitality' of Christianity depending upon such adaptation is dangerous, since it is to give to theological exposition, and in particular to an evolutionary exposition, an importance which revelation alone can have. An intelligent presentation of dogma well adapted to each age is indeed necessary, but the internal vitality of Christianity does not ultimately depend upon such presentation. For Teilhard, on the other hand, an evolutionary world-view is the *only* world-view, the sole framework, the sole mode of approach to reality, the sole criterion for solving all problems, whether scientific, philosophical, theological or spiritual. As a consequence all his affirmations tend to be cut from the same cloth, with little or insufficient distinction between various shades of assent. Truths of an experimental order, legitimate interpolations from scientific data, extrapolations of a purely conjectural order, philosophical speculation, truths revealed to Christian faith, opinions which are purely theological, all these are invariably presented with the same vigour and sometimes with the same unguarded assurance.

Teilhard, we have said, looked upon his synthesis as tentative and incomplete, and this is true. But that others must continue to work within the same evolutionary framework, this was a fact beyond discussion. There was never a doubt in his mind, for example, that the cosmic texts of St. Paul must be interpreted along the lines which he indicated, though he never pretended that his own interpretations were either normative or obligatory. All other views of these texts he dismissed 'purely and simply because they are less consistent with the spirit of St. Paul such as it animates the body of his letters, and less consistent also with my general view of the world.'[37] Teilhard's 'evolutionism' thus tends to narrow the field of research, to limit debate, to close out problems and to make virtually impossible any real objective evaluation of a certain number of basic questions.[38] It is this mentality which shocked Church authorities in Rome, where the greatest prudence and reserve have always been shown towards evolution, in spite of the fact that Catholic scientists have been given full freedom to use evolutionary data in explaining the origin of the human body.[39]

One final observation regarding this evolutionary outlook: a constant emphasis on the destiny of the human race as a whole risks losing sight of the supreme importance which each individual possesses in his own right. God's plan for mankind does not subordinate the person to the species, but governs the whole of human history in function of individual men whose worth is absolute and irreducible. This sense of the sacredness and mystery of every man is surely part of Teilhard's spiritual and theological outlook, but it is not a major part. Even love energy, that most personal of all realities, tends in his system to be treated exclusively in the context of its function for the species. This fact is most evident in regard to personal sin, whose essential character as a refusal of love is never explicitly treated at all. In the end, therefore, Teilhard's strong emphasis on the role of the human person involves an ironic tendency towards the impersonal, and this must be recognized as a real danger in his evolutionary system of thought.

The second risk involved in Teilhard's effort at synthesis is closely linked to the first and may be described as an extreme Incarnationism. Once again the risk comes from overemphasis. For no one would deny that Teilhard has elaborated in modern categories an authentic understanding of the Incarnation, one which is clearly present in the Greek Fathers and which sees in the God-

Man a dynamic unity between creation, redemption and man's ultimate salvation at the end of time. While creation thus becomes wholly Christological in character, Christ and his Church take on in their turn that cosmic dimension which they have in the writings of St. Paul. Christ is presented as still aggregating humanity 'physically' to himself, a task he will continue to accomplish until the completion of his Plenitude. In this sense his unchangeable human nature is still being conditioned by history and his Incarnation still being brought to fulfilment by God's continuous creation in time.[40] This close link between the Incarnation and the evolutionary process also links this process very closely to Christ's work of redemption. This explains why Teilhard's direct references to redemption are relatively infrequent, for as we saw in chapter five, the notion of redemption is implicitly present wherever he speaks of the Incarnation.[41]

Yet this strong emphasis on the Incarnation involves several dangers of which Teilhard himself seems to have been unaware. His key concept of Christ as physical Centre, for example, tends to distract one's attention from the fact that Christ gives meaning to evolution not through his passive physical omnipresence but primarily through the exercise of his freedom and love. This is in no way denied by Teilhard and is in fact implicitly understood, since it is to the Body-*Person* of Christ that humanity is organically united. Nevertheless, the strong dichotomy he sets up between the physical and the juridical in Christology somehow manages to throw into the shadows an all-important third element, the personal initiative of Christ. In the same way he ignores completely the fact that reparation for sin deals principally with the relationship of love between persons. Reparation is treated as if it were a purely juridical concept (as it may well have been in the theology which he was taught), and as such it is absorbed into an organic approach to the mystery of redemption. Perhaps what is responsible for this is Teilhard's constant search to elaborate a series of guarantees for evolution, which naturally meant that the element of contingency tended to be reduced, and therefore also the element of freedom. However the fact is to be explained, we must recognize that in Teilhard's treatment of the Body of Christ as a living organism, there is present once again that strange inclination towards the necessary and the impersonal.

Constant emphasis on the organic union of the universe with Christ is likewise responsible for the fact that Teilhard confines himself for the most part to a level of Christian revelation on which he could speak of the laws of human progress with serene assurance. This is the level of God's total plan for the universe, of the original goodness of the created world and of that primordial movement by which all things proceed from God and are infallibly destined eventually to return to their divine source. Seen from this level, the terrible mystery of evil is neutralized, its conquest assured by Christ's redemption and its eventual disappearance guaranteed. Teilhard's personal life was far from being lived on this optimistic level of God's total plan, as we have already had occasion to note, and he could write at times with disturbing force of the world's power to discourage and oppress.[42] Yet for the most part his theological writings are all characterized by a determined concentration upon the integral and definitive destiny of mankind. Christian revelation told him that ultimate success for humanity was a certainty because Christ is Man and all men are destined to form one Body with him.

'I feel resolutely determined,' he wrote in 1941, 'to devote myself by all possible means to the defence of the idea and the reality of a progress (collective and personalizing) against every secular and religious pessimism.' . . .'I would say boldly, "Get behind me, all pessimists, whether atheists or Christians." We must take up again, on a sounder scientific basis and as a more exact philosophical concept, the idea (or if you prefer the "myth") of progress. This is the essential setting in which I see the simultaneous renaissance of both humanism and Christianity.'[43] As a consequence we have an overall endeavour to sketch out in broad outline a set of universal laws for human progress and to explain how these laws find their full realization in Christ. For if Christ is at the centre of human history and cosmic development, then he must embody in himself all laws of progress, and it must be possible for the human mind to discover these, at least to some extent, by the simultaneous use of human reason and Christian revelation.[44]

Now this is a legitimate Christian attitude, and we have noted already its boldness and originality from both a scientific and theological point of view. But it runs the risk of remaining exclusively on the level of God's total plan, its beginning and end, and of never placing oneself on the level of immediate human experience. For on this level there is question of a theological judgment not on the definitive condition of the world but on its actual condition. Christian assurance of humanity's ultimate return to God becomes much less serene when faced with the drama and tragedy of human life, the sinfulness of man, his need of mercy and forgiveness, the mystery of the Cross and the Passion, and that mysterious power of Satan to pervert the good that men do into evil. On this level 'progress' is an ambiguous notion indeed, since the undeniable development of mankind on earth is inextricably entangled and confused with the moral 'regress' of individual men.[45] The grace of God enters the human heart through interior tension and conflict, and while the rupture of sin does not prevent God from completing mankind's return movement to himself, neither does the action of grace do away with continual human resistance.

On this level of immediate experience, then, the Christian tends to have far less intellectual assurance that he can discover those universal laws which govern humanity's movement towards the final Pleroma of Christ. Such laws exist in fact and *must* exist, for the order of creation and the order of salvation are one and the same in the mind of God. Yet man must be on his guard not to invade this divine sphere too rashly, for his proper attitude in this area is not one of curiosity but of reverence, hesitation and awe. A theology of history such as Teilhard wishes to construct must therefore beware of a too facile identification of man's knowable future on earth with that ultimate movement of mankind towards a destiny revealed in Christ. Faith tells us of God's total plan for the human race, but it says nothing about the concrete future of the world. 'I realize,' said Teilhard once, 'that it is always dangerous to predict and to extrapolate.'[46] The theologian can reasonably demand no more than that such a realization always qualify the relationship which Teilhard wishes to establish between human progress and the Incarnation of Christ.[47]

What we have just said concerning Teilhard's very strong stress on the implications of the Incarnation will enable us readily to appreciate the third area of risk in his Christology, namely that involved in his statements concerning the natural and the supernatural in Christ. 'Theologians forget that the practical reconciliation of the natural and supernatural in a single harmonious orientation of human activity is a problem a thousand times more acute than all the theoretical difficulties one can gather together on the essence of grace.'[48] For Teilhard this practical reconciliation means recognizing that 'the supernatural Plenitude of Christ receives support from the natural plenitude of the world,' and that 'Christ gives himself to us through a world which is to reach completion even on the natural level by reason of its relationship to him.' It means recognizing that, 'concretely speaking, there is only a single process of synthesis going on from the top to the bottom of the universe,' since 'the natural and supernatural fulfilments of the world envelop each other, the latter incorporating and transforming the former.' This means that 'God unites himself in such a way to the axis of the natural evolution of spirit; taken in its entirety, that Christogenesis appears as the sublimation of the whole of cosmogenesis.'[49]

Teilhard's great originality here is his insistence that the salvific action of God is also to be found at work in the natural energies of man, and, conversely, that the natural evolutionary process does not operate, and above all cannot reach its own natural fulfilment independently of Christ. Evolution (and by this word Teilhard means primarily the progress of radial energy towards higher spiritual consciousness) is thus situated squarely *within* the total supernatural movement from creation in Christ to the final Pleroma; the relationship is therefore that of part to whole, the distinction between the two movements being likewise that between part and whole. Through his Church, which he inserts as an organic phylum into evolution, Christ slowly takes possession of the natural process and through his supernatural influence upon radial energy, gradually relates the whole movement to a higher order of being. If it is detached from man's final destiny, therefore, evolution simply cannot be understood, for the divine purpose in cosmic history is ultimately salvation history. Christ is at the beginning and end of evolution precisely because he is at the beginning and end of salvation, and this is why Teilhard can, within his own system, boldly enumerate 'the following series of equal terms: cosmos = cosmogenesis = biogenesis = individual anthropogenesis = collective anthropogenesis = Christogenesis.'[50]

Such a conception of the relationship between natural and supernatural does not, it should be noted, involve the risk of minimizing the gratuity of grace. It simply insists that God's gratuitous interventions are so continual and so inseparably united to the natural in human activity, that one can never know in the concrete to what extent any given action is influenced by Christ and consequently ordered to a supernatural end. A certain freedom must be granted in this area, since the whole problem of how grace perfects nature, as well as the best way of understanding the fact of its gratuity, are questions which at present are still theologically very much open.[51] Nor is there any danger that the concept of divine transcendence will be neglected, since in Teilhard's thought the natural evolution-ary process is clearly destined to reach a supernatural termination. Christ is, moreover, consistently presented as a transcendent Centre for the universe, and that 'chosen' portion of humanity which freely breaks 'the death barrier' is obviously to be perfected in a way which transcends all natural powers.

What then is the risk in Teilhard's approach to this question? It consists in the fact that his explanations so emphasize the immanence of the divine action in the evolutionary process itself that a *sense* of its transcendence sometimes gets lost, even though the *concept* of transcendence itself is never absent. A case in point is Teilhard's approach to the mystery of the Cross. In his system it appears as something quite understandable, made inevitable, in a certain sense, by a world undergoing *genèse*—just as in the same world personal sin also appears as something ordinary and in a sense inevitable. This is all very true as far as it goes, but there is danger as soon as the aspect of 'otherness' in the Passion begins to be minimized, namely its ultimately sacred character as an impenetrable mystery of divine love, an object of adoration which cannot be fully understood simply by situating it within an evolutionary framework. The mysterious element of rupture through sin, so strong in Christian tradition regarding the Passion, tends likewise to get lost, for personal sin is never dealt with as a rupture between Christ and individual men (and therefore between Christ and evolution). The concept of rupture is surely not lacking in Teilhard's thought on hell, but in this case there is question of a definitive state outside of evolution and not of a rupture between God and man taking place here and now at the heart of the evolutionary process.

A lack of this sense of transcendence may also be seen in Teilhard's unqualified insistence on the Christian's commitment, and consequently the Church's commitment, to human values. He was reacting strongly here against a tendency in Christian thought which distrusts earthly achievement, as if an esteem for the world and its accomplishments could somehow detract from glory given to God. 'Christian faith,' he wrote, 'destroys neither man's rational mode of conquering the world nor his confidence in himself. . . . In conformity with faith in the integration of the natural and supernatural, . . . it brings to human effort, which it takes great care to preserve as a foundation, an unexpected completion; it directs it, organizes it and finally transforms it.'[52] This is quite true, and in his writings Teilhard has given new insight to this traditional Christian teaching.

An uncritical acceptance of everything human, however, entails the same type of risk as its uncritical rejection. Not everything which develops in the world is moved by the Spirit of Christ, nor is all human action a search for God. Consequently it is dangerous to state categorically that for the Christian it is a 'matter of life and death that the earth should flourish to the uttermost of its natural powers.'[53] Neither the Christian nor the Church can conceive their mission chiefly in terms of fostering evolution, even when this is seen to be growth in spirit and personal fulfillment in the realm of knowledge and love. In the life of the individual Christian as well as in the life of the Church as a whole there is an immediate and transcendent relationship to the Person of Christ which is independent of all human progress and which cannot be reduced to any mere human energy. Teilhard's desire to give a sacred character to all things profane without exception is a natural expression of his own mystical bent, as well as an understandable reaction against the severe dichotomy he encountered between sacred and profane in the lives of many Christians. Yet such a desire also involves risk, since its instinctive tendency is to suppress altogether a distinction which must never be too far from the Christian consciousness.

III

Before we close this study of Teilhard's Christology, we must insist once more that the three areas of risk which we have enumerated belong to the strictly theological order, that is to say, they concern the mode in which he understands and expresses the data of revelation. With the sole exception of his very tentative theory on original sin, all of his opinions fall within this area of free theological discussion. They concern change in the intelligence of faith, not in the faith itself. The final judgment of this present work, therefore, is that Teilhard's theological effort to rethink the mystery of Christ in terms of *genèse* constitutes a viable, though at times highly disputable, interpretation of Christian revelation. Whether one is favourable or hostile to it will depend in large measure upon one's theological temperament and education, one's susceptibility to change, and above all one's awareness of modern currents of thought in scientific and humanistic circles outside the Church. No one was more sensitive to these currents than Teilhard and he never tired of insisting that his mission was to show their compatibility with the Christian life.

All over the earth at this moment, at the heart of the new spiritual atmosphere created by the appearance of the idea

of evolution, there flow the currents of love of God and faith
in the world, the one current highly sensitive to the other. . . .
In me, by pure chance (temperament, education, milieu . . .),
the ratio of each has been favourable and their fusion has taken
place spontaneously,—too weak yet to be propagated with
explosive force, but still sufficient to make it clear that the
fusion itself is possible and that some day or other the chain
reaction will come.[54]

Ultimately the Christology of Teilhard de Chardin must be seen
as an attempt to explicitate in theological terms modern man's
anxiety and preoccupation in regard to his own destiny. It is thus
an effort to apply to immediate human needs the assertion of the
First Vatican Council that reason can 'reach a very fruitful understanding of [Christian] mysteries' by studying 'the links which
mysteries have with each other and with the destiny of man.'[55]
For Teilhard the most important of these links was the cosmic
function of Christ in the writings of St. Paul. This largely neglected
area he developed and interpreted until it became in his system the
point of contact between the Person of Christ and man's newly
discovered role in the universe. The result was a disconcerting
neglect of all other scriptural sources as well as the need to forge a
terminology quite foreign to traditional formulae, open to suspicion
and misunderstanding, and with very little theological precision.
His thought is therefore to be used with prudence and caution, and
counterbalanced always with a recognition that there are other
theologies and spiritualities equally Christian. The following
remarks of John Henry Newman are very much to the point here:

It is the very law of the human mind in its inquiry after, and
acquisition of, truth to make its advances by a process which
consists of many stages, and is circuitous. . . . Moreover, it is
not often the fortune of any one man to live through an
investigation; the process is one of not only many stages, but
of many minds. What one begins another finishes; and a true
conclusion is at length worked out by the co-operation of
independent schools and the perseverence of successive
generations. This being the case, we are obliged, under circum-

stances, to bear for a while with what we feel to be error, in consideration of the truth in which it is eventually to issue. . . .

Great minds need elbow-room, not indeed in the domain of faith, but of thought. And so indeed do lesser minds, and all minds. There are many persons in the world who are . . . gifted by nature with some particular faculty or capacity; and, while vehemently excited and imperiously ruled by it, they are blind to everything else. . . . Yet, if you insist that in their speculations . . . it is not enough that they should submit to the Church generally, and acknowledge its dogmas, but that they must get up all that divines have said or the multitude believed upon religious matters, you simply crush and stamp out the flame within them, and they can do nothing at all. . . .

Every human system, every human writer, is open to just criticism. Make him shut up his portfolio; good! and then perhaps you lose what, on the whole and in spite of incidental mistakes, would have been one of the ablest defences of revealed truth (directly or indirectly, according to his subject) ever given to the world. . . .[56]

One must recognize, therefore, that Teilhard de Chardin, like St. Paul, had an original vision of Christ's relationship to the cosmos. If the expression of his vision tends to be partial and incomplete, this is because the vision itself was limited by a highly personal spiritual experience as well as by a highly specialized world of science. If his terminology tends to be vague and imprecise, it is because the theology he knew gave him no words to express what he saw. If his spirit of conquest tends to be uncompromising, it is because he was fighting something equally strong, modern man's prevailing sense of being dominated by evil and a prey to ultimate defeat. He was quite aware that human progress had its limits and that there is an ultimate threshold beyond which it cannot reach without a divine force going before it. But the point he insists on always is that this divine force has already come in the Person of Jesus Christ, and that it is in and through him that the death and rebirth of the world are to take place, perhaps simultaneously, perhaps even now, in time.

Whatever dangers therefore are to be found in a broadening of traditional Christology, at least as this has been attempted in the works of Teilhard de Chardin, it should be repeated and clearly understood that the total effort is one of re-emphasis and completion, not of rejection or neglect. There is to be no question whatsoever of underestimating the immense mystery of evil; nor of confusing the spiritual mission of the Church with temporal progress; nor of minimizing Christ's role as Redeemer and the intensely personal relationship which must exist between him and the Christian. Rather, what is involved is an assertion that along with the gratuitous movement of God down towards man and the nature he created, there is likewise a movement of man and nature up, and that this second movement, seen with the eye of Christian faith, is not autonomous but has Christ also as its Centre and *raison d'être*.

In his *Agape and Eros* Anders Nygren has tried to show in another context that the Christian attempt to reconcile this double movement has thus far been a failure. If this is so, then the search for some synthesis must continue. The Copernican revolution shattered current notions of space; the Darwinian revolution is still shattering current notions of time; the technological revolution promises to shatter at long last man's sense of being imprisoned in a hostile universe. What should be the Christian's outlook on these extraordinary human achievements? How ought they affect his attitude towards the temporal order? Above all, what is the relationship of the Person of Christ to this determination of modern man to be master of the world in which he lives? These are the questions which troubled men like Teilhard de Chardin, and they should trouble the thoughtful Christian today. What he must develop in himself and in others is precisely a greater sensitivity to the fundamental good preserved by creation. Facile and sterile depreciation of the human still occurs too frequently, and it is usually accompanied by a scant awareness of Christian teaching that this sinful and wounded world is destined by the transforming grace of Christ to be made whole and entire once more. The problem is not that Christian hope in God is weak but that it engenders such little hope in man.

A constant theme running through both the Old and New Testaments is that temporal reality is the stage on which God works out his designs, and that these designs are always carried out in spite of every hostile force opposing them. May it not also be said that God's plan for the natural in his creation, for this movement of nature upwards, which he himself began and of which his Son is Centre, must likewise be inexorably successful? This is no irrelevant question for a world haunted by the thought that tomorrow's horizon may be darkened by a mushroom cloud. The ultimate destiny of man is indeed to live in 'the sphere of God', as Romano Guardini has said, but this must not blind the Christian to the seriousness and necessity of human endeavour while he yet lives in the sphere of man. To 'Christianize' the profane order does not mean to make it less profane. It means to help it become more completely itself. A Christian does not elevate the supernatural in him by neglecting its natural environment. To be a Christian does not dispense him from his duty to become a man.

NOTES

BIBLIOGRAPHY

INDEX

NOTES

ABBREVIATIONS

Archives—'Maurice Blondel et le Père Teilhard de Chardin; Mémoires échangés en décembre 1919, présentés par H. de Lubac', *Archives de Philosophie*, xxiv (1961), 123-56.

Cahiers—*Cahiers Pierre Teilhard de Chardin*, 4 volumes. (Paris, Seuil, 1958-63). Collections of essays by Teilhard eventually to appear in the *Oeuvres*, as well as brief essays by others on the significance of his life and work.

CM—*Le Coeur de la matière*, 1950. An unpublished essay.

Denzinger—Henricus Denzinger, *Enchiridion Symbolorum*, 32nd edition, ed. by Adolfus Schönmetzer, s.j. (Freiburg, Herder, 1963). The numeration of the earlier editions appears in brackets.

ET—*Ecrits du temps de la guerre, 1916-1919* (Paris, Grasset, 1965).

FM—*The Future of Man* (London & New York, Collins & Harper, 1964). Translation of volume v of the *Oeuvres*.

Genèse—*Genèse d'une pensée, lettres, 1914-1919* (Paris, Grasset, 1961). [Eng. trans., *The Making of a Mind* (London & New York, Collins & Harper, 1965).]

GZ—*Le Groupe zoologique humain*, 1949 (Paris, Michel, 1956). Also published as volume viii of the *Oeuvres* under the title of *La Place de l'homme dans la nature*.

HU—*Hymne de l'univers* (Paris, Seuil, 1961). Collection of early essays eventually to appear in the *Oeuvres*. [Eng. trans., *Hymn of the Universe* (London & New York, Collins & Harper, 1965).]

LV—*Lettres de voyage, 1923-1955* (Paris, Grasset, 1961). [Eng. trans., *Letters From a Traveller* (London & New York, Collins & Harper, 1962).]

MD—*Le Milieu divin*, 1927 (Paris, Seuil, 1957). [Eng. trans., *Le Milieu Divin* (London, Collins, 1960); *The Divine Milieu* (New York, Harper, 1960).]

MU—*Mon univers*, 1924. An essay published in volume ix of the *Oeuvres*.

Oeuvres—*Oeuvres de Pierre Teilhard de Chardin*, 9 volumes (Paris, Seuil, 1955-65). PH, MD, and GZ constitute volumes i, iv and viii; the other volumes are collections of writings from various periods.

PH—*Le Phénomène humain*, 1938-40 (Paris, Seuil, 1955). [Eng. trans., *The Phenomenon of Man* (London & New York, Collins & Harper, 1959; revised ed., 1965).] References below are to the revised edition.

NOTE: 1) There is a difference in pagination between the Collins and Harper English editions of *MD*. The pages of the Harper edition are given in parentheses after those of the Collins edition.

2) A small circle (°) before an item indicates material unpublished as of January 1966. References to these essays cannot always be accurate due to differences in pagination between various copies.

FOREWORD

1 *L'Ame du monde*, 1918, in *Ecrits du temps de la guerre, 1916-1919* (Paris, 1965), 221. Hereafter cited as *ET*.

2 Letter of January 10, 1953, in Claude Cuénot, *Pierre Teilhard de Chardin* (Paris, Plon, 1958), 442. [Eng. trans., *Teilhard de Chardin* (Baltimore & London, 1965), 363.]

3 *Le Milieu divin*, 1926-7, *Oeuvres de Pierre Teilhard de Chardin*, vol. iv (Paris, 1957), 33-4, 18. [Eng. trans., *Le Milieu Divin* (London), and *The Divine Milieu* (New York, 1960), 21, 11 (19,11).] Hereafter cited as *MD*.

CHAPTER I

1 *Le Phénomène humain*, 1938-40, *Oeuvres*, vol. i (Paris, 1955), 277. [Eng. trans., *The Phenomenon of Man* (London and New York, revised edition, 1965), 249.] Hereafter cited as *PH*.

2 Claude Cuénot's indispensable bibliography lists over 500 separate items: *Teilhard de Chardin*, iii-xli. [Eng. trans., 409-84.] On Teilhard's need for unity see N. M. Wilders, O.F.M.CAP., *Teilhard de Chardin* (Paris, 1960), 7-11. This tiny book is without doubt the best introduction to Teilhard's thought.

3 °*Comment je crois*, 1934, 5.

4 Letter of December 13, 1918, in *Genèse d'une pensée, Lettres, 1914-1919* (Paris, 1961), 351. [Eng. trans., *The Making of a Mind* (London and New York, 1965), 269.] Hereafter cited as *Genèse*. The spiritual import of these letters has been analyzed by René d'Ouince, S.J., 'Vivre dans la plénitude du Christ', *Christus*, ix (1962), 239-47.

5 *Mon univers*, 1918, in *ET*, 278; *Le Milieu mystique*, 1917, in *ET*, 159.

6 *MD*, 25. [Eng. trans., 15(15).]

7 *PH*, 25, 29, [Eng. trans., 31, 35.] See also °*Le Christique*, 1955, 1.

8 The point has been well made by Henri de Lubac, S.J., *La Pensée religieuse*

du Père Teilhard de Chardin (Paris, 1962), 47ff. See also Madeleine Barthé-lémy-Madaule, 'Teilhard de Chardin, Marxism, Existentialism: A Con-frontation', *International Philosophical Quarterly*, i (1961), 657.

9 Pierre Leroy, s.j., *Pierre Teilhard de Chardin tel que je l'ai connu* (Paris, 1958), 64. [Eng. trans., in *Letters From a Traveller* (London and New York, 1962), 46.]

10 Letter of September 8, 1916, in *Genèse*, 157. [Eng. trans., 123.]

11 Letters of April 10 and March 19, 1934, in *Lettres de voyage, 1923-1955* (Paris, 1961), 176. [Eng. trans., *Letters From a Traveller*, 202.] Hereafter cited as *LV*.

12 *La Foi qui opère*, 1918, in *ET*, 313; *La Grande Monade*, 1918, in *Cahiers Pierre Teilhard de Chardin*, vol. ii (Paris, 1960), 43-4. During the war Teilhard was drafted as a stretcher-bearer and spent four years at the front. For bravery he received the Croix de Guerre, the Médaille Militaire and the Légion d'Honneur.

13 Letters of May 11 and September 12, 1923, in *LV*, 31, 48-9. [Eng. trans., 70, 88.]

14 *MD*, 172. [Eng. trans., 128-9 (117).]

15 *PH*, 251-254. [Eng. trans., 227-9.]

16 °*Le Coeur de la matière*, 1950, 32. Hereafter cited as °*CM*. References to the world as a prison where men are 'shut in' occur frequently in Teilhard. Besides those noted here, see also *L'Hominisation*, 1925, *Oeuvres*, vol. iii (Paris, 1957), 106, and *La Transposition 'conique' de l'action*, 1942, *Oeuvres*, vol. v (Paris, 1959), 119. [Eng. trans., *The Future of Man* (London and New York, 1964), 90. Hereafter cited as *FM*.]

17 *Les Singularités de l'espèce humaine*, 1954, *Oeuvres*, vol. ii (Paris, 1956), 295-6. Significantly enough, the fragility of the living world was a source of profound disquiet to him even as a child. Cf. °*CM*, 6.

18 °*Le Phénomène chrétien*, 1950, 5. Cf. chapter four for a further analysis of the problem of death as part of the general problem of evil.

19 *PH*, 154. [Eng. trans., 142.]

20 *ibid.*, 255-6. [Eng. trans., 231.]

21 *ibid.*, 258-9. [Eng. trans., 232-4.]

22 *ibid.*, 257. [Eng. trans., 232.] See *Mon univers*, 1924, *Oeuvres*, vol. ix (Paris, 1965), 70-1. Hereafter cited as *MU*.

23 *Le Groupe zoologique humain*, 1949 (Paris, 1956), 161. Hereafter cited as *GZ*.

24 *La Formation de la noosphère*, 1947, *Oeuvres*, v, 227. [Eng. trans., *FM*, 180.]

25 *L'Esprit de la terre*, 1931, *Oeuvres*, vol. vi (Paris, 1962), 50, note 1. Cf. letter of May 4, 1931: 'It[Jean's book] is the most explicit (and hence to me the most interesting) statement I know of the attitude diametrically opposed to my own, and in it you can see laid bare all the weaknesses (a complete mis-

understanding of the phenomenon of life) that distort his thought.' (*LV*, 148. [Eng. trans., 176.])

26 Cf. letter of February 15, 1955: 'Certain parts of his [Blondel's] thought have had considerable effect upon me: the meaning of action . . . and the notion of "pan-Christism".' See Cuénot, *Teilhard de Chardin*, 55-6. [Eng. trans., 39.] Teilhard's analysis in °*Comment je crois*, 1934, 11-13, acknowledges Blondel explicitly; in *MU*, 70-1, the acknowledgement is implicit but the context clearly marks it as an exposition of Blondel's thought. Christian d'Armagnac, s.j., has discussed at length the correspondence between Blondel's *Action* and *Le Phénomène humain* in 'De Blondel à Teilhard, nature et intériorité', *Archives de Philosophie*, xxi (1958), 298-312.

27 *Mon univers*, 1918, in *ET*, 267, 269, 270. As a young boy Teilhard was attracted by the solidity and weight of metal and stone because these qualities seemed to guarantee resistance and immunity from change. Cf. °*CM*, 4.

28 *MU*, 69.

29 *MD*, 39-41. [Eng. trans., 25-6 (23-4).]

30 °*CM*, 2.

31 *ibid.*, 2.

32 *ibid.*, 20.

33 *ibid.*, 21.

34 *Le Milieu mystique*, 1917, in *ET*, 164-5.

35 Letter of July 30, 1918, in *Genèse*, 290. [Eng. trans., 223.]

36 *Mon univers*, 1918, in *ET*, 272.

37 *Le Prêtre*, 1918, *ET*, 293. Cf. St. Augustine: 'By loving, a man becomes a member; and by love he fits into the structure of Christ's Body; and so there will be one Christ loving himself.' (*In Epist. ad Parthos*, x, Migne, *Patrologia Latina*, xxxv, 2055.)

38 °*CM*, 22-3. See letters of June 29, 1916, and March 31, 1917, in *Genèse*, 136, 249-50. [Eng. trans., 106, 192.]

39 de Lubac, *Pensée religieuse* . . . , 265. It should be noted that the Person of Christ had an altogether dominant influence upon the elaboration of what Teilhard termed in English his 'personalistic universe'. Personalism is indeed at the heart of his system and must command extensive treatment in any exposition of his Christology. 'We can hope for no progress without the primacy and triumph of the personal at the summit of spirit.' *PH*, 331, speaking of Christianity. [Eng. trans., 297.]

40 *PH*, 328. [Eng. trans., 294.]

41 °*Comment je vois*, 1948, 23.

42 °*Le Christique*, 1955, 7.

43 °*Le Sens humain*, 1929, 14-15.

44 °*Trois choses que je vois*, 1948, 6.

45 Letters of September 27, 1918, January 6, 1917, and April 9, 1916, in *Genèse*, 312, 212, 124. [Eng. trans., 239, 164, 98-9.]

46 *MD*, 172-3. [Eng. trans., 129 (117-18).]

47 Letter of January 9, 1917, in *Genèse*, 213. [Eng. trans., 165.]

48 *La Parole attendue*, 1940, in *Cahiers*, vol. iv (Paris, 1964), 27.

49 °*Le Christique*, 1955, 7. Cf. text cited in note 35 for a previous use of *élu*.

50 *L'Avenir de l'homme vu par une paléontologiste*, 1941, *Oeuvres*, v, 100. [Eng. trans., *FM*, 76.]

51 °Letter of August 22, 1925, to Father Auguste Valensin.

52 *Réflexions sur le bonheur*, 1943, in *Cahiers*, ii, 69; °*CM*, 20.

53 Letter of December 12, 1919, in *Archives de Philosophie*, xxiv (1961), 140. Hereafter cited as *Archives*. On this point cf. de Lubac, *Pensée religieuse ...*, 169.

54 *PH*, 343, note 1. [Eng. trans., 308, note 2.] The official English translation is negligent here in rendering the French. Whether or to what extent this statement is theologically correct can be determined only after an analysis of the whole of Teilhard's Christology, as well as the relation therein between the natural and the supernatural. What is being stressed here is simply Teilhard's personal conviction. The meaning of 'hominization and 'coiling' will be explained in the following chapter.

55 °*CM*, 24. Teilhard coined the two nouns *l'En-Haut* and *l'En-Avant* to express and contrast the double current of psychic energy which for him character-ized the action and the thinking of modern man. Between 1947 and 1955 these words recur continually and mark off a separate area of his speculation regarding the noosphere, as we shall see in chapter five.

56 Letter of March 15, 1916, in de Lubac, *Pensée religieuse. ...* That same year he said, 'My most cherished conviction is that we cannot base supernatural growth upon disengagement from what is naturally attractive and noble.' (*La Vie cosmique*, 1916, in *ET*, 8.) Nevertheless, Teilhard was realist enough to write at the end of the war that 'whatever we do in this regard, we are not going to arrive at any perfect reconciliation between God and the world. Christ will always be the "Sign of contradiction". But at least ... no one should be allowed to say that his reason for having nothing to do with God is that he wants to remain more truly human.' (*L'Ame du monde*, 1918, in *ET*, 231-2.)

57 Letter of December 12, 1919, in *Archives*, 138. This desire to have an awareness of growing in Christ is spoken of also in a letter of December 8, 1918, in *Genèse*, 343. [Eng. trans., 263.]

58 *MD*, 34-6. [Eng. trans., 22-3 (20-1).] As a young Jesuit Teilhard seriously considered renouncing completely his love of geological study, and was prevented from doing so only by 'the robust common sense' of his spiritual

director, who told him that God willed the development of his natural talents as well as his sanctification, 'but without explaining to me how or why.' (°*CM*, 24.)

59 °*CM*, 23, 25.

60 Letter of Holy Saturday, 1922, in de Lubac, *Pensée religieuse* . . . , 147.

61 Letters of October 23, 1923 and September 8, 1935, in *LV*, 61, 64, 186 [Eng. trans., 101, 104, 207.]; letter of March 1, 1948, in Cuénot, *Teilhard de Chardin*, 339. [Eng. trans., 280.]

62 See for example the texts cited above in notes 20, 23, 44 and 49, where *en avant* occurs explicitly in the French.

63 Letter of August 7, 1950, in *LV*, 298. [Eng. trans., 303.]

64 *Science et Christ*, 1921, *Oeuvres*, ix, 56-7; letter of January 9, 1917, in *Genèse*, 213 [Eng. trans., 165.]; letter of October 1934, in *LV*, 181. [Eng. trans., 206.]

65 *Sur les bases possibles d'un credo humain commun*, 1941, *Oeuvres*, v, 106. [Eng. trans., *FM*, 81.]

66 *MD*, 196-7. [Eng. trans., 147-8 (133-4).]

67 *La Messe sur le monde*, 1923, in *Hymne de l'Univers* (Paris, 1961), 36. [Eng. trans., *Hymn of the Universe* (London and New York, 1965), 36.] Hereafter cited as *HU*.

CHAPTER II

1 *Quelques réflexions sur la conversion du monde*, 1936, *Oeuvres*, ix, 161-2. Consequently it is quite misleading to link Teilhard's spirituality directly to his explanation of evolution, as does Pierre Smulders, s.j., *La Vision de Teilhard de Chardin* (Paris, 1964), 125; see also 273-5, where this relationship is evident from the principal divisions of his study. A great deal of Teilhard's theological thought appears in Smulders' appendices and his chapters on spirituality, but it is never presented as a unified whole. His approach, therefore, tends to lose the force of Teilhard's own dialectic in which a theology is based upon a hyperphysics of evolution and becomes in turn the basis for a spirituality. The work of Smulders is nonetheless one of the few excellent studies of Teilhard.

2 °*Comment je vois*, 1948, 25.

3 *PH*, 22. [Eng. trans., 30.]

4 On the influence of paleontology on Teilhard's thinking, see *L'Avenir de l'homme vu par un paleontologiste*, 1941, *Oeuvres*, v, 85-100. [Eng. trans., *FM*, 61-76.] Cf. also Cuénot, *Teilhard de Chardin*, 33-59 [Eng. trans., 17-42.]; Bruno de Solages, 'La Pensée chrétienne face à l'évolution', *Bulletin de Littérature Ecclésiastique*, xlviii (1947), ciii-cxvi. [Eng. trans., 'Christianity and Evolution', *Cross Currents*, i (1951), 26-7.]

5 *PH*, 49-50. [Eng. trans., 53.] The originality of the method outlined in this passage has been analyzed at length by Christian d'Armagnac, s.j., 'Philosophie de la nature et méthode chez le Père Teilhard de Chardin', *Archives de Philosophie*, xx (1957), 5-41. Note that the word 'phenomenology' in Teilhard's sense of 'generalized physics' or 'hyperphysics' has a totally different meaning from the same word as applied to the philosophical methodology elaborated by Edmond Husserl and Martin Heidegger in Germany and by Maurice Merleau-Ponty and Paul Ricoeur in France. On this point Teilhard was explicit: 'My phenomenology is not that of Husserl and Merleau-Ponty.' (Letter of April 11, 1953, in Cuénot, *Teilhard de Chardin*, 311. [Eng. trans., 255.])

6 *Le Phénomène humain*, 1930, in *Oeuvres*, iii, 228-9.

7 *PH*, 53, note 1. [Eng. trans., 57, note 1] Olivier Rabut, o.p., has noted that this use of 'consciousness' corresponds to Aristotle's 'immanence', which he saw to be present in all living things. See *Dialogue avec Teilhard de Chardin* (Paris, 1958), 40. [Eng. trans., *Dialogue with Teilhard de Chardin* (London, 1961), 38.]

8 There is an unfortunate rendering of *psychique* as 'physical' in the first edition of the official English translation of *PH*, page 64—(page 62 in the French). —The reason for this apparently arbitrary presumption will become clear later, sc. all energy, even the most crassly material, is ordered to that highest form of psychic energy which is love. See *PH*, 257, note 1. [Eng. trans., 232, note 1.]

9 *PH*, 78. [Eng. trans., 78.] For Teilhard the genesis of life on earth belongs to the category of absolutely unique events which, once they have happened, are never repeated. See *ibid.*, 100-7. [Eng. trans., 96-102.] See also *GZ*, 5.

10 °*On the Trend and Significance of Human Socialization*, 1948, 2. A lecture in English delivered in New York. There is a similar affirmation at the end of *PH*, 334 [301], called by Teilhard 'the substance of these long pages.' See also *PH*, 62, note 1 [Eng. trans., 65, note 1.]: 'Let it be noted in passing that the less an element is "centred" (i.e. the feebler its radial energy) the more will its tangential energy reveal itself in powerful mechanical effects.'

Attention is here called to the fact that Teilhard himself chose the English 'coiling' to describe what in French he usually calls *enroulement*, sometimes *reploiement*. In the official English translation of *PH*, these words are usually translated as 'involution'. This creates an unfortunate ambiguity, since in its strict biological sense of 'retrograde development', the word 'involution' conveys exactly the opposite of Teilhard's meaning. See, for example, *PH*, 71, 72, 288, 304, 333, 334, 337, 343, note 1, 347. [Eng. trans., 72, 73, 259, 273, 300, 301, 304, 308 note 2, 313.] There is sometimes the translation 'furling back'. See, for example, *PH*, 269, 302. [Eng. trans.,

243, 272.] In *PH* Teilhard uses the French word *involution* in the sense of *enroulement* only on page 341 [Eng. trans., 307.] In *FM* the translation is usually 'coiling', but sometimes 'in-folding', as for example pages 245ff.

11 *PH*, 199. [Eng. trans., 180-1.] 'Orthogenesis' is the biological term for the law on controlled complication. 'My considered opinion is that the word is essential and indispensable for singling out and affirming the manifest property of living matter to form a system in which terms *succeed each other* experimentally, following the constantly increasing degrees of centro-complexity.' *ibid.*, 114, note 1. [Eng. trans., 108, note 1.] On the opinion of modern science regarding the relation of psychism to organic complexity, see Dr. Paul Chauchard, *L'Etre humain selon Teilhard de Chardin* (Paris, 1959), 57-102. [Eng. trans., *Man and Cosmos* (New York, 1965), 47-83.] Joseph F. Donceel, s.j., has dealt at length with the apparent disagreement of Teilhard with many palaeontologists on the subject of orthogenesis in 'Teilhard de Chardin: Scientist or Philosopher?' *International Philosophical Quarterly*, v (1965), 248-66.

12 *PH*, 186, note 1. [Eng. trans., 169, note 1.] The same point is made by Teilhard regarding scientific knowledge of monogenism, i.e., the origin of the human race from a single couple. 'The problem of monogenism in the strict sense of the word . . . seems to *elude* science as such by its very nature. At those depths of time when hominization took place, the movements of a unique couple are positively ungraspable. . . . Accordingly one can say that there is room *in this interval* for anything that a trans-experimental source of knowledge might demand.' *ibid.*, 206, note 1. [Eng. trans., 186, note 1.] Fossil data either proving or disproving monogenism can never be found precisely because the first tentative expressions of a species mutation are the weakest and vanish quickly. Only the gradually improving forms grow to full maturity and so have the strength to survive as fossils. This phenomenon is known as the 'suppression of peduncles'. See *ibid.*, 128-30 [Eng. trans., 120-2.]; *GZ*, 81-3; *Le Paradoxe transformiste*, 1925, *Oeuvres*, iii, 131-2.

13 *Le Paradoxe transformiste*, 1925, *Oeuvres*, iii, 142, note 1; °*Note sur les modes de l'action de Dieu dans l'univers*, 1920, 4. See also *PH*, 79 [Eng. trans., 79.]: 'Seen from the outside and materially, the best we can say at the moment is that life properly speaking begins with the cell.' What Teilhard is affirming here is a concomitance ('seen from the *outside* and *materially*') not a total reproduction. Confer the principle enunciated in *Que faut-il penser du transformisme?*, 1930, *Oeuvres*, iii, 216: 'In transformism the scientific plane (of experimental succession in time) and the philosophical plane (of ultimate causality) are not to be confused.' On this question see the excellent treatment of John L. Russell, s.j., 'The Phenomenon of Man', *The Heythrop Journal*, ii (1961), 4-5.

14 *PH*, 184. [Eng. trans., 168.]

15 *ibid.*, 188. [Eng. trans., 171.] Olivier Rabut does not take sufficient account of this point in his criticism of Teilhard. See his *Dialogue* . . . , 105-7. [Eng. trans., 121-3.]

16 *L'Esprit de la terre*, 1931, *Oeuvres*, vi, 55; *MU*, 76; *MD*, 173 [Eng. trans., 129 (118).]; *La Crise présente*, 1937, published as 'Sauvons l'humanité', in *Cahiers*, iii (Paris, 1962), 78. See also *Esquisse d'un univers personnel*, 1936, *Oeuvres*, vi, 69-114, and letter of January 6, 1917, in *Genèse*, 210. [Eng. trans., 163.] Teilhard twice uses the English phrase 'a personalistic universe', once in 1936 as a gloss on the title of *Esquisse d'un univers personnel*, and once in 1944 as a subtitle at the start of °*Introduction à la vie chrétienne*.

17 *Le Phénomène humain*, 1930, *Oeuvres*, iii, 231; *PH*, 202-3. [Eng. trans., 183-4.]

18 *PH*, 244, 247. [Eng. trans., 221, 223.] See also *La Formation de la 'noosphère'*, 1947, *Oeuvres*, v, 201-31 [Eng. trans., *FM*, 155-84.]; *GZ*, 129-62; *Du cosmos à la cosmogénèse*, 1951, *Oeuvres*, vii (Paris, 1963), 261-77.

19 *PH*, 265. [Eng. trans., 239.] See on this question François Russo, s.j., 'La Socialisation selon Teilhard de Chardin', *Revue de l'Action Populaire*, xii (1962), 1157-70.

20 To avoid confusion we should note two points regarding Teilhard's use of this image. First, he uses it uniquely to describe that stage of the evolutionary process which began with the emergence of *homo sapiens* and the crossing of the threshold of reflection. It is never used to describe the evolutionary process as such. For this his favourite image is that of a cone, the lower part of which extends itself indefinitely while the upper part converges towards a point. Cf. *Le Cône du temps*, 1942, *Oeuvres*, v, 111-17. [Eng. trans., *FM*, 83-9.] Secondly, the zone of convergence after the equator is out of all chronological proportion when applied to man. 'By analogy with other living layers its duration would run into millions of years.' *PH*, 212, with diagram. [Eng. trans., 192.] Teilhard says 'thousands or even millions of years' in *La Planétisation humaine*, 1945, *Oeuvres*, v, 169. [Eng. trans., *FM*, 133.]

21 *PH*, 288. [Eng. trans., 259.] See also *Les Singularités de l'espèce humaine*, 1954, *Oeuvres*, ii, 322-37; *La Structure phylétique du groupe humain*, 1951, *Oeuvres*, ii, 217; *PH*, 265-71. [Eng. trans., 239-45.] A common expression used by Teilhard to express the same idea is the 'totalization' of humanity upon itself. See *Le Rebondissement humain de l'évolution*, 1947, *Oeuvres*, v, 253. Also *GZ*, 132-4.

22 *PH*, 287, 289, 291, 292 [Eng. trans., 259, 260, 262, 263.]; *La Crise présente*, 1937, in *Cahiers* iii, 78; *La Grande option*, 1939, *Oeuvres*, v, 75. [Eng. trans., *FM*, 54.] See also the lengthy analysis of Teilhard's personalism in de Lubac, *Pensée religieuse* . . . , 201-14. The phrase 'union differentiates' is frequent in

Teilhard. For example, °*Comment je crois*, 1934, 16, note 1; *L'Energie humaine*, 1937, *Oeuvres*, vi, 179; *La Grande option*, 1939, *Oeuvres*, v, 74, 76 [Eng., trans., *FM*, 54, 55.]; *La Centrologie*, 1944, *Oeuvres*, vii, 122. See also chapter five, note 81.

23 *Super-humanité, super-Christ, super-charité*, 1943, *Oeuvres*, ix, 93, note 1.

24 *PH*, 279. [Eng. trans., 251-2.] See *MU*, 112: 'In some way the men of the future will form but a single consciousness.' Cf. also the lengthy treatment in *Les Singularités de l'espèce humaine*, 1954, *Oeuvres*, ii, 338-66, esp. 354, and the clear statement in °*Trois choses que je vois*, 1948, 3, note 1.

25 *Super-humanité, super-Christ, super-charité*, 1943, *Oeuvres*, ix, 196-7. Emphasis added. See also *PH*, 337. [Eng. trans., 303.] On this hypothetical nature of evolutionary convergence cf. de Lubac, *Pensée religieuse . . .* , 250-62, and Christian d'Armagnac, s.j., 'La Pensée du Père Teilhard de Chardin comme apologétique moderne', *Nouvelle Revue Théologique*, lxxxiv (1962), 604, 613.

26 *PH*, 258. [Eng. trans., 233.] See also °*Comment je vois*, 1948, 23.

27 Letter of January 1, 1954, in Cuénot, *Teilhard de Chardin*, 482. [Eng. trans., 400.]

28 *PH*, 316. [Eng. trans., 284.]

29 Anything else would take us far afield into his metaphysics of 'creative union', by which he sought to explain the mystery of spirit by analyzing the link between matter and reflective consciousness. We shall deal with this theory at the end of chapter five, since it is meant to be 'a philosophical extension of faith in the Incarnation' (*MU*, 82) and logically forms a conclusion to Teilhard's Christology.

30 °*Comment je crois*, 1934, 2. 'Faith in the world, . . . faith in spirit, . . . faith in immortality, . . . faith in personality.' (*ibid.*, 3, 6, 10, 13.) See also *Quelques réflexions sur la conversion du monde*, 1936, *Oeuvres*, ix, 158-9.

31 *PH*, 238, 243. [Eng. trans., 215, 219.] See also *Du cosmos à la cosmogénèse*, 1951, *Oeuvres*, vii, 275-7.

32 *PH*, 255, 257. [Eng. trans., 230, 232.] Teilhard's italics have been retained for the last clause although they do not appear in the first edition of the official English translation. The English expression 'self-evolution' appears in *Les Singularités de l'espèce humaine*, 1954, *Oeuvres*, ii, 349, and in °*Contingence de l'univers et goût humain de survivre*, 1953, 1. On the uncertainty introduced into evolution by human freedom, see *PH*, 250, 342 [Eng. trans., 225-6, 307.]; *GZ*, 140-4; *L'Hominisation*, 1925, *Oeuvres*, iii, 106-7. See also the development of this idea in chapter four.

33 *PH*, 253. [Eng. trans., 228.] See also *L'Atomisme de l'esprit*, 1941, *Oeuvres*, vii, 56-8.

34 *PH*, 254. [Eng. trans., 229.] See Teilhard's lengthy analysis of this phen-

NOTES TO PP. 52-4

omenon of modern anxiety and fear in *Un phénomène de contre-évolution en biologie humaine ou la peur de l'existence*, 1949, *Oeuvres*, vii, 189-202.

35 *PH*, 254, 259. [Eng. trans., 229, 234.]

36 *ibid.*, 285. [Eng. trans., 257.] There have been several efforts to link the thought of Teilhard with that of Karl Marx, most notably that of the French Marxist Roger Garaudy in *Perspectives de l'homme* (Paris 1961), 170-223. This large subject cannot be treated at present, but it should be clearly noted that Teilhard was poles apart from a deterministic view of history. For him man has in no sense lost control of his destiny on earth. On the contrary, it is man who is master of evolution, not vice-versa, and this by reason of his freedom. See the excellent critique of Garaudy by George Morel, s.j., 'Karl Marx et le P. Teilhard de Chardin', *Etudes*, ccciv (1960), 80-7.

37 Teilhard has developed at some length the role in his system of thought of what he calls 'the sexual sense'. 'The mutual attraction of the sexes is so fundamental a fact that any explanation of the world which does not succeed in incorporating it *structurally*, as an *essential* part of its edifice, is virtually condemned.' (*Esquisse d'un univers personnel*, 1936, *Oeuvres*, vi, 91.) Besides the lengthy treatment in *Esquisse*, there is also that of °*L'Evolution de la chasteté*, 1934. See also *La Lutte contre la multitude*, 1917 ,in *ET*, 125; *L'Union créatrice*, 1917, in *ET*, 192-5; *Note pour servir à l'évangélisation des temps nouveaux*, 1919, in *Cahiers*, iv, 18-19; *L'Eternel féminin*, 1918, in *ET*, 253-62.

38 *PH*, 295-6. [Eng. trans., 266-7.] On 'amorization' and a fuller analysis of the meaning of love in this cosmic sense, see *L'Energie humaine*, 1937, *Oeuvres*, vi, 180-98; *Esquisse d'un univers personnel*, 1936, *Oeuvres*, vi, 101-5; *L'Esprit de la terre*, 1931, *Oeuvres*, vi, 39-47; *La Centrologie*, 1944, *Oeuvres*, vii, 125-6.

39 *PH*, 297-8. [Eng. trans., 267-8.]

40 *GZ*, 162. Emphasis added.

41 *PH*, 299-300. [Eng. trans., 269.] See letter of January 19, 1929: 'The supreme Centre must be both lovable and loving'. (*LV*, 118. [Eng. trans., 151.]) In a letter of October 18, 1940, Teilhard said of the war: '. . . the root of the evil is not in the apparent conflicts, but very far away from them, it seems, in the inner fact that men have despaired of God's personality.' See *LV*, 262. [Eng. trans., 269.] Cf. also *Comment concevoir et espérer que se réalise sur terre l'unanimisation humaine?*, 1950, *Oeuvres*, v, 373. [Eng. trans., *FM*, 286-7.]

42 *L'Esprit de la terre*, 1931, *Oeuvres*, vi, 53. See Teilhard's earlier analysis of the problem of action in *PH*, 251-9. [Eng. trans., 226-34.], and the treatment of this theme in chapters one and four.

43 *PH*, 301. [Eng. trans., 270-1.] The study of Olivier Rabut manages to convey

the false impression that in Teilhard's mind the *real* Omega is somehow the product of natural evolution. He fails to distinguish clearly between the Omega of Teilhard's initial hypothesis of probability, which would indeed be the product of natural evolution, and the *real* Omega of his second hypothesis, which is already in existence and consequently transcends the evolutionary process. (*Dialogue. . .* , 101ff. [Eng. trans., 115ff.])

44 '*Tout tient par en haut*'. (*MU*, 78.) An indication of the coherence and consistency of Teilhard's thought is the fact that these same words are used, though without the terseness, both at the beginning and at the end of *The Phenomenon of Man*. See *PH*, 37 and 301. [Eng. trans., 43 and 271.] The same expression with slight variations is to be found in *La Foi qui opère*, 1918, in *ET*, 322, *L'Elément universel*, 1919, in *ET*, 410, note 8, and °*Comment je crois*, 1934, 13.

45 *PH*, 301, 341. [Eng. trans., 271, 307.] On the transcendence of Omega see *L'Esprit de la terre*, 1931, *Oeuvres*, vi, 52-7. Teilhard himself felt that he was giving here a valid proof from reason for the existence of God (*Vie et Planètes*, 1945, *Oeuvres*, v, 153, note 1 [Eng. trans., *FM*, 120, note 1.]), but not all critics agree. For opposing views, see Rabut, *Dialogue. . .* , 101-15 [Eng. trans., 115-34.], and Bruno de Solages, 'Les Preuves teilhardiennes de Dieu', in *L'Homme devant Dieu*, vol. iii (Paris, 1964), 125-32.

46 °*Comment je vois*, 1948, 14. A more detailed treatment of Teilhard's understanding of evolution may be found in the excellent analysis of Smulders in *La Vision. . .* , 39-125. The decisive role of Teilhard's 'psychological act of faith' is implied in Smulders' development (123-5) but never explicitly stated.

47 °*Panthéisme et Christianisme*, 1923, 8.

48 *PH*, 323. [Eng. trans., 290.] On this need of 'Someone' instead of 'something' at the end of evolution, see also *Esquisse d'un univers personnel*, 1936, *Oeuvres*, vi, 101; *L'Avenir de l'homme vu par un paléontologiste*, 1941, *Oeuvres*, v, 99-100 [Eng. trans., *FM*, 75-6]; *Comment concevoir et espérer que se réalise sur terre l'unanimisation humaine?*, 1950, *Oeuvres*, v, 374. [Eng. trans., *FM*, 287-8.]

49 °*Le Dieu de l'évolution*, 1953, 3. This is the precise point which Teilhard criticizes most in the philosophy of Henri Bergson: 'By the mere fact that one sees in universal becoming a pattern of convergence, one eliminates the Bergsonian idea of a vital thrust without finality, a *vis a tergo*. A dynamism such as his allows indeed for a centre of divergence at its starting point, but I do not see how it would produce a fusion of the elements which it drives before it.' (*L'Union créatrice*, 1917, in *ET*, 181.) Nevertheless, as we know from °*CM*, 8-9, reading Bergson before the first world war was a strong catalyst for Teilhard's first intuitions on the relationship between matter, energy and spirit. The two thinkers are contrasted with

admirable clarity by Madeleine Barthélémy-Madaule in *Bergson et Teilhard de Chardin* (Paris, 1963), 236–99. See chapter five below, note 60, on this contrast between the two men.

50 *L'Esprit de la terre*, 1931, *Oeuvres*, vi, 59.

51 *Les Directions et les conditions de l'avenir*, 1948, *Oeuvres*, v, 304 [Eng. trans., *FM*, 236.]; °*Le Christique*, 1955, 7; *MU*, 81.

52 See texts cited above in notes 1 and 34.

53 *L'Ame du monde*, 1918, in *ET*, 227–8; letter of September 23, 1947, in *LV*, 290. [Eng. trans., 294–5.]

54 *Hérédité sociale et progrès*, 1938, *Oeuvres*, v, 51. [Eng. trans., *FM*, 34.] See also °*Comment je vois*, 1948, 15.

55 °*Le Christique*, 1955, 7; *Super-humanité, super-Christ, super-charité*, 1943, *Oeuvres*, ix, 210; *L'Energie humaine*, 1937, *Oeuvres*, vi, 192; °*Essai d'intégration de l'homme dans l'univers*, 1930, 4th lecture, 11.

56 *PH*, 343, note 1. [Eng. trans., 308, note 2.] The official English translation is negligent here in rendering the French.

57 *Les Directions et les conditions de l'avenir*, 1948, *Oeuvres*, v, 305. [Eng. trans., *FM*, 237.] The words in brackets were added by Teilhard in a footnote to the word 'condition'. Almost the same formulation appears a year later in *Le Coeur du problème*, 1949, *Oeuvres*, v, 348. [Eng. trans., *FM*, 268.]

58 de Lubac, *Pensée religieuse* . . . , 100. See the excellent treatment of Teilhard's confrontation of these two sources of knowledge in d'Armagnac, 'La pensée du Père Teilhard . . . ', 603–4. See also °*Trois choses que je vois*, 1948, 4.

59 *PH*, 332, note 1. [Eng. trans., 298, note 1.]

60 *Ma position intellectuelle*, 1948, published as 'La Pensée du P. Teilhard de Chardin par lui-même', *Les Etudes Philosophiques*, x (1955), 581. Teilhard makes the same distinction between the two sources of knowledge in *Esquisse d'une dialectique de l'esprit*, 1946, *Oeuvres*, vii, 155: a response to revelation is called an 'act of *recognition* . . . the emergence of theological faith under the influence of grace.'

61 *Science et Christ*, 1921, *Oeuvres*, ix, 59–60, 62.

62 *Ma position intellectuelle*, 1948, *Les Etudes Philosophiques*, 581. See also °*Trois choses que je vois*, 1948, 4.

63 °*Comment je vois*, 1948, 1.

64 'Science et révélation', appendix to *Barrière de la mort et co-réflexion*, 1955, *Oeuvres*, vii, 428. On this orientation of Teilhard's thought see Georges Crespy, *La Pensée théologique de Teilhard de Chardin* (Paris, 1961), 63.

65 *Note sur le progrès*, 1920, *Oeuvres*, v, 34–5. [Eng. trans., *FM*, 22.]

66 °*Comment je crois*, 1934, 23, note 2.

67 °*Comment je vois*, 1948, 16. The words in brackets were added by Teilhard in a footnote to the word 'necessary'. See also his remark that same year in

°*Trois choses que je vois*, 4: 'The point of human maturation' is 'a condition (not indeed sufficient and determinative but necessary)' for 'the point of the Parousia of Christ.'

68 °*Comment je vois*, 1948, 25.

69 Letter of January 1, 1951, in Cuénot, *Teilhard de Chardin*, 330, note 3. [Eng. trans., 273.] See *L'Etoffe de l'univers*, 1953, *Oeuvres*, vii, 405: 'It is impossible to think of Christ as the source of evolution without at the same time having to rethink the whole of Christology.'

70 °*Le Christique*, 1955, 8.

71 *PH*, 330–1. [Eng. trans., 297.]

72 See texts cited above in notes 28 and 30. The three strata of which we are here speaking should not be confused with the three directions of Teilhard's thought indicated in the text cited in note one. It will be readily seen that the first direction indicated in that text includes the first two strata now under discussion.

73 *PH*, 263. [Eng. trans., 237.]

74 The word is Julian Huxley's and is used in his perceptive Introduction to the English edition of *The Phenomenon of Man*, pages 18 and 27. Huxley sees quite clearly (page 19) that a personal Omega cannot legitimately be postulated from scientific data, since on the strict level of phenomena there is no basis for 'personifying the non-personal elements of reality.' On the other hand he does not seem to recognize the central importance of love in Teilhard's explanation of evolution, which is the key concept in his 'psychological act of faith'.

75 See *PH*, 328: [Eng. trans., 294.] 'Doubtless I should never have ventured to envisage the latter [i.e. Omega] or formulate the hypothesis rationally if, in my consciousness as a believer, I had not found not only its speculative model but also its living reality.

76 °*Comment je vois*, 1948, 23.

77 Letter of September 6, 1953, in *LV*, 346. [Eng. trans., 344.] Claude Tresmontant justly remarks that most misunderstandings of Teilhard result from a failure to take into account the level or stratum of thought on which a given text was composed. It does not follow, however, as Tresmontant would seem to suggest, that these distinct strata can be fully understood independently of each other or that they were ever really separated in Teilhard's mind. See his *Introduction à la pensée de Pierre Teilhard de Chardin* (Paris, 1956), 122. [Eng. trans., *Pierre Teilhard de Chardin, His Thought* (Baltimore, 1959), 99.]

CHAPTER III

1 *PH*, 244. [Eng. trans., 221.] See Teilhard's clear summary in *Agitation ou Genèse?*, 1947, *Oeuvres*, v, 275-84. [Eng. trans., *FM*, 214-22.]

2 *Hérédité sociale et progrès*, 1938, *Oeuvres*, v, 51. [Eng. trans., *FM*, 34.]

3 *La Mystique de la science*, 1939, *Oeuvres*, vi, 220-1. The same problem is approached in almost the same way in 'Catholicisme et science', *Esprit*, xiv (1946), 253-4.

4 *La Vie cosmique*, 1916, in *ET*, 39-40, 47.

5 °*Panthéisme et Christianisme*, 1923, 8.

6 *MD*, 117. [Eng. trans., 86 (77-8).]

7 *ibid.*, 140-1. [Eng. trans., 104-5 (95).] Cf. °letter of December 31, 1926, to Father Auguste Valensin: 'Without an historical revelation Our Lord evaporates.'

8 °*Comment je crois*, 1934, 24-5; °*Quelques vues générales sur l'essence du Christianisme*, 1939, 2: *La Parole attendue*, 1940, in *Cahiers*, iv, 28.

9 °*Introduction à la vie chrétienne*, 1944, 5.

10 °*Christianisme et évolution*, 1945, 6-7. Cf. *Esquisses d'une dialectique de l'esprit*, 1946, *Oeuvres*, vii, 157-8: 'For a mind *already Christian* it is positively difficult to think of Omega . . . without perceiving that its collective, unifying function implies as a consequence that it be in one way or another partially involved in the world.'

11 °*CM*, 30.

12 *L'Union créatrice*, 1917, in *ET*, 195.

13 *MU*, 84.

14 *Forma Christi*, 1918, in *ET*, 341-2; °letter of January 10, 1920, to Father Auguste Valensin; letter of December 12, 1919, in *Archives*, 139-40.

15 Letter of December 29, 1919, in *Archives*, 154.

16 *La Vie cosmique*, 1916, in *ET*, 49; *L'Ame du monde*, 1918, in *ET*, 228; *MD*, 200-1 [Eng. trans., 151 (137).]; °*Christologie et évolution*, 1933, 10.

17 *Super-humanité, super-Christ, super-charité*, 1943, *Oeuvres*, ix, 209-10. The same formulation appears almost verbatim in °*Note sur la notion de perfection chrétienne*, 1942, 2, after which Teilhard asks: 'Faced with this [i.e. the idea of a 'bicephalous' universe] what would be the reply of St. Paul and a whole chorus of Greek Fathers?'

18 *Du cosmos à la cosmogénèse*, 1951, *Oeuvres*, vii, 272.

19 *Note sur le Christ universel*, 1920, *Oeuvres*, ix, 39.

20 °*Comment je crois*, 1934, 23 and note 1.

21 *Super-humanité, super-Christ, super-charité*, 1943, *Oeuvres*, ix, 210-11. Teilhard makes the same point regarding a juridical as opposed to a 'physical' con-

ception of Christ's Kingship in *La Parole attendue*, 1940, in *Cahiers*, iv, 27, and in *La Transposition 'conique' de l'action*, 1942, *Oeuvres*, v, 123-4. [Eng. trans., *FM*, 94-5.]

22 Letter of December 29, 1919, in *Archives*, 156. A brief summary of this exchange of letters may be found in Christopher F. Mooney, s.j., 'Blondel and Teilhard de Chardin', *Thought*, xxxvii (1962), 543-62.

23 *L'Union créatrice*, 1917, in *ET*, 196.

24 *Forma Christi*, 1918, in *ET*, 239. 'Every unity in the world, provided it be a natural unity, is a monad.' (*MU*, 75.)

25 °Letter of May 25, 1923, to Father Auguste Valensin; *MD*, 141. [Eng. trans., 105 (95).] See also his remark on reading *Les Grands Initiés* of Edouard Schuré: 'In reading Schuré I have put my finger on the error of all false mysticism: it confuses planes, looks for mystery on the plane of phenomena, strains objective reality as well as the imagination of its advocates, and mixes together the ether, the sphere of the "stars", and the true sphere of the spirit.' (Letter of December 13, 1918, in *Genèse*, 350. [Eng. trans., 268.])

26 *MU*, 86-7, 106 note 1.

27 *MD*, 137, 150, 162, 196. [Eng. trans., 102, 112, 121, 147 (92, 101, 110, 133).] As the editor of the English translation has noted, the word *milieu* has no exact equivalent in English. It implies at one and the same time both centre and environment.

28 *Esquisse d'un univers personnel*, 1936, *Oeuvres*, vi, 113.

29 *MD*, 43-4. [Eng. trans., 28-9 (26).]

30 *MU*, 90.

31 *Le Christ dans la matière*, 1916, in *HU*, 50. [Eng. trans., 48.]

32 *Le Prêtre*, 1918, in *ET*, 287. The essay of the previous year is *Le Milieu mystique*, 1917, in *ET*, 164-5: 'From the moment that you said "This is my Body", not only the bread and wine on the altar but to a certain extent everything in the universe became yours which nourishes in our souls the life of grace and the spirit.' See also *La Puissance spirituelle de la matière*, 1919, in *HU*, 67. [Eng. trans., 64.]

33 °*Panthéisme et Christianisme*, 1923, 12.

34 *La Messe sur le monde*, 1923, in *HU*, 23, 24, 34, 36. [Eng. trans., 24, 25, 34, 37.]

35 *MU*, 93, 104.

36 *MD*, 150-2. [Eng. trans., 112-13 (101-2).]

37 *ibid.*, 153-4. [Eng. trans., 114-15 (103-4).]

38 *ibid.*, 136. [Eng. trans., 102 (91).]

39 *PH*, 327-8, 331. [Eng. trans. 293-4, 297.] Compare Teilhard's treatment here with Yves Congar's attempt to come to grips with the same problem within the framework of scholastic theology: 'Sur l'inclusion de l'humanité

dans le Christ', *Revue des Sciences Philosophiques et Théologiques*, xxv (1936), 489-5.

40 °*Introduction à la vie chrétienne*, 1944, 10.

41 °*Le Christique*, 1955, 8-9.

42 *MD*, 24. [Eng. trans., 14 (14).]

43 A recent example of a lengthy and well-reasoned refutation of a position which Teilhard never held is Leo Scheffczyk's 'Die "Christogénèse" Teilhard de Chardins und der Kosmische Christus bei Paulus', *Tübinger Theologische Quartalschrift*, cxliii (1963), 136-174. Professor Scheffczyk seems to interpret the 'physical' relationship of Christ to the universe as an immanence which is wholly natural and which therefore would exclude all that is personal and supernatural. He then goes on to show without difficulty that such a relationship is nowhere to be found in St. Paul.

44 A thorough summary of both the Greek and Latin traditions on this question may be found in Emile Mersch, S.J., *Le Corps mystique du Christ, Etudes de théologie historique*, 2 vol. (Bruxelles, 3e éd., 1951). [Eng. trans., *The Whole Christ* (Milwaukee, 1938).]

45 Teilhard has the following footnote to this sentence: 'See especially in St. Paul: Rom. 8:18ff, 14:7-9; I Cor. 4:22, 6:15ff, 10:16, 12:12ff, 15:23-9, 39ff; II Cor. 3:18, 4:11, 5:4, 19; Gal. 3:27-8; Eph. 1:10, 19-23, 2:5, 10, 13-14, 3:6, 18, 4:9, 12-13, 16; Phil. 2:10, 3:10-11, 20-1; Col. 1:15-20, 28, 2:9-10, 12, 19, 3:10; I Thes. 4:17; Heb. 2:7-8.'

46 *MU*, 82. Teilhard frequently cites *Ephesians* 4:9, but he obviously means 4:10. The texts which appear most frequently in his writings are Colossians 1:17, 'and in him all things subsist', cited six times, always in its Latin translation; and I Corinthians 15:28, 'so that God may be all in all', cited thirteen times, usually in the Greek original, *en pasi panta Theos*. Other favourite texts are Acts 17:28, 'In him we live and move and have our being', Romans 8:22, 'The whole of nature has been groaning until now in an agony of birth', and Ephesians 4:10, 'He has ascended high above all the heavens in order to fill all things with his presence.'

47 Lucien Cerfaux, *La Théologie de l'Eglise suivant Saint Paul* (Paris, 2e éd., 1948) 206, 209, 210, 212, 254-9. [Eng. trans., *The Church in the Theology of St. Paul* (New York, 1959), 265, 269, 270, 274, 337, 344.] Pierre Benoit, O.P., 'Corps, Tête et Plérôme dans les épîtres de la captivité', *Revue Biblique*, lxiii (1956), 7-11, 20-1; J. A. T. Robinson, *The Body* (London 1952), 49-83.

48 For example, Th. Zapelena, 'Vos Estis Corpus Christi', *Verbum Domini*, xxxvii (1959), 78-95, 162-70. A clear reply to Zapelena as well as an excellent statement of the relationship between Paul and *Mystici Corporis* has been given by J. Havet, 'La doctrine Paulinienne du "Corps de Christ", essai de mise au point', *Littérature et théologie Paulinienne*, (Louvain, 1950), 186-216.

On the same problem see also P. Erbich, 'Mystischer oder Auferstandener Leib Christi', *Orientierung*, xxiii (1959), 193-5, 204-7.

49 Benoit, 'Corps, Tête . . .', 18; J. A. T. Robinson, *The Body*, 26-8. In his monumental study, *Gnosis, La Connaissance religieuse dans les épîtres de Saint Paul* (Bruges, 1949), Jacques Dupont, o.s.b., after weighing all the evidence, concludes that Paul's primary influence in developing 'Body of Christ' was Semitic and not Hellenistic (pp. 440-50).

50 H. W. Robinson, 'The Hebrew Concept of the Corporate Personality', in *Werden und Wesen des Alten Testaments*, ed. by J. Hempel (Berlin, 1936) 58ff. See also Jean de Fraine, s. j., *Adam et son lignage: Etudes sur la notion de 'personalité corporative' dans la Bible* (Bruges, 1959).

51 J. A. T. Robinson, *The Body*, 58. See also the extended treatment of the relation between the Eucharist and Paul's theology of the Body by A. E. J. Rawlinson 'Corpus Christi', in *Mysterium Christi*, ed. by G. Bell and A. Deissmann (Berlin, 1931), 275-96.

52 Cerfaux, *Théologie de l'Eglise* . . . , 215. [Eng. trans., 277.] This is also the conclusion of Benoit, 'Corps, Tête . . .', 13-18. See the excellent study of the major epistles by Barnabas Ahern, c.p., 'The Christian's Union with the Body of Christ in Cor., Gal. and Rom.' *Catholic Biblical Quarterly*, xxiii (1961), 199-209.

53 Cerfaux, *Théologie de l'Eglise* . . . , 143-57 [Eng. trans., 187-206.] gives a full treatment of texts. Some commentators find the ecumenical meaning weakly asserted in three or four early passages, especially I Corinthians 12-27ff.

54 Benoit, 'Corps, Tête . . .', 23-9. Cf. I Corinthians 6:15, 10:17, 12:7-11, and Romans 12:6-8 for previous use of the Body theme.

55 Ephesians 1:23 is explicit, while Ephesians 5:23 is implicit from the use of 'Church and 'Body' in a parallelism.

56 Benoit, 'Corps, Tête . . .', 21; Cerfaux, *Théologie de l'Eglise* . . . , 259. [Eng. trans., 344.] 'To say that the Church is the Body of Christ because the life of grace and the life of Christ are alike is not enough. To say that there is an identity of life and therefore an identity of the Church and the Body is too much.' (*ibid.*, 258 note 4. [Eng. trans., 343 note 35.]) A fuller development of the above analysis may be found in Christopher F. Mooney, s.j., 'Paul's Vision of the Church in "Ephesians" ', *Scripture*, XV (1963), 33-43.

57 Cerfaux is of the opinion that for Paul the Incarnation had no salvific value at all and that the Greek Fathers corrected his too rigid synthesis. See *Le Christ dans la théologie de Saint Paul* (Paris, 1951), 130, 132, 135. [Eng. trans., *Christ in the Theology of Saint Paul* (New York, 1959), 166, 168, 172.] Others favour the view that in Paul's mind the whole of Jesus' life is redemptive, including therefore the Incarnation. See, for example, Joseph Bonsirven,

s.j., *L'Evangile de Paul* (Paris, 1948), 157-9; Felix Malmberg, s.j., *Ein Leib-Ein Geist* (Freiburg, 1960), 239-41; Benoit, 'Corps, Tête . . . ', 38. Yves de Montcheuil, s.j. holds that the Eucharist in Paul's mind is related to the whole of humanity and therefore the whole of creation precisely because of the Incarnation. See his 'L'Unité du sacrifice et du sacrement dans l'Eucharistie', in *Mélanges Théologiques* (Paris, 1946) 49-70.

58 Henri Bouillard, s.j., *Blondel et le Christianisme* (Paris, 1961), 162-3. The recent study of Oscar Cullmann, *La Christologie du Nouveau Testament* (Paris, 1958), is practically silent on these Pauline texts.

59 I Corinthians 15:28. The explanation as well as the translation of the Romans text has been taken from Stanislaus Lyonnet, s.j., 'La Rédemption de l'univers', *Lumière et Vie*, ix (1960) 41-62; A. Viard, o.p., 'Expectatio Creaturae (Rom. viii, 19-22)', *Revue Biblique*, lix (1952), 337-54; and Paul Henry, s.j., *Philosophie religieuse de l'épître aux Romains* (Paris, 1950, manuscript), Chapter vii, 7-9.

60 Benoit, 'Corps, Tête . . .', 31-40; Dupont, *Gnosis*, 453-576. The same opinion is developed with slight differences by Victor Warnach, o.s.b., 'Kirche und Kosmos', in *Enkainia*, ed. Hilarius Emonds, o.s.b. (Düsseldorf, 1956), 184-96; and Heinrich Schlier, *Der Brief an die Epheser* (Düsseldorf, 3.Aufl., 1962), 96-8. For the Old Testament concept of God's creative presence, see the references in Benoit (36-7) and the lengthy treatment of André Feuillet, 'L'Eglise plérôme du Christ d'après Eph.', *Nouvelle Revue Théologique*, lxxviii (1956), 446-72, 596-610.

61 Joseph Huby, s.j., *Les Epîtres de la captivité* (Paris, 1935), 40. The expression of J. B. Lightfoot is from his *St. Paul's Epistles to the Colossians and to Philemon* (London, 1904), 148. Exegetes have noted that whenever Paul speaks of the pre-existence of Christ, as in Colossians, he is always thinking of the concrete, historical God-Man and never of the Word independent of his humanity. Cf. for example Joseph Bonsirven, s.j., *Théologie du Nouveau Testament* (Paris, 1951), 254 [Eng. trans., *Theology of the New Testament* (Westminster, 1963), 232.]: 'St. Paul knows nothing of this Word existing in the bosom of the Trinity; when he envisages a pre-existence, he is always speaking of Jesus Christ, who was consequently mediator of creation, for example, even before his appearance on earth.' See also B. Brinkmann, 'Die kosmische Stellung des Gottmenschen in Paulinischer Sicht', *Wissenschaft* und *Weisheit*, xiii (1950), 6-33, especially 8-9; F. X. Durrwell, c.ss.r., 'Le Christ, premier et dernier', *Bible et Vie Chrétienne*, ix (1963), 16-28, especially 22-5; A. Grillmeier, s. j., 'Zum Christusbild der Heutigen Katholischen Theologie', in *Fragen der Theologie Heute*, ed. J. Feiner, J. Trütsch, F. Böckle (Einsiedeln, 1957), 269-70.

62 The interpretation given here is based on the following: Heinrich Schlier,

'Kephalē, Anakephalaioomai', in *Theologisches Wörterbuch zum Neuen Testament*, ed. by Gerhard Kittel, vol. iii (Stuttgart, 1938) 681-2; *idem*, 'Die Kirche nach dem Briefe an die Epheser', in *Die Zeit der Kirche* (Freiburg, 1956), 171-2; Cerfaux, *Le Christ* . . . , 318-19 [Eng. trans., 424-5.]; Warnach, 'Kirche . . .', 189-90; Benoit, 'Corps, Tête . . .', 40-4; Dupont, *Gnosis*, 425-6.

63 In a lengthy study Franz Mussner has vigorously contested many of the interpretations given here: *Christus, das All und die Kirche* (Trier, 1955). See also the article by Leo Scheffczyk cited in note 43 above.

64 Besides those mentioned already, see the works of the following Protestant theologians: L. S. Thornton, *The Incarnate Lord* (London, 1928), 28-110; E. C. Rust, *Nature and Man in Biblical Thought* (London, 1953), 197-303; Allen D. Galloway, *The Cosmic Christ* (London, 1951), 3-56; E. L. Mascall, *Christian Theology and Natural Science* (London, 1956), 36-46; Ernest Best, *One Body in Christ* (London, 1955), 83-159.

65 °Letter of December 17, 1922, to Father Auguste Valensin.

66 °*Essai d'intégration de l'homme dans l'univers*, 1930, 4th lecture, 12; *MD*, 153. [Eng. trans., 114 (103).]

67 *Commentarium in IV Sent.*, lib. III, dist. V, ques. I, art. II, ad 6: 'Another reason [that the flesh of Christ is said to be divinized] is that it is a quasi-instrument through which the divine power works out our salvation; for it was by touching the leper with his flesh that he cured him through the power of Divinity, and it was by dying in the flesh that he conquered death through the power of Divinity. But the power of the agent is somehow in the instrument by means of which it acts.'

68 *Summa Theologica*, pars III, ques. 48, art. 6, ad 2.

69 *ibid.*, pars III, ques. 79, art. 1, ad 1: 'This sacrament has power to confer grace of itself; nor does anyone have grace prior to the reception of this sacrament, except by reason of some *votum* for it.'

70 Ladislaus Boros, s.j., *Mysterium Mortis, Der Mensch in der Letzten Entscheidung* (Freiburg, 1962), 154-6. Cf. Mk. 5:25-34; Lk. 9:43-8.

71 Cf., for example, the text cited above in note 24, and the lengthy development of the whole subject in *The Phenomenon of Man*.

72 Maurice Blondel, *Une énigme historique, le 'Vinculum Substantiale' d'après Leibnitz et l'ébauche d'un réalisme supérieur* (Paris, 1930). This is a French adaptation of his Latin thesis of 1893. See especially pages 105-6, where in speaking of Christ as the *Vinculum*, he appeals to the Eucharist as an illustration of his theory. Confer also the remarks of Yves de Montcheuil, s.j., 'Les Problèmes du "Vinculum" Leibnitzien d'après M. Blondel', in *Mélanges Théologiques* (Paris, 1946), 294. Teilhard said himself that he was considerably influenced by Blondel's 'pan-Christism' (letter of February 15, 1955, in

Cuénot, *Teilhard de Chardin*, 55-6 [Eng. trans., 39.]) and it is quite possible that he came in contact very early with Blondel's original Latin thesis through Father Auguste Valensin, who was a close mutual friend; but there is no record to this effect.

73 Letter of December 15, 1919, in *Archives*, 129. Cf. Blondel's *Lettre sur l'apologétique de 1896*, in *Les Premiers écrits de Maurice Blondel*, vol. ii (Paris, 1956), 80-1, for a development of these same ideas. On the nature of Blondel's 'pan-Christism', see Bouillard, *Blondel et le Christianisme*, 160-5, and Jean Rimaud, s.j., 'Vie spirituelle et philosophie: Maurice Blondel', *Christus*, ix (1962), 272-88.

74 Karl Rahner, s.j., *Zur Theologie des Todes* (Freiburg, 1958), 19-20. [Eng. trans., *On the Theology of Death* (London, 1961), 26-7.]

75 *Idem, Sendung und Gnade* (Innsbruck, 1959), 61. [Eng. trans., *Mission and Grace*, vol i (London, 1963), 73.]

76 *Idem*, 'Probleme der Christologie von Heute', *Schriften zur Theologie*, vol. i (Einsiedeln, 1954), 187-8. [Eng. trans., *Theological Investigations*, vol. i (London, 1960), 165.] We might note here a rare theological essay on the cosmic dimensions of the Eucharist by Ladislaus Boros, s. j., 'Meditationen über die Eucharistie', *Orientierung*, xxvii (1963), 117-19, 134-6. Hans Urs von Balthasar, in his recent study on the theology of history, *Das Ganze im Fragment* (Einsiedeln, 1964), 330-32, agrees that Teilhard's approach to the Eucharist is correct, even though he is in strong disagreement with Teilhard's evolutionary presuppositions.

CHAPTER IV

1 *PH*, 342. [Eng. trans., 307-8.]
2 °*Le Christ évoluteur*, 1942, 6-7.
3 *Esquisse d'un univers personnel*, 1936, *Oeuvres*, vi, 105.
4 *La Transposition 'conique' de l'action*, 1942, *Oeuvres* v, 119. [Eng. trans., *FM*, 90.]
5 *PH*, 347. [Eng. trans., 313.]
6 *ibid.*, 346. [Eng. trans., 312.]
7 °*Comment je vois*, 1948, 19-20. This text is taken from an elaboration of Teilhard's theory of creative union, which we shall deal with in chapter five. We shall then see more clearly the full implications of what is said here concerning creation and multiplicity. The thought of this text and in some cases the same words appear in a slightly different guise in *PH*, 346 [Eng. trans., 312.]; *MD*, 87-8 [Eng. trans., 64-5 (57-8).]; °*CM*, 28. A much longer development is to be found in *La Lutte contre la multitude*, 1917, in *ET*, 113-22.
8 *La Signification et la valeur constructrice de la souffrance*, 1933, *Oeuvres*, vi, 63. The

explanations given thus far are repeated in different form in *Esquisse d'un univers personnel*, 1936, *Oeuvres*, vi, 106-7; °*Quelques vues générales sur l'essence du Christianisme*, 1939, 1; *L'Atomisme de l'esprit*, 1941, *Oeuvres*, vii, 57; °*Le Néohumanisme moderne et ses réactions sur le Christianisme*, 1948, 5; *Du cosmos à la cosmogénèse*, 1951, *Oeuvres*, vii, 267-8.

9 *MD*, 83-4. [Eng. trans., 60-1 (54).] The official English translation is negligent here in rendering the French.

10 *PH*, 300. [Eng. trans., 270.]

11 These expressions are to be found in °*Comment je crois*, 1934, 2; *L'Energie humaine*, 1937, *Oeuvres*, vi, 173; *PH*, 263, 299, 337. [Eng. trans., 237, 269, 304.] See the lengthier analysis of this psychological problem in chapter one.

12 It is interesting to compare Teilhard's argumentation here with that of St. Thomas based on man's natural desire for final beatitude; especially the succinct statement from *In Boetium de Trinitate*, ques. 6, art. 4, ad 5: 'Although man is naturally drawn towards his ultimate end, he cannot obtain it naturally but only through grace; and the reason for this is the pre-eminence of this end.' The same position is developed at greater length in *Contra Gentiles*, lib. iii, cap. 50; *Compendium Theologiae*, ch. 104; *Summa Theologica*, pars i, ques. 12, art. 1; *De Veritate*, ques. 8, art. 1. On this question see the excellent article of Guy de Broglie, s.j. 'De la place du surnaturel dans la philosophie de Saint-Thomas', *Recherches de Science Religieuse*, xiv (1924), 193-245.

13 *PH*, 265. [Eng. trans., 239.] For the relationship between the two energies see *ibid.*, 62-4 [Eng. trans., 64-6.]; °*CM*, 27; as well as the treatment of the question at the start of chapter two.

14 *PH*, 302. [Eng. trans., 272.] 'In the measure that the conscious becomes centred upon itself, it gradually detaches itself from that frame of complexity needed to begin and to support its convergence.' (*Barrière de la mort et co-réflexion*, 1955, *Oeuvres*, vii, 423, note 1.)

15 *PH*, 302. [Eng. trans., 272.] The relationship of this passage to Teilhard's theory regarding the end of the world will be treated in the following chapter.

16 *ibid.*, 78. [Eng. trans., 78.] See the treatment of 'critical points' in the early part of chapter two. See also *Le Rebondissement humain de l'évolution*, 1947, *Oeuvres*, v, 261-2 [Eng. trans., *FM*, 203-4.] for the relationship between technical progress and true progress.

17 *Esquisse d'un univers personnel*, 1936, *Oeuvres*, vi, 108-9. The phrase 'death barrier' occurs in *Barrière de la mort et co-réflexion*, 1955, *Oeuvres*, vii, 419-29. There is likewise a second threshold of reflection for the species. See *PH*, 338-41 [Eng. trans., 304-7.] and the treatment of this question in chapter five.

18 Letter of November 13, 1916, in *Genèse*, 186–7 [Eng. trans., 145.]; °letter of
   May, 1920 [*sic*] to Father Auguste Valensin. See also *Le Milieu mystique*,
   1917, in *ET*, 151, for the same reaction to death. Among others, Karl
   Rahner has treated at length this new relationship of the separated soul to
   the whole of the universe, calling it *pancosmic* as opposed to *cosmic*, in his
   Zur Theologie des Todes (Freiburg, 1958), 20–5. [Eng. trans., *On the Theology
   of Death* (London, 1961), 26–34.]

19 °*Comment je vois*, 1948, 19, note 31.

20 Leroy, *Teilhard de Chardin*, 43–4. [Eng. trans., in *Letters from a Traveller*, 35–6.]

21 *MD*, 137, 83. [Eng. trans., 102, 60 (92, 53–4).] See also *ibid.*, 171–3. [Eng.
   trans., 128–9 (117–18).]

22 *L'Energie spirituelle de la souffrance*, 1950, Oeuvres, vii, 256–7.

23 *MD*, 168–9. [Eng. trans., 126 (114–15).] See *La Foi qui opère*, 1918, in *ET*, 323.

24 *MD*, 84–5, 92, 112–13. [Eng. trans., 61, 67, 83 (54–5, 60, 74).]; *La Lutte
   contre la multitude*, 1917, in *ET*, 130.

25 *Agitation ou genèse?*, 1947, Oeuvres, v, 285, note 1. [Eng. trans., *FM*, 223,
   note 1.]

26 *MD*, 93–4. [Eng. trans., 68–9 (61).] See *MU*, 91: 'From a Christian viewpoint
   the function of human death is to give life in virtue of the death of Jesus.'

27 *MD*, 128, note 1, 117, 47. [Eng. trans., 94, note 1, 86, 31 (86, note 1, 78, 28).]

28 Letter of January 9, 1917, in *Genèse*, 214 [Eng. trans., 165–6.]; letters of December 12 and December 29, 1919, in *Archives*, 135–6, 155, 140. See also *La
   Messe sur le monde*, 1923, in *HU*, 31 [Eng. trans., 31.]: 'In order for my
   being to be really and truly joined to yours, not only the monad has to die
   in me but the world as well. In other words, I have to pass through a phase
   of diminishment which will be heart-rending and for which there will be
   no tangible compensation.'

29 *MD*, 127–8, 123. [Eng. trans., 93–4, 90 (85–6, 82).] The comparison with a
   current deflecting a ship from its course is not made explicitly by Teilhard,
   but is contained implicitly in the French word *dérive* which refers to a ship's
   leeway or drift. Cf. *ibid.*, 113, note 1 [83, note 1 (75, note 1).]: '. . . to get
   the maximum spiritual yield from the objects which surround us,—which
   is what the kingdom of God really consists in.' See also letter of January 9,
   1917, in *Genèse*, 215 [Eng. trans., 166.]: 'The sanctification of the universe
   is true progress, the real extension of the labour which has given us the
   human brain and its power to think.'

30 *MD*, 49–50, 115. [Eng. trans., 33, 84–5 (30, 76).]

31 Letters of September 27, 1918 and January 9, 1917, in *Genèse*, 312, 213. [Eng.
   trans., 239, 165.] On use of *élu* in the context of purification, see also *La
   Lutte contre la multitude*, 1917, in *ET*, 131; °*Panthéisme et Christianisme*, 1923,
   9–10; letter of July 30, 1918, in *Genèse*, 290. [Eng. trans., 223.]

32 *MD*, 56, 96 [Eng. trans., 38, 70 (35, 62).]; *MU*, 92-3. On the Eucharist see, for example, *Le Christ dans la matière*, 1916, in *HU*, 50 [Eng. trans., 49.]; *Le Prêtre*, 1918 in *ET*, 287; *MD*, 171, 153-4 [Eng. trans., 128, 114-15 (116-17, 103-4).]; °*Introduction à la vie chrétienne*, 1944, 10; °*Le Christique*, 1955, 9. These texts have already been treated at length in chapter three.

33 *MD*, 118-19. [Eng. trans., 86-87 (78-79).] This same explanation of redemption's relationship to cosmic evolution is repeated in slightly different form in *La Vie cosmique*, 1916, in *ET*, 56; *La Signification et la valeur constructrice de la souffrance*, 1933, *Oeuvres*, vi, 65-6; °*Quelques vues générales sur l'essence du Christianisme*, 1939, 2; °*Ce que le monde attend en ce moment de l'Eglise de Dieu*, 1952, 4-5.

34 *MU*, 90.

35 °*Essai d'intégration de l'homme dans l'univers*, 1930, 4th lecture, 13, 15; *MD*, 116, 119. [Eng. trans., 85, 87-8 (77, 79).]

36 *MD*, 97-9. [Eng. trans., 71-3 (63-6).] See also *ibid.*, 85-7 [Eng. trans., 62-3 (55-6).]; *MU*, 100-2; *La Signification et la valeur constructrice de la souffrance*, 1933, *Oeuvres*, vi, 64-5. One of the reproaches levelled by Teilhard against all eastern religions is precisely the total passivity they encourage before the misfortunes of human life. See °*La Route de l'Ouest*, 1932, 14-15.

37 °*Christologie et évolution*, 1933, 7-8.

38 The teaching of Scotus on the motive for the Incarnation is well summarized by P. Ramond, 'Duns Scot', *Dictionnaire de théologie catholique*, vol. 4 (Paris, 1911), 1891. See also Wildiers, *Teilhard de Chardin*, 92-5; Robert North, S.J., 'Teilhard and the Problem of Creation', *Theological Studies*, xxiv (1964), 595-7. Teilhard himself mentions Scotus explicitly only once, in *Esquisse d'une dialectique de l'esprit*, 1946, *Oeuvres*, vii, 158.

39 Cf. text cited earlier in note 2.

40 St. Thomas felt that redemption from sin was the sole purpose of the Incarnation and that all discussion must begin from what God has actually done in the present order of creation (*Summa Theologica*, pars iii, ques. 1, art. 3.). The unreal question of what God would have done in some other order is 'not of great importance' (*In1^{am} ad Tim.*, cap. I, lectio iv).

41 *MU*, 90. The consequences of this 'kenosis' of Christ spoken of by Paul in Philippians 2:6-11 have been analyzed at great length by Paul Henry, S.J., 'Kénose', *Dictionnaire de la Bible, Supplément*, vol. v (Paris, 1950), 7-161; recent developments on this text are treated by Paul Lamarche, S.J., 'L'hymne de l'épître aux Philippiens et la kénose du Christ', in *L'Homme devant Dieu*, vol. i (Paris, 1964), 147-58. See also Felix Malmberg, S.J., *Über den Gottmenschen* (Freiburg, 1960), 19-22. The meaning of the phrase 'redemptive Incarnation' is well discussed by L. Richard, *Le Mystère de la rédemption* (Paris, 1959), 237-57.

42 In *Etudes*, cclxvi (1950), 284. The occasion was the review of an anonymous attack upon him entitled *L'Evolution rédemptrice du P. Teilhard de Chardin*. 'I do not recognize here the expression of my thought, not even in the title, which insinuates that I attribute a properly salvific power to the cosmic process.'

43 *PH*, 251, 257, 306. [Eng. trans., 226, 233, 275.] Italics in original. See also *GZ*, 140-4; *L'Hominisation*, 1925, *Oeuvres*, iii, 106-7; *La Foi en l'homme*, 1947, *Oeuvres*, v, 237-9. [Eng. trans., *FM*, 187-9.]

44 *PH*, 321. [Eng. trans., 288.]

45 *Note sur le progrès*, 1920, *Oeuvres*, v, 31, 33. [Eng. trans., *FM*, 19, 21.] At this early stage of his thought Teilhard believed that it could be the *whole* of humanity which would decide either for or against Omega. This decision he referred to as 'the final option'. See *ibid.*, 31.

46 *PH*, 321-3. [Eng. trans., 288-9.] On man's capacity for refusal of true progress towards growth in spirit, see *L'Hominisation*, 1925, *Oeuvres*, iii, 106ff.

47 *La Grande option*, 1939, *Oeuvres*, v, 75 [Eng. trans., *FM*, 54.]; *L'Esprit de la terre*, 1931, *Oeuvres*, vi, 42; *Esquisse d'un univers personnel*, 1936, *Oeuvres*, vi, 90. Teilhard has often explained his understanding of love as the sole energy capable of furthering true human progress. See, for example, *PH*, 293-8 [Eng. trans., 264-8.]; *L'Energie humaine*, 1937, *Oeuvres*, vi, 180-96.

48 *Réflexions sur le bonheur*, 1943, in *Cahiers*, ii, 64.

49 *Le Phénomène spirituel*, 1937, *Oeuvres*, vi, 134, and note 2.

50 °*CM*, 27. Teilhard makes the same point in *La Lutte contre la multitude*, 1917, in *ET*, 129, and in *Esquisse d'un univers personel*, 1936, *Oeuvres*, vi, 104, 110.

51 *MD*, 84, 119. [Eng. trans., 61, 87 (54, 79).]; °*Christologie et évolution*, 1933, 8. See also *La Vie cosmique*, 1916, in *ET*, 57.

52 *MU*, 109, note 2. Teilhard applied the word 'physical' equally, though analogously, to the material and the personal as well as to the natural and supernatural. See the lengthy analysis of this concept in chapter three.

53 *PH*, 345. [Eng. trans., 311.]

54 °*Comment je vois*, 1948, 20. See previous citation of this text in more complete form earlier in this chapter.

55 *MD*, 89 and note 1. [Eng. trans., 65 and note 1 (58 and note 1).] See also °*Note sur les modes de l'action divine dans l'univers*, 1920, 10-11.

56 Henricus Denzinger, *Enchiridion Symbolorum*, 32nd edition, ed. Adolfus Schönmetzer, s.j. (Freiburg, 1963), no. 1521 [793]. Hereafter cited as Denzinger. On St. Thomas, see *Summa Theologica*, pars I-II, ques. 109, art. 8.

57 *Ma position intellectuelle*, 1948, in *Les Etudes Philosophiques*, 1955, 581; *PH*, 117, 346. [Eng. trans., 110, 312.]

58 For example, Smulders, *La Vision . . .* , 149, 164-5.

59 *MD*, 173 [Eng. trans., 129 (118).]; *MU*, 76-7.

60 By original sin, says Maximus the Confessor, 'the one nature was shattered into a thousand pieces.' *Ubi peccata ibi multitudo* is the classic formula of Origen. Henri de Lubac has assembled these and other patristic texts in the first chapter of his *Catholicisme* (Paris, 1937). [Eng. trans., *Catholicism* (London, 1950).]

61 *Les Directions et les conditions de l'avenir*, 1948, Oeuvres, v, 303 [Eng. trans., *FM*, 235.]; *PH*, 347 [Eng. trans., 313.]; *MD*, 117. [Eng. trans., 86 (77).]

62 *Note sur le progrès*, 1920, Oeuvres, v, 33. [Eng. trans., *FM*, 21.] See the previous citation of this passage in note 45 as well as its development in the main body of the chapter.

63 *La Maîtrise du monde et le Règne de Dieu*, 1916, in *ET*, 82; *Forma Christi*, 1918, in *ET*, 349-50; *Terre promise*, 1919, in *ET*, 395. For similar references from the same period to outer darkness and man's refusal of love, see *Le Christ dans la matière*, 1916, in *HU*, 51 [Eng. trans., 49.]; *L'Union créatrice*, 1917, in *ET*, 195; *Le Prêtre*, 1918, in *ET*, 289.

64 *MD*, 187-8, 191. [Eng. trans., 140-1, 143 (128-9, 131).] For a similar use of *élu* see *ibid.*, 139. [Eng. trans., 104 (93).] The word or its equivalent, *choisi*, is found especially in Teilhard's early essays in this context of man's freedom and Christ's role as Judge. See, for example, *La Vie cosmique*, 1916, in *ET*, 52, 59; *La Maîtrise du monde et le Règne de Dieu*, 1916, in *ET*, 67; *La Lutte contre la multitude*, 1917, in *ET*, 131; *Le Prêtre*, 1918, in *ET*, 298. In the light of these texts it is difficult to understand the remark of George Crespy, *La Pensée théologique* . . . , 218: 'In Teilhard's world there is place for Christ the Conqueror but no place for Christ the Judge.'

65 °*Introduction à la vie chrétienne*, 1944, 9.

66 This is precisely the point which is not seen by Olivier Rabut in his *Dialogue* . . . , 157-61. [Eng. trans., 186-92.] He continually equates the words 'creation' and 'physical' with 'natural' and 'material'. Hence his understandable difficulty in seeing how the supernatural action of Christ (i.e. the movements of grace) can be connected with the natural evolutionary process.

67 *La Maîtrise du monde et le Règne de Dieu*, 1916, in *ET*, 82-3; *La Lutte contre la multitude*, 1917, in *ET*, 124. See letter of June 17, 1917, in *Genèse*, 256 [Eng. trans., 197.]: 'For our peace as well as for our taste for God, etc., we are at the mercy of grace. I liken this to the state of an object illuminated by a ray of light from a projector. It cannot force the ray of light either to come closer or to remain. The difference with us is that we are able to pray for help and, as you say, to have certitude that the light will not abandon us.'

68 *MD*, 19, 29, 164, 169, 179, 190. [Eng. trans., 12, 17, 122, 126, 134, 142 (12, 17, note 1, 111, 115, 122, 130).]

69 *PH*, 326 [Eng. trans., 293.]; *Catholicisme et science*, 1946, Oeuvres, ix, 241.

70 *PH*, 343, note 1, from the postcript written in 1948 [Eng. trans., 308, note 2.]; *Les Directions et les conditions de l'avenir*, 1948, Oeuvres, v, 305. [Eng. trans., *FM*, 237.] See the previous citation of these texts in chapter two, notes 50 and 56.

71 *Le Goût de vivre*, 1950. Oeuvres, vii, 251.

72 *MD*, 88, 89, 93, 124. [Eng. trans., 64, 65, 68, 91 (57, 58, 61, 83).] Hence it cannot be said, as does Smulders (*La Vision . . .*, 157-67), that Teilhard's ultimate purpose is to elaborate an infra-cosmic guarantee of evolution's success. Smulders is quite correct in saying that, in his rational analysis of moral evil, Teilhard is seeking every possible reason for optimism regarding the outcome of evolution. But in order to equate such an effort with a personal conviction of the existence of an infra-cosmic guarantee, one has to separate Teilhard's rational analysis from what he says regarding the whole positive aspect of redemption. Such a separation is both gratuitous and unfaithful to Teilhard's avowed purpose of seeking a vision of reality which unites the two sources of knowledge. It is true that Teilhard usually treats the two sources separately and that the data of one source is not the data of the other. Yet his thought is nonetheless a whole, and no definitive conclusion may be drawn from the consideration of one part only.

73 °*Ce que le monde attend en ce moment de l'Eglise de Dieu*, 1952, 5. See also °*Introduction à la vie chrétienne*, 1944, 8.

74 °*Christologie et évolution*, 1933, 7, note 1.

75 *La Vie cosmique*, 1916, in *ET*, 60-1.

76 In 'Die Spiritualität Teilhards de Chardin', *Wort und Wahrheit*, xvii (1963) 339-50, Hans Urs von Balthasar points out clearly the consistency of Teilhard's failure to emphasize in any way the negative aspect of redemption. His critique, however, suffers from a strong and rather unfair prejudice against the starting point of Teilhard's theological enquiry, namely the desire to rethink the data of revelation in the context of scientific data concerning cosmic and organic evolution.

77 Original sin and monogenism are mentioned together explicitly only twice, in °*Chute, rédemption et géocentrie*, 1920, 1, and in °*Note sur quelques représentations historiques du péché originel*, 1924, 2. Twice also Teilhard states explicitly that on its own level science is incapable of passing judgment on the subject of monogenism; see *PH*, 206, note 1 [Eng. trans., 186, note 1] and °*Monogénisme et monophylétisme*, 1950, 1. Further elaboration of this point has been given above in chapter two, note 12. Teilhard's personal conviction was that the scientific evidence pointed rather to monophyletism, or the origin of all men from a single branch or phylum. See

below, note 89, for the significance of the Encyclical *Humani Generis* in this regard. The present scientific state of the question is treated at length by Edouard Boné, s.j., 'Polygénisme et polyphylétisme', *Archives de Philosophie*, xxiii (1960), 99-141. See also Smulders, *La Vision* . . . , 201-9; Cyril Vollert, s.j., 'Human Evolution and Theological Implications', *Proceedings, Catholic Theological Society of America*, vi (1951), 122-45, and Johannes Hürzeler, 'Evolution und Monogenismus/Polygenismus', *Orientierung*, xxviii (1964), 196-7.

78 *Note sur le Christ universel*, 1920, *Oeuvres*, ix, 41; °*Chute, Rédemption et géocentrie*, 1920, 1, 5; °*Note sur quelques représentations historiques du péché originel*, 1924, 8.

79 °*Réflexions sur le péché originel*, 1947, 3.

80 °*Christologie et évolution*, 1933, 3, 4, note 1; °*Réflexions sur le péché originel*, 1947, 1; excerpt on original sin from letter of June 19, 1953 to Mme. Jean Carlhian. For the influence of the cult of the Heart of Christ on Teilhard's own spiritual life, confer °*CM*, 21-3, as well as the treatment of this subject in chapter one. See also the comment on Pius XI's 1928 Encyclical on reparation in °*Le Sens humain*, 1929, 16, and Teilhard's essay *L'Incroyance moderne*, 1933, *Oeuvres*, ix, 152-3.

81 Ephesians 2:10. For Ephesians 3:9 most manuscripts read . . . God, who created all things through Jesus Christ'. On this point see Evode Beaucamp, o.f.m., *La Bible et le sens religieux de l'univers* (Paris, 1959), 104 [Eng. trans., *The Bible and the Universe* (Westminster, 1963), 86.] 'Wherever the fact of creation is evoked in the Bible, it is always placed in relation to one aspect or other of the drama of salvation.'

82 *De Veritate*, ques. 14, art. 11. He also says that Adam had explicit faith in the Incarnation of Christ before the fall (*Summa Theologica*, pars II-II, ques. 2, art. 7).

83 On this large question see the excellent treatment by Smulders, *La Vision* . . . , 175-89. Cf. also C. Dumont, s.j., 'La Prédication du péché originel', *Nouvelle Revue Théologique*, lxxxiii (1961), 113-34; A. M. Dubarle, o.p., *Le Péché originel dans l'écriture* (Paris, 1958), 122-49 [Eng. trans., *The Biblical Doctrine of Original Sin* (London, 1964), 45-87.]; Hans Küng, *Rechtfertigung* (Einsiedeln, 1957), 150-70 [Eng. trans., *Justification* (New York, 1964), 148-70.].

84 On the relationship between death as a biological end to life and death as a consequence of sin, see Gustave Martelet, s.j., *Victorie sur la mort* (Paris, 1962), 97-113; Louis Ligier, s.j., *Péché d'Adam et péché du monde*, vol. i (Paris, 1960), 201-10, vol. ii (Paris, 1961), 266-73; Rahner, *Zur Theologie des Todes*, 31-45 [Eng. trans., 40-57]; Roger Troisfontaines, s.j., *Je ne meurs pas* (Paris, 1960), 153-68. [Eng. trans., *I Do Not Die* (New York, 1964), 189-207.]

85 'One could wonder if true human sin might not be that of man arrived much later at a fullness of consciousness, as it were, at a full sense of his responsibility . . .' (°*Quelques vues générales sur l'essence du Christianisme*, 1939, 2.)

86 See Smulders, *La Vision* . . . , 190–4; also Stanislaus Lyonnet, s.j., 'Le Péché originel et l'exégèse de Rom. 5:12–14,' *Recherches de Science Religieuse*, xliv (1956), 63–84; de Fraine, *Adam et son lignage*, 90–3; P. Schoonenberg, s.j., 'Erbsünde und Sünde der Welt', *Orientierung*, xxvi (1962), 65–9; Louis Bouyer, 'Les deux économies du gouvernement divin, Satan et le Christ', *Initiation théologique*, ed. A.-M. Henry, o.p., vol. ii (Paris, 1952), 503–35. [Eng. trans., *God and His Creation* (Chicago, 1955), 466–96.]

87 °*Note sur quelques représentations historiques du péché originel*, 1924, 6; °*Réflexions sur le péché originel*, 1947, 6; °*Comment je vois*, 1948, 20, note 32; °*Quelques vues générales sur l'essence du Christianisme*, 1939, 2; *La Vie cosmique*, 1916, in *ET*, 61; *L'Etoffe de l'univers*, 1953, *Oeuvres*, vii, 405. See also °*Chute, rédemption et géocentrie*, 1920, 3. In some of the above essays Teilhard considers another solution which, though in itself 'valid' because it makes original sin a transhistoric reality, is for him too 'gratuitous and fantastic'. This was the view inspired by St. Gregory of Nyssa and the Alexandrian school, which conceived the fall of man as taking place before the beginning of time, and hence capable of embracing the whole of history because altogether prior to the existence of this present world. This is the solution which Teilhard mentions when he writes for the first time of original sin in a letter of October 7, 1915, in *Genèse*, 92 [Eng. trans., 74.] and in *Les Noms de la matière*, 1919, in *ET*, 426–7. See also *MU*, 109, note 1.

88 This distinction between 'cosmic fundament' and 'historical actuation' is made in °*Le Christ évoluteur*, 1942, 9.

89 Pius XII, *Humani Generis*, in Denzinger, 3879 [2328]. These words of the Encyclical merely give a résumé of what was said by the Council of Trent. Cf. Denzinger, 223 [102], 327 [175], 1513 [790]. In regard to monogenism, it might be noted that the precise problem here is that it is still not clear whether Trent was implicitly *teaching* the individuality of Adam, or whether it was simply *presupposing* it spontaneously because of the mode of presentation found in Scripture. See the extended treatment of this question by Karl Rahner, s.j., 'Theologisches zum Monogenismus', *Schriften zur Theologie*, vol. i (Einsiedeln, 1954), 265–71. [Eng. trans., *Theological Investigations*, vol. i (London, 1961), 240–7.] The historical background to Trent's deliberations on original sin may be studied in A. Vanneste, 'La Préhistoire du décret du Concile de Trente sur le péché originel', *Nouvelle Revue Théologique*, lxxxvi (1964), 355–68, 490–510.

90 °*Le Christ évoluteur*, 1942, 8; °*Réflexions sur le péché originel*, 1947, 1, note 1; letter of April 28, 1954, in T. V. Fleming, s.j., 'Two Unpublished Letters of

Teilhard', *The Heythrop Journal*, vi (1965), 36. Teilhard's doubts were all the more real because, as he said, he was 'perfectly aware of the solemn canons of the Council of Trent', and consequently was 'quite aware of the changes these new views would be introducing'. (°*Christologie et évolution*, 1933, 8.)

91 See texts cited above in notes 55, 61 and 72.

92 The first to publish a just and balanced judgment on this radical deficiency in Teilhard has been Louis Cognet, *Le Père Teilhard de Chardin et le pensée contemporaine* (Paris, 1952), 117-20. His judgments on the correlative questions of grace and divine initiative, however, appear to this writer much too severe in the light of the textual evidence. Teilhard's tendency to depersonalize sin does not in fact, as Cognet would seem to suggest, fit logically into his total approach to freedom, love, personal responsibility, and the mystery of hell.

93 *PH*, 346. [Eng. trans., 311.]

94 Diary for November 29, 1947, in de Lubac, *Pensée religieuse* . . . , 161.

95 *La Lutte contre la multitude*, 1917, in *ET*, 124; °*Le Christ évoluteur*, 1942, 9; °*Le Christique*, 1955, 11. Smulders is therefore not correct when he says (*La Vision* . . . , 169-72) that Teilhard is primarily interested in elaborating an apologetics of hope independently of supernatural hope in Christ. One could only conclude this if one were to take Teilhard's treatment of the subject on the level of reason as the sole norm of judgment, and ignore the whole third stratum of his thought based upon the data of revelation. See above, note 72.

96 °Letter of January 10, 1926 to Father Auguste Valensin.

97 °*Comment je crois*, 1934, 26-7. See the texts cited early in chapter one for further indications of Teilhard's natural inclination towards pessimism.

CHAPTER V

1 °*CM*, 31. Other examples of the Ephesians text in the context of the Resurrection are to be found in *MU*, 92, and *MD*, 149. [Eng. trans., 111-12 (100-1).] 'When, faced with a universe whose physical and spiritual immensity tends to stagger us more and more, we become afraid of the ever growing weight of energy and glory which the Son of Mary must bear in order to continue to receive our adoration, let us think of the Resurrection.' (*MU*, 92.)

2 'What shortsightedness to present creation as an instantaneous act long past which would have produced . . . essences which the divine power now merely supports and conserves!' (*Le Milieu mystique*, 1917, in *ET*, 149.) See also the lengthy explanation in *Les Fondements et le fond de l'idée de l'évolution*, 1926, *Oeuvres*, iii, 186-190. The misunderstanding here is obviously due to the unreal and superficial distinction (unfortunately insisted upon too

strongly by later scholastic theology) between creation and conservation, which are in reality one and the same divine action. See St. Thomas, *Summa Theologica*, pars I, ques. 45, art. 3, ad 3, and ques. 104, art. 1, ad 4. See also his *De Potentia*, ques. 3, art. 3, ad 6.

3 *La Vie Cosmique*, 1916, in *ET*, 39; *MD*, 181 [Eng. trans., 136 (124).]; °*Introduction à la vie chrétienne*, 1944, 1; °*CM*, 31; °*Le Christique*, 1955, 5-6.

4 *La Vie Cosmique*, 1916, in *ET*, 41, 42, 48, 51-2.

5 *ibid.*, 53-4.

6 *La Maîtrise de Monde et le Règne de Dieu*, 1916, in *ET*, 81; *L'Elément universel*, 1919, in *ET*, 411; *Forma Christi*, 1918, in *ET*, 344. See also *Mon univers*, 1918, in *ET*, 275 and *La Lutte contre la multitude*, 1917, *ET*, 125-6. In *Forma Christi* (343) Teilhard deliberately changes St. Paul's words in Romans 8:28 to '*Credenti, omnia convertuntur "in Christum"*.'

7 Letter of December 12, 1919, in *Archives*, 140; *Note sur le progrès*, 1920, *Oeuvres*, v, 35. [Eng. trans., *FM*, 22.] See also *La Maîtrise du monde et le Règne de Dieu*, 1916, in *ET*, 80, and *Terre promise*, 1919, in *ET*, 395, for the same idea.

8 °*Panthéisme et Christienisme*, 1923, 11; *MU*, 96; *Les Fondements et le fond de l'idée d'évolution*, 1926, *Oeuvres*, iii, 193. See also *L'Union créatrice*, 1917, in *ET*, 195; *Note pour servir à l'évangélisation des temps nouveaux*, 1919, in *Cahiers*, iv, 20; *L'Elément universel*, 1919, in *ET*, 411.

9 *MD*, 44, 47-52, 56. [Eng. trans., 29, 31-5, 38 (27, 29-32, 35).]

10 *MD*, 52-5. [Eng. trans., 35-7 (32-4).] See also p. 187 [140 (128)]: 'Jesus, Saviour of human activity to which you have given meaning. . . .' On this relationship between human effort and holiness in Teilhard's thought see J. M. Le Blond, s.j., 'Consacrer l'effort humain', *Etudes*, ccxcvi (1958), 58-68; and George Vass, s.j., 'Teilhard de Chardin and Inward Vision', *The Heythrop Journal*, ii (1961), 237-49.

11 *MD*, 39, 66. [Eng. trans., 25, 46 (23, 42).] Cf. *ibid.*, 135, note 1 [101, note 1 (90, note 1)]: 'I grasp [God] at the centre of the beautiful and the good in the measure that I pursue these ever further with faculties which are ceaselessly purified.' For other references to the importance of a morality of intention for Teilhard, see *ibid.*, 166, 175 [124, 131 (113, 119)], and the lengthy appendix in de Lubac, *Pensée religieuse* . . . , 364-70. See also letter of February 8, 1940, in *LV*, 250. [Eng. trans., 257.]

12 *MD*, 182-4. [Eng. trans., 136-8 (125-6).] See also *ibid.*, 51-2 [35 (32)]: 'The very sincerity with which we desire and pursue success for God's sake reveals itself as a new factor . . . of our more perfect union with the all-powerful One who animates us. . . . We unite ourselves with him now in the shared love of the goal to which we are giving birth.'

13 See *L'Esprit de la terre*, 1931, *Oeuvres*, vi, 39-47; *Esquisse d'un univers personnel*,

1936, *Oeuvres*, vi, 101–105; *L'Energie humaine*, 1937, *Oeuvres*, vi, 180–98.

14 °*Christologie et évolution*, 1933, 13; *Quelques réflexions sur la conversion du monde*, 1936, *Oeuvres*, ix, 162.

15 Letter of October 15, 1916, in *Genèse*, 169 [Eng. trans., 132.]; letter of December 29, 1919, in *Archives*, 156.

16 °Letter of January 10, 1926 to Father Auguste Valensin; *MD*, 140, 142 [Eng. trans., 104, 106 (94, 95).].; letter of June 16, 1929, in de Lubac, *Pensée religieuse*, 71, note 3.

17 *L'Energie humaine*, 1937, *Oeuvres*, vi, 193–4. Compare these ideas with those in *Note sur le progrès*, 1920, *Oeuvres*, v, 29–30. [Eng. trans., *FM*, 17–18.]

18 *L'Energie humaine*, 1937, *Oeuvres*, vi, 194–5. See also *Hérédité sociale et progrès*, 1938, *Oeuvres*, v, 49. [Eng. trans., *FM*, 33.] It is interesting to compare Teilhard's thought here with Karl Rahner's analysis of the role played in the life of the Church by canonized saints. See his 'Die Kirche der Heiligen', *Schriften zur Theologie*, vol. iii (Einsiedeln, 1956), 111–26, especially 124–6.

19 *PH*, 123, 125. [Eng. trans., 115, 117–18.]

20 *ibid.*, 123–4. [Eng. trans., 116.]

21 *ibid*, 329, 331, 332. [Eng. trans., 296, 297, 298.] The same development is to be found in °*Le Christique*, 1955, 5.

22 °*Introduction à la vie chrétienne*, 1944, 1, 2, 11. For later references confer letters of August 16, 1951 and November 15, 1953, in Cuénot, *Teilhard de Chardin*, 446 [Eng. trans., 367.]: 'I still feel that the Church is essential as a phylum for the fulfilment of the human [phylum].' . . .'Correctly understood, Christianity and it alone should itself be able to stimulate human energy fully and completely.'

23 °*Christianisme et évolution*, 1945, 10; Letter of November 9, 1948, in de Lubac, *Pensée religieuse* . . . , 277; letter of October 7, 1948, in *LV*, 294. [Eng. trans., 299.]

24 Letter of October 10, 1950, in de Lubac, *Pensée religieuse* . . . , 340, note 4; °*CM*, 20; *Le Goût de vivre*, 1950, *Oeuvres*, vii, 249, note 1.

25 See on this question the essay by René d'Ouince, s.j., who was Teilhard's immediate religious superior for a number of years: 'L'Epreuve de l'obéissance dans la vie du Père Teilhard de Chardin', in *L'Homme devant Dieu*, vol iii, 331–46. References to the 'Roman phylum' and the 'Roman axis', from letters written in 1950, are to be found on p. 343. See also letters of August 16, 1951, and March 14, 1954, in Cuénot, *Teilhard de Chardin*, 446–7 [Eng. trans., 367.]: 'I feel no trace of bitterness from this situation.' . . .'I must continue to struggle from the *inside*, without bitterness and with an immense confidence. Nothing can withstand a love of the "Christic phylum" growing ever greater.'

26 °*Le Christique*, 1955, 5.

27 *Hérédité sociale et progrès*, 1938, Oeuvres, v, 50-1. [Eng. trans., *FM*, 34.]

28 *La Mystique de la science*, 1939, Oeuvres, vi, 221; *PH*, 330-1. [Eng. trans., 297.]

29 °*Note sur la notion de perfection chrétienne*, 1942, 2.

30 *Réflexions sur le bonheur*, 1943, in *Cahiers*, ii, 69-70. See also the statement in *PH*, 331 [Eng. trans., 297.]: 'Literally to be able to say to God that one loves him, not only with all one's body, all one's heart and all one's soul, but with every fibre of the universe moving towards unification, that is a prayer that can only be made in space-time.'

31 *Super-humanité, super-Christ, super-charité*, 1943, Oeuvres, ix, 213-17. Similar statements on love are to be found in *Sur les bases possibles d'un credo humain commun*, 1941, Oeuvres, v, 105 [Eng. trans., *FM*, 79.]; *La Transposition 'conique' de l'action*, 1942, Oeuvres, v, 124-5 [Eng. trans., *FM*, 95-6.]; *Quelques réflexions sur le retentissement spirituel de la bombe atomique*, 1946, Oeuvres, v, 187 [Eng. trans., *FM*, 148.]; *Le Rebondissement humain de l'evolution*, 1947, Oeuvres, v, 267. [Eng. trans., *FM*, 208.]

32 °*Introduction à la vie chrétienne*, 1944, 10.

33 °*Christianisme et évolution*, 1945, 6; *Catholicisme et science*, 1946, Oeuvres, ix, 239-40.

34 *Esquisse d'une dialectique de l'esprit*, 1946, Oeuvres, vii, 156. This is the only instance when Teilhard calls the Church a cone, his usual designation being an axis or phylum. The image of the cone is nonetheless his favourite to describe the evolutionary process as a whole. See *Le Cône du temps*, 1942, Oeuvres, v, 111-17. [Eng. trans., *FM*, 82-9.]

We might note here both the similarity and the difference between Teilhard's image of the cone with three centres and the image employed by Oscar Cullmann in *Christus und die Zeit* (Zürich, 1946), 166-70. [Eng. trans., *Christ and Time* (London, 3rd ed., 1962), 185-90.] For Cullmann the Church is related to the world as an inner to an outer circle, Christ being the Centre who reigns over the entire surface but is more closely related to the inner surface. Cullman, however, in fidelity to his own Protestant tradition, would vigorously deny any organic relationship between the history of the Church and that of the world, and especially any possibility that Christian action in the world could serve as a preparation for the coming of the Parousia.

35 *Agitation ou genèse?*, 1947, Oeuvres, v, 285. [Eng. trans., *FM*, 223.] Once more Teilhard insists, p. 286 [224]: 'It is literally, not metaphorically, that the believer can lead and prolong in Christogenesis the genesis of the universe around him.'

36 See texts cited above in notes 30 and 31.

37 °*Introduction à la vie chrétienne*, 1944, 4; *Agitation ou genèse*, 1947, Oeuvres, v,

287 [Eng. trans., *FM*, 224.]; *La Foi en l'homme*, 1947, *Oeuvres*, v, 242. [Eng. trans., *FM*, 192.]

38 *Sur la valeur religieuse de la recherche*, 1947, *Oeuvres*, ix, 260-1. Faith in this context again refers to an intellectual conviction in regard to man's future, along with a personal commitment to such a conviction. On this point see °*Comment je crois*, 1934, 2; °*Comment je vois*, 1948, 23; *Le Coeur du problème*, 1949, *Oeuvres*, v, 346. [Eng. trans., *FM*, 266.] See also the treatment of Teilhard's 'psychological act of faith' in chapter two, and the treatment in chapter one of what Teilhard calls the conflict between his Christic and his cosmic sense.

39 °*Trois choses que je vois*, 1948, 4. This same statement occurs almost verbatim in *Les Directions et les conditions de l'avenir*, 1948, *Oeuvres* v, 305 [Eng. trans., *FM*, 237.]; °*Comment je vois*, 1948, 16; °*Le Néo-humanisme moderne et ses réactions sur le Christianisme*, 1948, 3.

40 *Le Coeur du problème*, 1949, *Oeuvres*, v, 348-9. [Eng. trans., *FM*, 268-9.] The word 'salvation' in this text is obviously to be understood in its eschatological sense. In *Quelques réflexions sur la conversion du monde*, 1936, *Oeuvres*, ix, 163, there is likewise a denial that some compromise is being sought between Christianity and the world. See also °*Le Néo-humanisme moderne et ses réactions sur le Christianisme*, 1948, 2-3.

41 *La Singularité du phénomène chrétien*, 1954, *Oeuvres*, ii, 373-4; °*Trois choses que je vois*, 1948, 7, note 1; °*Comment je vois*, 1948, 17. The French for 'intensity of its charity' in the last text is *super-charité*. The ambiguity of a literal translation has been avoided by following Teilhard's statement that this prefix, 'is employed to indicate not a difference of *nature*, but a *degree* of more advanced realization and perception.' (*Super-humanité, super-Christ, super-charité*, 1943, *Oeuvres*, ix, 93, note 1.)

42 *Réflexions sur l'ultra-humain*, 1951, *Oeuvres*, vii, 288; °*Le Christique*, 1955, 8. For similar statements see °*Trois choses que je vois*, 1948, 6; °*Comment je vois*, 1948, 24; *Réflexions sur l'ultra-humain*, 1951, *Oeuvres*, vii, 290.

43 *Diary* for April 7, 1955, reproduced in *Oeuvres*, v, 404-5. [Eng. trans., *FM*, 309.] The 'three verses' refer to I Corinthians 15:26-8. The Greek here is the original of verse 28: 'so that God may be all in all.'

44 Besides essays already cited, see °*CM*, 23-9; *Du cosmos à la cosmogénèse*, 1951, *Oeuvres*, vii, 274-5; Letter of March 2, 1952, in *LV*, 322-3 [Eng. trans., 323-4.]; °*Ce que le monde attend en ce moment de l'Eglise de Dieu*, 1952, 1; *L'Etoffe de l'univers*, 1953, *Oeuvres*, vii, 404; °*Le Christique*, 1955, 10-11.

45 A recent scriptural study by André Feuillet, 'Le Temps de l'Eglise d'après le quatrième Evangile et l'Apocalypse', *La Maison-Dieu*, lxv (1961), 60-79, emphasizes that the time of the Church, coming between the Resurrection and Parousia, signifies principally the presence in history of the risen Christ.

He notes also that the woman clothed with the sun in the Apocalypse, while primarily a symbol of the Sion of the prophets which is changed by Christ into his Church, signifies also Christ's Mother, seen as an incarnation of God's people and an image of the Church.

Teilhard, interestingly enough, though he sees the Church in exactly this light, sees Mary rather as symbol of the earth, 'the Blessed Virgin Mary, Queen and Mother of all things, the true Demeter'. (*La Vie cosmique*, 1916, 30.) This explains why a whole chapter of *The Phenomenon of Man* is entitled 'Demeter'. Teilhard describes therein, on a phenomenological level, the earth's labour to bring forth thought, but on the level of revelation this birth of thought is for him simply one of the steps preparing for the birth of Christ.

46 This explains the sense in which Teilhard can say that for the Christian it is 'a matter of life and death that the earth should flourish to the uttermost of its natural powers.' *MD*, 61. [Eng. trans., 42 (38).] Jean Mouroux has explained with great originality some of the implications of this participation of both the Church and the Christian in Christ's creative and redemptive work, though his perspective is slightly different from that of Teilhard. See his *Le Mystère du temps* (Paris, 1962), 212-16, 238-45 [Eng. trans., *The Mystery of Time* (New York, 1964), 232-6, 263-70.].

47 *La Parole attendue*, 1940, in *Cahiers*, iv, 26.

48 *La Vie cosmique*, 1916, in *ET*, 48; *Science et Christ*, 1921, *Oeuvres*, ix, 60; *MU*, 89, 108; °*Contingence de l'univers et goût humain de survivre*, 1953, 4. Teilhard also speaks of Christ as 'Alpha and Omega' in *Note sur le Christ universel*, 1920, *Oeuvres*, ix, 39.

49 Cf. the texts and authors cited in chapter three, notes 60 and 61, and chapter four, note 81. To this list may be added the following: E. B. Allo, *Première épître aux Corinthiens* (Paris, 1934), 201; F. M. M. Sagnard, O.P., 'A propos de I Cor. viii, 6', *Ephemerides Theologicae Louvanienses*, xxvi (1950), 54-8; Leo Scheffczyk, 'Die Idee der Einheit von Schöpfung und Erlösung', *Tübinger Theologische Quartalschrift*, cxl (1960), 19-37; Mouroux, *Le Mystère du Temps*, 82-3, 95-9, 156-62 [Eng. trans., 85-89, 101-6, 170-6.]; Bonsirvin, *L'Evangile de Paul*, 86-8; Emile Mersch, S.J., *La Théologie du Corps Mystique*, vol. i (Bruxelles, 4e éd., 1954), 163-70 [Eng. trans., *The Theology of the Mystical Body* (St. Louis, 1952), 135-41.]; Küng, *Rechtfertigung*, 130-50. [Eng. trans., 125-47.] The unity of creation and salvation has also been shown to be a major theme of the Old Testament. See Lucien Legrand, 'La Création, triomphe cosmique de Yahvé', *Nouvelle Revue Théologique*, lxxxiii (1961), 449-70.

50 °*Comment je vois*, 1948, 4, note 4, 21, note 35. Hans Küng has attempted an explanation of Christ's pre-existence by making use of Cullman's study of

the New Testament mode of conceiving time and eternity. See *Recht-fertigung*, 277-95 [Eng. trans., 285-301.], and Cullmann's *Christus und die Zeit*, 52-9 [Eng. trans., 61-8.]. In the *Summa Theologica* (pars III, ques. 24, art. 1-4) St. Thomas relates Christ to the totality of time and space by reason of his eternal predestination. And Karl Rahner has recently observed that, on the scale of an evolution which should continue millions of years, the Incarnation actually took place at the beginning of true human history, that is to say, when man had just commenced taking charge of the world in which he found himself in order to shape his own destiny. See 'Die Christologie innerhalb einer evolutiven Weltanschauung', *Schriften zur Theologie*, vol. v (Einsiedeln, 1962), 218.

51 Claude Tresmontant so treats and so distorts the theory of creative union in his *Introduction . . .*, 112-15. [Eng. trans., 89-93.] See also his 'Le Père Teilhard de Chardin et la théologie', *Lettre*, i (1962), 11-38. Teilhard's references to the Pleroma are not, as Tresmontant says, forced into his theory, but constitute its starting point. Pierre Smulders, who has not read all of Teilhard's unpublished essays and who consequently follows here the interpretation of Tresmontant, admits that references to the Pleroma in this context puzzle him greatly and are seemingly without explanation. (*La Vision . . .*, 93, 95, note 17.)

52 *MU*, 82. The first text is from *L'Union créatrice*, 1917, in *ET*, 196. When Teilhard says (in *MU*, 72) that his theory is simply the result of his reflection upon the relationship between matter and spirit, what he omits to tell the reader is that he is thinking here as a Christian and is therefore making use of two sources of knowledge.

53 *La Vie cosmique*, 1916, in *ET*, 49; *L'Union créatrice*, 1917, in *ET*, 196; *La Lutte contre la multitude*, 1917, in *ET*, 128; °*Panthéisme et Christianisme*, 1923, 11; °*Essai d'intégration de l'homme dans l'univers*, 1930, 4th lecture, 13.

54 °*Comment je vois*, 1948, 17. Teilhard's earlier extended treatment of creative union is to be found in *MU*, 72-6, preceeded by an exposition of his philosophic option only. The theory was broached in its most elementary form in °*L'Union créatrice*, 1917, *passim*, and is mentioned explicitly or alluded to in numerous other essays which we shall have occasion to cite in the notes which follow.

55 Creative union may also be situated within the more limited context of Teilhard's approach to the mystery of evil, and this is the approach of George Crespy (*Pensée théologique . . .*, 113-22). Teilhard does this himself occasion-ally, although in this context the theory loses some of its force as a clarifica-tion of Christogenesis. The best extended analysis of creative union as a metaphysical theory is that of Madeleine Barthélémy-Madaule, *Bergson et Teilhard de Chardin*, 599-618. The author recognizes that Teilhard's con-

cepts have been inspired for the most part from revelation, but confines her examination to the value they have in themselves as philosophic categories.

56 °*Comment je vois*, 1948, 17, and note 26. In the same note Teilhard puts his two formulas 'more clearly' in Latin: '*Plus esse=plus plura unire*' and '*Plus esse=plus a pluribus uniri.*'

57 The words in brackets were added by Teilhard as a footnote to the word 'freedom'. The French *multiple* in this and the following texts is translated either as 'multiplicity' or as 'many', depending on the context.

58 *ibid.*, 18-19.

59 de Lubac, *Pensée religieuse* . . . , 282-9. While occasional expressions like 'positive nothingness' do not make things any easier for Teilhard's interpreters, they hardly justify the conclusion of Tresmontant that Teilhard fell victim to the ancient myth of a Chaos which opposed God until vanquished by the act of creation. See his *Introduction* . . . , 115-16. [Eng. trans., 93-4.]

60 *La Place de l'homme dans l'univers*, 1942, *Oeuvres*, iii, 323-4. The allusion is to the 'creative evolution' of Henri Bergson, with whom Teilhard differed greatly, as we have seen in chapter two, note 49. Other references to Bergson are to be found in *La Vie cosmique*, 1916, in *ET*, 15; *La Réflexion de l'énergie*, 1952, *Oeuvres*, vii, 339, note 2; *Les Singularités de l'espèce humaine*, 1954, *Oeuvres*, ii, 358. In regard to the Person of Christ the difference is radical: Teilhard always speaks of Christ as an object of faith; Bergson always as an object of philosophy. See Henri Gouhier, *Bergson et le Christ des Evangiles* (Paris, 1961), 98-9, 164, 191.

61 *Summa Theologica*, pars I ques. 45, art. 6 deals with the interior life of the Trinity as motive and image of creation, while art. 7 deals with the reflection of the Trinity in every creature; ques. 93, art. 1 and 2 deal with man as God's image. Pars I-II, ques. 1, art. 7 and 8 deal with the necessary movement of all things created towards their own highest unity, which means union with God who is One in an absolute sense; see also ques. 2, art. 8. On this point see Smulders, *La Vision* . . . , 94.

62 °*Le Christique*, 1955, 8, note 3.

63 *MU*, 73-4; *MD*, 149. [Eng. trans., 111 (100).] We might note here that in °*Le Christique*, 1955, 9, Teilhard speaks of the Pleroma as able to 'complete' God, but adds immediately 'in a true sense [of the word]', a phrase which in French always means that the expression being used is poor but the idea is correct.

64 °*La Route de l'Ouest*, 1932, 20. At the end of his life he writes again: 'In conformity with the spirit of St. Paul I am led now to see [in the world] a mysterious production which completes and fulfills the Absolute Being himself. . . . [Creation is] participated being which pleromizes and converges.' (°*CM*, 30.)

65 *MD*, 61-2. [Eng. trans., 43 (39).] Cf. Pius XII's encyclical on the Mystical Body, nos. 54-5 (America Press edition, 20): 'Yet this too must be held, marvellous though it appear: Christ requires his members. . . . This is not because he is indigent or weak, but rather because he has so willed it for the greater glory of his unspotted Spouse.'

66 °*Christianisme et évolution*, 1945, 4; °*Comment je vois*, 1948, 19; °*Contingence de l'univers et goût humain de survivre*, 1953, 3-4. These same ideas are to be found in slightly different form in °*Christologie et évolution*, 1933, 6, and note 1; *Action et activation*, 1945, Oeuvres, ix, 227-8; *Du cosmos à la cosmogénèse*, 1951, Oeuvres, vii, 271-2 and 273, note 1.

67 See the texts cited in chapter two, notes 59 and 60, and chapter three, notes 12 and 13. In *Du cosmos à la cosmogénèse*, 1951, Oeuvres, vii, 272, there is yet another affirmation of this 'ultra-gratuity' of the present supernatural order. Teilhard simply insists, here as before, that within his system such ultra-gratuity means that the function of Centre of the universe has been assumed by God himself, and not given to some intermediary between God and the world.

68 °*Comment je vois*, 1948, 20-1. An almost identical statement appears in °*Christianisme et évolution*, 1945, 7-8, although here Teilhard states explicitly what we have added in brackets in the text just quoted: 'Without creation something is strictly lacking to God considered in his Plenitude, i.e. in his act of union, not in his being.'

69 *L'Ame du monde*, 1918, in *ET*, 231; °*Réflexions sur le péché originel*, 1947, 7. See also °*Quelques vues générales sur l'essence du Christianisme*, 1939, 1-2; *Du cosmos à la cosmogénèse*, 1951, Oeuvres, vii, 272. In this sense the mystery of original sin would also be inseparable from this 'mystery of mysteries', since the first sin of man exists from eternity in God's foreknowledge of the Incarnation and redemption. This is not, however, the way Teilhard wishes to universalize original sin; for him it is not moral evil at all, as we have seen in chapter four, but the physical imperfection of the cosmos at the moment of creation.

70 °*Introduction à la vie chrétienne*, 1944, 3. This perspective of Teilhard explains for the most part expressions such as the following: '. . . the work of man's salvation in which creation consists.' (*ibid.*, 9); 'By the Incarnation, which has saved mankind . . .' (*La Vie cosmique*, 1916, in *ET*, 49); 'Like creation, of which it is the visible surface, the Incarnation is coextensive with the duration of the world.' (*MU*, 92); '. . . the mystery which summarizes Christianity: the Incarnation.' (°*Comment je crois*, 1934, 22); 'The essence of Christianity is neither more nor less than belief in the world's unification in God by the Incarnation.' (*Esquisse d'un univers personnel*, 1936, Oeuvres, vi, 113); 'the redeeming Incarnation' (*PH*, 327 [Eng. trans., 293]); 'The

achievement of the ultra-human . . . coincides concretely with the con-summation which all Christians expect for the Incarnation.' (*Le Coeur du problème*, 1948, *Oeuvres*, v, 348).

71 *Super-humanité, super-Christ, super-charité*, 1943, *Oeuvres*, ix, 211.

72 °*Le Christique*, 1955, 7; °*Comment je crois*, 1934, 24. A third form of the same affirmation appears in °*Introduction à la vie chrétienne*, 1944, 3.

73 Cf. on this point *L'Etoffe de l'Univers*, 1953, *Oeuvres*, vii, 399.

74 Of all these expressions, 'the universal Christ' is most common. Examples of its use may be found in *L'Elément universel*, 1919, in *ET*, 410; *Note sur le Christ universel*, 1920, *Oeuvres*, ix, passim; *MD*, 141 [Eng. trans., 105 (95).]; °*Comment je crois*, 1934, 22, 24; *La Parole attendue*, 1940, in *Cahiers*, iv, 27; °*Introduction à la vie chrétienne*, 1944, 3, 5; °*Le Christique*, 1955, 9. etc. In regard to 'the Soul of the world', Teilhard prudently says 'quasi-Soul' in *L'Elément universel*, 1919, in *ET*, 410; and in *MU*, 90, he says he means that Christ has been chosen 'to animate the universe'. See de Lubac's treatment of this problem in *Pensée religieuse* . . . , 86–7.

75 °*Comment je vois*, 1948, 21; °*Le Christique*, 1955, 7–8. Behind Teilhard's use of such expressions as 'third nature' was his desire for some terminology which would clearly express Christ's Lordship over rational beings who might be discovered on other planets. See letter of January 14, 1955, in de Lubac, *La Prière du Père Teilhard de Chardin* (Paris, 1964), 53–4.

76 In °*Panthéisme et Christianisme*, 1923, 10, Teilhard states clearly: 'This idea of a "hypostatic union" extended to the whole universe (which, we might note, would simply be the pantheism of Spinoza), while not in itself ridiculous or contradictory, is opposed to the whole Christian outlook on individual freedom and personal salvation.' On the theological problems involved in speaking of a 'continuing Incarnation' see Yves Congar, O.P., 'Dogme Christologique et Ecclésiologie', in *Das Konzil von Chalkedon*, ed. A. Grillmeier, s.j., and H. Bacht, s.j., vol iii (Würzburg, 1954), 262–8.

77 *Le Christ dans la matière*, 1916, in *HU*, 56 [Eng. trans., 53.]; °*Panthéisme et Christianisme*, 1923, 3; °*CM*, 7–8.

78 On at least ten different occasions this text is either cited or alluded to in the context of the Pleroma of Christ. *Le Christ dans la matière*, 1916, in *HU*, 56 [Eng. trans., 53.]; *Panthéisme et Christianisme*, 1923, 13; *MU*, 113; *MD*, 139 [Eng. trans., 104 (94).]; °*La Route de l'Ouest*, 1932, 15; *PH*, 327, 344 [Eng. trans., 294, 310.]; °*Introduction à la vie chrétienne*, 1944, 1, 13; *Réflexions sur deux formes inverses d'esprit*, 1950, *Oeuvres*, vii, 232, 234; °*Quelques remarques 'pour y voir clair' sur l'essence du sentiment mystique*, 1951, 1; *Diary* for April 7, 1955, reproduced in *Oeuvres*, v, 404–5. [Eng. trans., *FM*, 309.]

79 *Réflexions sur deux formes inverses d'esprit*, 1950, *Oeuvres*, vii, 234; *PH*, 327.

[Eng. trans., 294.] Teilhard uses the term 'pan-Christism' to indicate a Christian pantheism in *MU*, 87; °*Comment je crois*, 1934, 24; °*Quelques réflexions sur la conversion du monde*, 1936, 10; °*Introduction à la vie chrétienne*, 1944, 13. The source of the term was Maurice Blondel; see chapter three, note 72.

80 *MD*, 139. [Eng. trans., 104 (93-4).] The same mode of distinguishing between these two forms of pantheism is to be found with slight variations in the texts cited in the previous note as well as in the following: *Note sur l'Elément universel du monde*, 1918, in *ET*, 359-62; *L'Elément universel*, 1919, in *ET*, 403-9; °*Panthéisme et Christianisme*, 1923, 9-13; °*Quelques vues générales sur l'essence du Christianisme*, 1939, 3; *La Parole attendue*, 1940, in *Cahiers*, iv, 28; °*Quelques remarques 'pour y voir clair' sur l'essence du sentiment mystique*, 1951, 1-2.

81 On the phrase 'union differentiates' see chapter two, note 22. To the texts cited there we may also add the following: *MU*, 74, 87; *Le Phénomène spirituel*, 1937, Oeuvres, vi, 129, 130; *Les Unités humaines naturelles*, 1939, Oeuvres, iii, 292; *GZ*, 154; *La Fin de l'espèce*, 1952, Oeuvres, v, 394, note 1. [Eng. trans., *FM*, 302, note 1.]

82 This superiority of Christianity over all Eastern religions is treated at length in °*La Route de l'Ouest*, 1932, 1-21, and *L'Apport spirituel de l'Extrême-Orient*, 1947, in *Revue de la pensée juive*, ii (1950), 105-13. See also *Le Christianisme dans le monde*, 1933, Oeuvres, ix, 137-41; °*Comment je crois*, 1934, 19-22; *PH*, 233-235 [Eng. trans., 210-212.]; °*Comment je vois*, 1948, 21-3; *Réflexions sur deux formes inverses d'esprit*, 1950, Oeuvres, vii, 227-36.

83 See texts cited above in note 39, and in chapter two, notes 57 and 67. Hans Urs von Balthasar has criticized severely the 'acosmic' character of Catholic eschatology since the 16th century by which the 'last things' have been regarded simply as a relationship between the creature and a *Deus nudus*. See 'Eschatologie', in *Fragen der Theologie Heute*, 403-21.

84 See texts cited in chapter two, notes 22, 24, and 25.

85 *La Messe sur le monde*, 1923, in *HU*, 30. [Eng. trans., 31.] See chapter two, note 75. See also de Lubac, *Pensée religieuse . . .*, 309-12. One thing which de Lubac does not point out must be insisted upon here: it is not possible for Teilhard to conceive of a 'super-humanity' within history. The reason is that planetary maturation is to be brought about by contact with Omega, as is clear from *PH*, 302, 341 [Eng. trans., 272, 307.]; and Omega for Teilhard is always the Person of Christ, whose Parousia will bring an end to human history and whose Pleroma is clearly a transhistoric reality. On this belief in a unique Centre for evolution see texts cited in chapter three, notes 12, 13, 14, 15, 16 and 17. Teilhard, moreover, says explicitly that 'human history develops *between* two critical points of re-

flection, the one inferior and individual, the other superior and collective.'
PH, 320, note 1. [Eng. trans., 287, note 1.] Emphasis added. The same
statement appears ten years later in °*Trois choses que je vois*, 1948, 3, note 1.

86 °*Trois choses que je vois*, 1948, 3. See also Abel Jeannière, s.j., 'L'Avenir de
l'Humanité d'après Teilhard de Chardin', *Revue de l'Action Populaire*, xii
(1962), 5-12; Dominique Dubarle, o.p., 'L'Homme et la fin de l'humanité',
Lumière et Vie, ii (1953), 24-38; J. Edgar Bruns, 'Cosmogenesis and Theology', in *The World of Teilhard*, ed. Robert T. Francoeur (Baltimore,
1961), 167-85.

87 *La Fin de l'espèce*, 1952, *Oeuvres*, v, 393-4 [Eng. trans., *FM*, 302.]; *PH*, 320.
[Eng. trans., 287-8.] This same idea is expressed in *MD*, 93 [Eng. trans.,
68 (61).]; *L'Atomisme de l'esprit*, 1941, *Oeuvres*, vii, 51-2; °*Comment je vois*,
1948, 14 ('to succeed in piercing the phenomenal web of space-time . . .');
Du cosmos à la cosmogénèse, 1951, *Oeuvres*, vii, 270; *L'Activation de l'énergie
humaine*, 1953, *Oeuvres*, vii, 415 ('. . . a point of escape beyond time and
space'). See also the many texts of transformation cited in chapter four.

88 *Le Coeur du problème*, 1948, *Oeuvres*, v, 348 [Eng. trans., *FM*, 268.]; letter of
December 23, 1952, in de Lubac, *Pensée religieuse* . . . , 191, note 3; *Réflexions
sur deux formes inverses d'esprit*, 1950, *Oeuvres*, vii, 234. Other brief references
to this fundamental defect of Marxism are to be found in °*Le Néo-
humanisme moderne et ses réactions sur le Christianisme*, 1948, 3; °*Trois choses
que je vois*, 1948, 5; °*Le Christique*, 1955, 10. 'The only means of overcoming
Communism,' said Teilhard, 'is to present Christ as he ought to be presented:
not as an opium or derivative of hominization, but as its chief Mover.'
—Letter of October 14, 1952, in Cuénot, *Teilhard de Chardin*, 448. [Eng.
trans., 368.] See chapter two, note 36, on further contrast between Marx
and Teilhard.

89 *La Fin de l'espèce*, 1952, *Oeuvres*, v, 394-5 [Eng. trans., *FM*, 303.]; *PH*, 322.
[Eng. trans., 289.] Man's fundamental desire for 'more-being' is mentioned
again in *Réflexions sur l'ultra-humain*, 1951, *Oeuvres*, vii, 290; letter of
November 21, 1952, in de Lubac, *Pensée religieuse* . . . , 54; *Recherche,
travail et adoration*, 1955, *Oeuvres*, ix, 284. Note also Teilhard's formulation
of creative union in the text cited above in note 56.

90 *MD*, 143-4. [Eng. trans., 107 (96-7).]

91 *PH*, 321-2. [Eng. trans., 289.] See texts cited in chapter four, notes 44, 45,
46, 63, 64 and 65.

92 *L'Esprit de la terre*, 1931, *Oeuvres*, vi, 57; *MU*, 112.

93 Letter of December 12, 1919, in *Archives*, 135; *La Messe sur le monde*, 1923, in
HU, 37 [Eng. trans., 37.]; *MU*, 91, 102; °*Note sur la notion de perfection
chrétienne*, 1942, 3. On this total transformation of the cosmos see the
lengthy chapter in de Lubac, *Pensée religieuse* . . . , 185-200. The same idea

appears in many other texts; for example: *Archives*, 149, 151; *MD*, 108, 184, 198 [Eng. trans., 79, 138, 149 (71, 126, 135).]; *HU*, 30-1 [Eng. trans., 30-1:]; *La Grande option*, 1939, *Oeuvres*, v, 77 [Eng. trans., *FM*, 56.]; letter of February 15, 1940, in Cuénot, *Teilhard de Chardin*, 300. [Omitted in Eng., trans.]

94 See on this question M. E. Boismard, o.p., 'Le Retour du Christ', *Lumière et Vie*, ii (1953), 53-76. Neither theology nor exegesis has reached any satisfying conclusions regarding these two distinct traditions in the New Testament. What is quite clear is that all images of cosmic cataclysm are to be treated with great caution and prudence. For example, according to André Feuillet ['La Synthèse eschatologique de Saint-Matthieu (xxiv-xxv)', *Revue Biblique*, lvi (1939), 340-64; lvii (1950), 62-91, 180-211.] the only actual destruction spoken of in Matthew's eschatological discourse is that of Jerusalem, the section dealing with the end of the world being concerned primarily with Christian morality and charity. Even the Old Testament, although it speaks of the 'Day of Yahweh' as one of ultimate change in the existing order, nevertheless conceives this change as a continuation of the line of history and hence not a total destruction. See H. Wheeler Robinson, *Inspiration and Revelation in the Old Testament* (Oxford, 1946), 106-59; A. Gelin, 'Jours de Yahvé et Jour de Yahvé', *Lumière et Vie*, ii (1953), 39-52.

95 *MU*, 113-14, reproduced in *Oeuvres*, v, 402-3. [Eng. trans., *FM*, 307-8.] See also Teilhard's comment on the presentation of the Parousia in Scripture in °*Trois choses que je vois*, 1948, 3.

96 *MD*, 164. [Eng. trans., 123 (112).] See the perceptive treatment of this point by Abel Jeannière, s.j., 'Approches Christologiques', *Essais sur Teilhard de Chardin, Recherches et Débats*, Numéro 40 (Paris, 1962), 92-5.

97 °*Trois choses que je vois*, 1948, 7, note 1. Teilhard implies here as elsewhere that, as the world draws to a close, it will be the task of the Church to supply through the charity of its members that love which a whole segment of humanity may refuse.

CHAPTER VI

1 Josef Pieper, *Scholastik* (München, 1960), 221. [Eng. trans., *Scholasticism* (New York, 1960), 161.] The recent study of Emile Rideau, s.j., *La Pensée du Père Teilhard de Chardin* (Paris, 1965), has tried to capture all these various elements in a very balanced presentation of all the aspects of Teilhard's work.

2 Letter of October 12, 1951, in Leroy, *Teilhard de Chardin*, 55-7. [Eng. trans., 42-3.]

3 *GZ*, 158. Teilhard is speaking here of the ascent of life towards higher consciousness.

4 *PH*, 286. [Eng. trans., 257-8.]

5 °*CM*, 1; °*Le Christique*, 1955, 1. Ladislaus Boros has tried to show in a lengthy study that Teilhard's whole system is an attempt to translate into modern terms the Christian experience of 'finding God in all things': 'Evolutionismus and Spiritualität', *Der Grosse Entschluss*, xv (1960), 254-9, 301-3, 346-50, 399-403.

6 *MU*, 65-6.

7 *LV*, 91-2. [Eng. trans., 127.]

8 Letter of July 22, 1916, in de Lubac, *Pensée religieuse* . . . , 352; *Note pour servir à l'évangélisation des temps nouveaux*, 1918, in *Cahiers*, iv, 20-1; *MU*, 67. The apologetic aspect of Teilhard's thought has been treated in depth by the article of d'Armagnac, 'La Pensée du Père Teilhard . . .', 590-621, and in a much more personal vein by de Lubac, *Pensée religieuse* . . . , 332-5.

9 °Letter of August 22, 1925, to Father Auguste Valensin. 'Hominization' refers to the title of an essay written that same year; 'divinization' refers to the first draft of *The Divine Milieu*.

10 *Note pour servir à l'évangélisation des temps nouveaux*, 1919, in *Cahiers*, iv, 13.

11 Letters of September 18, 1916, and October 15, 1916, in *Genèse*, 163 and 170. [Eng. trans., 128 and 133.]

12 *Mon Univers*, 1918, in *ET*, 267; *MU*, 65-6; °*Christologie et évolution*, 1933; °letter of December 28, 1933, to Father Auguste Valensin.

13 *PH*, 30, 22, 323. [Eng. trans., 35, 30, 290.]

14 Letter of March 24, 1917, in *Genèse*, 245 [Eng. trans., 189.]; °*Comment je vois*, 1948, 17.

15 °*Christianisme et évolution*, 1945, 1; letters of April 13, 1940 and December 10, 1952, in Cuénot, *Teilhard de Chardin*, 301 and 482. [Eng. trans., 244 and 400.]

16 *L'Union créatrice*, 1917, in *ET*, 176.

17 Letter of July 26, 1917, in de Lubac, *Pensée religieuse* . . . , 354. Teilhard stated a number of times that his basic religious vision never changed, in contrast to his ideas of the cosmos and its phenomenological interpretation, which changed gradually over the years. See °*CM*, 26; °*Le Christique*, 1955, 2, quoted at the end of *MD*, 202-3. [Eng. trans., 153 (139).]

18 Letter of September 25, 1947, in d'Ouince, 'L'Epreuve de l'obéissance . . .', 342. It has frequently been suggested that permission to publish his major works during his lifetime, by exposing them early to public scrutiny and criticism, would have forced Teilhard to defend and so to clarify many areas of his thought.

19 Karl Rahner, s.j., *Über die Schriftinspiration* (Freiburg, 1959), 16. [Eng. trans., *Inspiration in the Bible* (London, 1961), 8.]

20 °*Le Christique*, 1955, 12.

21 °*Le Christ évoluteur*, 1942, 1. See on this point the perceptive article of Dominique Dubarle, O.P., 'L'Entreprise scientifique moderne et sa mise en accusation religieuse', *Signes du Temps*, i (1960), 9-12.

22 °*Note sur le Christ universel*, 1920, 5. See the same observation in °*Christologie et évolution*, 1933, 1-2.

23 See °*Le Sens humain*, 1929, 13. Teilhard was well aware that professional philosophers and theologians tend to integrate into their own systems, sometimes by ingenious artifice, any factual data whatsoever, without in the least modifying their own mental outlook. On the question of modern theology's renewal from Teilhard's viewpoint, see Gaston Fessard, S.J., 'La Vision religieuse et cosmique de Teilhard de Chardin', in *L'Homme devant Dieu*, vol. iii, 223-48; Crespy, *Pensée théologique . . .*, 220-1; Wildiers, *Teilhard de Chardin*, 83-9; William Donnelly, 'The Thought of Teilhard de Chardin', *The Clergy Review*, xlv (1960), 324-49.

24 *Acta Apostolica Sedis*, liv (1962), 792.

25 *Le Milieu mystique*, 1917, in *ET*, 159; °*Le Christ évoluteur*, 1942, 5. This theme is taken up again at some length in °*Recherche, travail et adoration*, 1955, 1-3.

26 See, for example, Joseph Ratzinger, 'Theologia Perennis?' *Wort und Wahrheit*, xv (1960), 179-88; Gérard Philips, 'Deux tendences dans la théologie contemporaine', *Nouvelle Revue Théologique*, lxxxv (1963), 225-38; Peter Fransen, S.J., 'Three Ways of Dogmatic Thought', *The Heythrop Journal*, iv (1963), 3-24.

27 See on this point the remarks of Crespy, *Pensée théologique . . .*, 169.

28 Franz Cardinal König, 'Les Taches de l'intellectuel catholique dans le monde d'aujourd'hui', *Union Catholique des Scientifiques Français*, July-August, 1961, 18.

29 The Holy Office in Rome recently issued a warning to Catholics concerning ambiguities and even serious errors of a philosophical and theological nature in the works of Teilhard, though none of his writings were condemned or forbidden to be read. See *Osservatore Romano*, July 1, 1962, page 1.

30 Besides works already cited we may note the following. From a scientific viewpoint: Wolfgang Kuhn, 'Teilhard de Chardin und die Biologie', *Stimmen der Zeit*, clxxii (1963), 246-63; Paulinus F. Forsthoefel, S.J., 'Beneath the Microscope', in *The World of Teilhard*, 98-113. From a philosophical viewpoint: Dominique Dubarle, O.P., 'A propos du "Phénomène humain" du P. Teilhard de Chardin', *La Vie Intellectuelle*, xxvii (1956), 6-25; August Brunner, S.J., 'Pierre Teilhard de Chardin', *Stimmen der Zeit*, clxv (1959), 210-22; Léopold Malevez, S.J., 'La Méthode du P. Teilhard de Chardin et la phénoménologie', *Nouvelle Revue Théologique*, lxxxix (1957), 579-99. From a theological viewpoint: Philippe de la Trinité, O.C.D., 'Teilhard de Chardin, synthèse ou confusion?' *Divinitas*, iii (1959), 285-329; Cyril

Vollert, s.j., 'Towards Omega: Man in the Vision of Teilhard de Chardin', *The Month*, xxiii (1960), 261-9; Charles Journet, 'La Vision teilhardienne du monde', *Divinitas*, iii (1959), 330-44.

31 An exhaustive treatment of the present scientific state of the question is given by Paul Overhage, s.j., *Das Problem der Hominisation* (Freiburg, 1961), 99-374. See also the summary of the same data by J. Franklin Ewing, s.j., 'Human Evolution', *Anthropological Quarterly*, xxix (1956), 91-139.

32 See on this point Jean Danielou, s.j., 'Signification de Teilhard de Chardin', *Etudes*, cccxii (1962), 146-49; Ladislaus Boros, s.j., 'Evolution und Metaphysik', *Orientierung*, xxv (1961), 237-41. Teilhard defends himself strongly against the charge of materialism in *Du cosmos à la cosmogénèse*, 1951, *Oeuvres*, vii, 267.

33 *In Boetium de Trinitate*, ques. 2, art. 3.

34 See Dominique Dubarle, o.p., 'Concept de la matière et discussions sur le matérialisme', *Science et Matérialisme* (Paris, 1962), 37-57, and the same author's 'A propos . . .', 18-20. Cf. the interesting observation of Russell, 'The Phenomenon . . .', 274-5, to the effect that 'where Aristotle regarded his system primarily as a philosophical interpretation of scientific data so far as these were known to him, the scholastics tended more and more to regard it as a conclusion rigorously deduced from self-evident metaphysical principles. . . . The original keystone of the Aristotelian "steadystate" universe was the immutable nature of the heavenly bodies and their cyclic movements. This theory became discredited in the seventeenth century; however, the steady-state universe remained, supported now by metaphysical rather than physical principles.' See also the same author's 'The Principle of Finality in the Philosophy of Aristotle and Teilhard de Chardin', *The Heythrop Journal*, iii (1962), 347-57; iv (1963), 32-41.

35 Letter of August 21, 1919, in *Genèse*, 295. [Eng. trans., 302.] Consequently when Teilhard says in *PH*, 21 [Eng. trans., 29.] that his book 'must not be read as a work on metaphysics', it is metaphysics in this pejorative sense of which he is speaking. See also *La Centrologie*, 1944, *Oeuvres*, vii, 105-6.

36 *Catholicisme et science*, 1946, *Oeuvres*, ix, 240; °*Christologie et évolution*, 1933, 1-2.

37 *MU*, 83.

38 Both those favourable and those hostile to Teilhard's thought have pointed out this defect; for example, Russell in 'The Phenomenon . . .', 13, and Scheffczyk in 'Die "Christogénèse" . . .', 147.

39 Confer the encyclical *Humani Generis* of Pius XII, which speaks, of course, of evidence available in 1950: 'The teaching of the Church leaves the doctrine of evolution an open question, as long as it confines its speculations to the development, from living matter already in existence, of the human body—

for the Catholic faith obliges us to hold that souls are immediately created by God. In the present state of scientific and theological opinion, this question may legitimately be canvassed by research and by discussion between experts on both sides. At the same time, the reasons for and against either view must be weighed and judged with all seriousness, fairness and restraint. . . . There are some who take rash advantage of this liberty of debate, by treating the subject as if the whole matter were closed . . .'. Denzinger, 3896 [2327].

40 There is no question here, it should be noted, of denying the unchangeableness of each man's nature, but simply of emphasizing the fact that unchangeable essences undergo development in the course of time. This is especially true of the unchangeable human nature of Christ whose Body-Person is continually being affected by its physical union with new members of the Church in the course of time. See on this point Pius XII, *Humani Generis*, in Denzinger, 3878 [2306]; also Malmberg, *Über den Gottmenschen*, 23-6.

41 See chapter five, note 70. As a sampling of the vast literature on the Greek approach to the Incarnation, we may list the following: J. Gross, *La Divinisation du Chrétien d'après les Pères Grecs* (Paris, 1938); Roger Leys, S.J., *L'Image de Dieu chez St. Grégoire de Nysse* (Paris, 1951); G. Isaye, S.J., 'L'Unité de l'opération divine dans les écrits de Saint Grégoire de Nysse', *Recherches de Science Religieuse*, xxvii (1937), 422-39; Léopold Malevez, S.J., 'L'Eglise dans le Christ', *Recherches de Science Religieuse*, xxv (1935), 257-91, 418-43.

42 For example, see texts cited in chapter one, notes 10 to 17, chapter four, notes 19 to 22, 28, and 97.

43 Letters of January 11 and 12, 1941, in *LV*, 268-269. [Eng. trans., 276-277.]

44 The question of a theology of history has received extraordinary attention in recent years. See the excellent summary of the present state of the question by Jakob David, 'Theologie der irdischen Wirklichkeiten', in *Fragen der Theologie Heute*, 549-68, with extensive bibliography. The discussion was launched in full by the two volumes of Gustave Thils, *Théologie des réalités terrestres* (Paris, 1947 and 1949).

45 Teilhard admits as much when he says that by 'progress' he means not that man is becoming morally better but that as a species he is moving towards a higher state of complexity and consciousness. See *Note sur le progrès*, 1920, *Oeuvres* v, 29-30 [Eng. trans., *FM*, 17-18], and *L'Etoffe de l'univers*, 1953, *Oeuvres*, vii, 403. The need to maintain this ambiguous understanding of progress, as well as the mystery of God's transcendence, has been vigorously asserted by Hans Urs von Balthasar in his *Theologie der Geschichte* (Basle, 1950), 52-64. [Eng. trans., *A Theology of History*, (London, 1964), 111-48.]

46 °*Le Dieu de l'évolution*, 1953, 5.

47 This whole question has been treated with great insight in the delicately nuanced study of Dominique Dubarle, O.P., *Optimisme devant ce monde* (Paris, 1949). See also Malevez, 'La Vision chrétienne de l'histoire', *Nouvelle Revue Théologique*, lxxxi (1949), 244-64.

48 *Note pour servir à l'évangélisation des temps nouveaux*, 1919, in *Cahiers*, iv, 19.

49 Letter of December 12, 1919, in *Archives*, 139-40; °*Christologie et évolution*, 1933, 10; °*Note sur la notion de perfection chrétienne*, 1942, 2. See the use of these and many other texts in the early part of chapter three, as well as the lengthy explanation of Christogenesis in chapter five. See also de Lubac, *Pensée religieuse* . . . , 174-7.

50 °*Trois choses que je vois*, 1948, 4, note 1. The only theologian who has developed a similar understanding of the relationship between the natural and supernatural is Karl Rahner, in *Sendung und Gnade*, 52-75. [Eng. trans., 59-94.] It is extraordinary how the whole point of Teilhard's approach to this question can be missed by such an otherwise perceptive critic as Olivier Rabut. See his *Dialogue* . . . , 157-61, 181, note 1. [Eng. trans., 186-92, 217-18, note 1.]

51 See the survey of the present state of the question, including an abundant bibliography, by Karl Rahner, s.J., 'Natur und Gnade', *Fragen der Theologie Heute*, 209-30. [Eng. trans., in *Nature and Grace* (London, 1963), 3-50.] An excellent survey is also given by Juan Alfaro, s.J., 'Natur und Gnade' *Lexikon für Theologie und Kirche*, vol. vii (Freiburg, 1962) 830-5. Among original speculative studies the following should especially be noted: Henri Bouillard, s.J., 'L'idée de surnaturel et le mystère chrétien', in *L'Homme devant Dieu*, vol. iii, 153-6; Karl Rahner, s.J., 'Über das Verhältnis von Natur und Gnade', *Schriften zur Theologie*, vol. i, 323-45 [Eng. trans., *Theological Investigations*, vol. i, 297-317.]; Léopold Malevez, s.J., 'L'Esprit et le désir de Dieu', *Nouvelle Revue Théologique*, lxix (1947), 3-31.

52 *La Foi qui opère*, 1918, in *ET*, 325.

53 *MD*, 61. [Eng. trans., 42 (38).] Nevertheless, this text can be so interpreted that risk is reduced to a minimum; see chapter five, note 46.

54 °*Le Christique*, 1955, 13. See the same sentiment expressed almost thirty years before: 'Instinctively, especially during the last ten years, I have always offered myself to Our Lord as a sort of field of experience where the fusion between the two great loves of God and the world would take place in a small way, a fusion without which I am convinced the coming of the Kingdom of God is not possible.' (°Letter of December 31, 1926, to Father Auguste Valensin.)

55 Denzinger, 3016 [1796].

56 John Henry Newman, 'Christianity and Scientific Investigation', *The Idea of a University*, 4th ed. (London, 1875), 474-7.

BIBLIOGRAPHY

I WORKS OF PIERRE TEILHARD DE CHARDIN

NOTE: Only works cited in this present study are included here. A complete bibliography of Teilhard's writings, including over 500 items, is to be found in the biography by Claude Cuénot listed below in section II. A small circle (°) before an item indicates material unpublished as of January 1966. The abbreviations 's.s.' and 'd.s.' indicate whether the typing of an unpublished item is single or double space. A list of other abbreviations will be found on the first page of the Notes.

A Books and Articles

1916—*La Vie cosmique*, in *ET*, 5-61.
—*La Maîtrise du monde et le règne de Dieu*, in *ET*, 67-84.
—*Le Christ dans la matière*, in *HU*, 39-58 [Eng. trans., 41-55.], and *ET*, 91-107.
1917—*La Lutte contre la multitude*, in *ET*, 113-32.
—*Le Milieu mystique*, in *ET*, 137-67.
—*L'Union créatrice*, in *ET*, 175-97.
1918—*L'Ame du monde*, in *ET*, 221-32.
—*La Grande Monade*, in *Cahiers*, ii, 39-49, and *ET*, 237-48.
—*L'Eternel féminin*, in *ET*, 253-62.
—*Mon univers*, in *ET*, 267-79.
—*Le Prêtre*, in *ET*, 285-302.
—*La Foi qui opère*, in *ET*, 307-29.
—*Forma Christi*, in *ET*, 335-53.
—*Note sur l'Elément universel du monde*, in *ET*, 359-62.
1919—*Note pour servir à l'évangélisation des temps nouveaux*, in *Cahiers*, iv, 11-21, and *ET*, 367-81.
—*Terre promise*, in *ET*, 387-96.
—*L'Elément universel*, in *ET*, 401-13.
—*La Puissance spirituelle de la matière*, in *HU*, 59-75 [Eng. trans., 59-71.], and *ET*, 437-46.

—*Les Noms de la matière*, in *ET*, 419-32.

1920—*Note sur le Christ universel*, in *Oeuvres*, ix, 39-44.

—°*Note sur les modes de l'action divine dans l'univers*, d.s. 13 pp.

—°*Chute, rédemption et géocentrie*, s.s. 5 pp.

—*Note sur le progrès*, in *Oeuvres*, v, 23-37. [Eng. trans., *FM*, 11-24.]

1921—*Science et Christ*, in *Oeuvres*, ix, 47-62.

1923—°*Panthéisme et christianisme*, s.s. 13 pp.

—*La Messe sur le monde*, in *HU*, 17-37. [Eng. trans., 19-37.]

1924—*Mon univers*, in *Oeuvres*, ix, 65-114.

—°*Note sur quelques représentations historiques du péché originel*, d.s. 8 pp.

1925—*Le Paradoxe transformiste*, in *Oeuvres*, iii, 115-42.

—*L'Hominisation*, in *Oeuvres*, iii, 77-111.

1926—*Les Fondements et le fond de l'idée d'évolution*, in *Oeuvres*, iii, 165-97.

1926-7—*Le Milieu divin*, *Oeuvres*, iv. [Eng. trans., *Le Milieu Divin* (London, 1960) and Fontana ed. (London, 1964); *The Divine Milieu* (New York, 1960).]

1929—°*Le Sens humain*, s.s. 16 pp.

1930—*Que faut-il penser du transformisme?*, in *Oeuvres*, iii, 213-23.

—*Le Phénomène humain*, in *Oeuvres*, iii, 227-43.

—°*Essai d'integration de l'homme dans l'univers*, 4th lecture, d.s. 17 pp.

1931—*L'Esprit de la terre*, in *Oeuvres*, vi, 23-57.

1932—°*La Route de l'Ouest*, d.s. 21 pp.

1933—*La Signification et la valeur constructrice de la souffrance*, in *Oeuvres*, vi, 59-66.

—*L'Incroyance moderne*, in *Oeuvres*, ix, 149-53.

—*Le Christianisme dans le monde*, in *Oeuvres*, ix, 131-45.

—°*Christologie et évolution*, s.s. 14 pp.

1934—°*L'Evolution de la chasteté*, s.s. 17 pp.

—°*Comment je crois*, s.s. 27 pp.

1936—*Esquisse d'un univers personnel*, in *Oeuvres*, vi, 67-114.

—*Quelques réflexions sur la conversion du monde*, in *Oeuvres*, ix, 157-66.

—*La Crise présente*, in *Cahiers*, iii, 69-97, and *Oeuvres*, ix, 169-91.

1937—*Le Phénomène spirituel*, in *Oeuvres*, vi, 115-39.

—*L'Energie humain*, in *Oeuvres*, vi, 141-200.

1938—*Hérédité sociale et éducation*, in *Oeuvres*, v, 41-53. [Eng. trans. in *FM*, 25-36.]

1938-40—*Le Phénomène humain*, *Oeuvres*, i. [Eng. trans., *The Phenomenon of Man* (London and New York,) 1959) and Fontana ed. (London, 1965).]

1939—*La Mystique de la science*, in *Oeuvres*, vi, 201-23.

—*Les Unités humaines naturelles*, in *Oeuvres*, iii, 273-301.

—°*Quelques vues générales sur l'essence du christianisme*, s.s. 3 pp.

—*La Grande option*, in *Oeuvres*, v, 57-81. [Eng. trans., *FM*, 37-60.]

1940—*La Parole attendue*, in *Cahiers*, iv, 22-9.

1941—*L'Avenir de l'homme vu par un paléontologiste*, in Oeuvres, v, 85-100. [Eng. trans., *FM*, 61-76.]

—*Sur les bases possibles d'un credo humain commun*, in Oeuvres, v, 101-6. [Eng. trans., *FM*, 76-81.]

—*L'Atomisme de l'esprit*, in Oeuvres, vii, 29-63.

1942—°*Note sur la notion de perfection chrétienne*, s.s. 4 pp.

—*Le Cône du temps*, in Oeuvres, v, 111-17. [Eng. trans., *FM*, 83-9.]

—*La Transposition 'conique' de l'action*, in Oeuvres, v, 118-26. [Eng. trans., *FM*, 89-96.]

—°*Le Christ évoluteur*, s.s. 9 pp.

—*La Place de l'homme dans l'univers*, in Oeuvrès, iii, 305-26.

1943—*Super-humanité, super-Christ, super-charité*, in Oeuvres, ix, 193-218.

—*Réflexions sur le bonheur*, in Cahiers, ii, 53-70.

1944—°*Introduction à la vie chrétienne*, s.s. 13 pp.

—*La Centrologie*, in Oeuvres, vii, 104-34.

1945—*Action et Activation*, in Oeuvres, ix, 221-33.

—°*Christianisme et évolution*, s.s. 10 pp.

—*La Planétisation humaine*, in Oeuvres, v, 159-75. [Eng. trans., *FM*, 124-39.]

1946—*Catholicisme et science*, in Oeuvres, ix, 237-41.

—*Quelques réflexions sur le retentissement spirituel de la bombe atomique*, in Oeuvres, v, 179-87. [Eng. trans., *FM*, 140-8.]

—*Esquisse d'un dialectique de l'esprit*, in Oeuvres, vii, 1948-58.

1947—*La Formation de la 'noosphère'*, in Oeuvres, v, 201-31. [Eng. trans., *FM*, 155-84.]

—*La Foi en l'homme*, in Oeuvres, v, 235-43. [Eng. trans., *FM*, 185-92.]

—°*Réflexions sur le péché original*, s.s. 7 pp.

—*L'Apport spirituel de l'Extrême-Orient*, in Revue de la pensée juive, ii (1950), 105-13.

—*Sur le valeur religieuse de la recherche*, in Oeuvres, ix, 257-63.

—*Le Rebondissement humain de l'évolution et ses conséquences*, in Oeuvres, v, 253-71. [Eng. trans., *FM*, 196-213.]

—*Agitation ou genèse?*, in Oeuvres, v, 275-89. [Eng. trans., *FM*, 214-26.]

1948—*Les Directions et les conditions de l'avenir*, in Oeuvres, v, 293-305. [Eng. trans., *FM*, 227-37.]

—°*Trois choses que je vois*, s.s. 7 pp.

—°*On the Trend and Significance of Human Socialisation*, d.s. 7 pp.

—*Ma position intellectuelle*, published in Les Etudes Philosophiques, x (1955), 580-1, under the title, 'La pensée du Père Teilhard de Chardin par lui-même'.

—°*Comment je vois*, s.s. 26 pp.

—°*Le Néo-humanisme moderne et ses réactions sur le christianisme*, s.s. 6 pp.

1949—*L'Humanité se meut-elle biologiquement sur elle-même?*, in *Oeuvres*, v, 319-36. [Eng. trans., *FM*, 244-59.]

—*Un phénomène de contre-évolution en biologie humaine ou la peur de l'existence*, in *Oeuvres*, vii, 189-202.

—*Le Groupe zoologique humain* (Paris, 1956). Also published as *Oeuvres*, viii, under the title of *La Place de l'homme dans la nature*.

—*Le Coeur du problème*, in *Oeuvres*, v, 339-49. [Eng. trans., *FM*, 260-9.]

1950—°*Monogénisme et monophylétisme*, s.s. 2 pp.

—*Comment concevoir et espérer que se réalise sur terre l'unanimisation humaine?*, *Oeuvres*, v, 367-74. [Eng. trans., *FM*, 281-8.]

—°*Le Phénomène chrétien*, s.s. 6 pp.

—*Réflexions sur deux formes inverses d'esprit*, in *Oeuvres*, vii, 225-36.

—°*Le Coeur de la matière*, s.s. 34 pp.

—*Le Goût de vivre*, in *Oeuvres*, vii, 239-54.

1951—*La Structure phylétique du groupe humain*, in *Oeuvres*, ii, 187-234.

—*Du cosmos la cosmogénèse*, in *Oeuvres*, vii, 261-77.

—°*Quelques remarques 'pour y voir clair' sur l'essence du sentiment mystique*, s.s. 2 pp.

—*L'Energie spirituelle de la souffrance*, in *Oeuvres*, vii, 255-7.

—*Réflexions sur l'ultra-humain*, in *Oeuvres*, vii, 281-91.

1952—*La Réflexion de l'énergie*, in *Oeuvres*, vii, 335-53.

—°*Ce que le monde attend en ce moment de l'église de Dieu*, s.s. 5 pp.

—*La Fin de l'espèce*, in *Oeuvres*, v, 389-95. [Eng. trans., *FM*, 298-303.]

1953—°*Contingence de l'univers et le goût humain de survivre*, s.s. 5 pp.

—*L'Etoffe de l'univers*, in *Oeuvres*, vii, 397-406.

—°*Le Dieu de l'évolution*, s.s. 6 pp.

—*L'Activation de l'énergie humaine*, in *Oeuvres*, vii, 409-16.

1954—*Un Sommaire de ma perspective 'phénoménologique' du monde*, in *Les Etudes Philosophiques*, x (1955), 569-71.

—*Les Singularités de l'espèce humaine*, in *Oeuvres*, ii, 295-369.

—*La Singularité du phénomène chrétien*, an appendix to the previous essay, in *Oeuvres*, ii, 371-4.

1955—*Barrière de la mort et co-réflexion*, in *Oeuvres*, vii, 419-29.

—°*Le Christique*, s.s. 13 pp.

—*Recherche, travail et adoration*, in *Oeuvres*, ix, 283-9.

B *Letters*

1914-1919—*Genèse d'une pensée* (Paris, 1961). [Eng. trans., *The Making of a Mind* (London and New York, 1965).]

1919—'Maurice Blondel et le Père Teilhard de Chardin; Mémoires échangés en décembre 1919, présentés par H. de Lubac,' *Archives de Philosophie*, xxiv (1961), 123-56.

1917-34—°Letters to Father Auguste Valensin.

1923-55—*Lettres de Voyage* (Paris, 1961). [Eng. trans., *Letters from a Traveller*, (London and New York, 1962).]

II WORKS ON THE THOUGHT OF TEILHARD DE CHARDIN

NOTE: Only works cited in the present study have been listed below. An exhaustive bibliography in all languages, published each year since 1956, appears in the July-December issue of *Archivum Historicum Societatis Jesu* under the section entitled 'Bibliographia de historia, S.J.'.

A *Books*

BARTHELEMY-MADAULE, MADELEINE, *Bergson et Teilhard de Chardin* (Paris, Editions du Seuil, 1963).

CHAUCHARD, PAUL, *L'Etre humain selon Teilhard de Chardin* (Paris, Gabalda, 1959). [Eng. trans., *Man and Cosmos* (New York, Herder and Herder, 1965).]

COGNET, LOUIS, *Le Père Teilhard de Chardin et la pensée contemporaine* (Paris, Flammarion, 1952).

CRESPY, GEORGES, *La Pensée théologique de Teilhard de Chardin* (Paris, Editions Universitaires, 1961).

CUENOT, CLAUDE, *Pierre Teilhard de Chardin* (Paris, Plon, 1958). [Eng. trans., *Teilhard de Chardin* (Baltimore, Helicon Press, and London, Burns Oates, 1965).]

GARAUDY, ROGER, *Perspectives de l'homme, existentialisme, pensée catholique, marxisme* (Paris, Presses Universitaires, 1961).

LEROY, PIERRE, S.J., *Pierre Teilhard de Chardin tel que je l'ai connu* (Paris, Plon, 1958). [Eng. trans. in *Letters from a Traveller* (London, Collins, and New York, Harper, 1962), 15-47 and in *Le Milieu Divin* (London, 1964) Fontana ed., 13-42.]

DE LUBAC, HENRI, S.J., *La Pensée religieuse du Père Teilhard de Chardin* (Paris, Aubier, Montaigne, 1962).

—*La Prière du Père Teilhard de Chardin* (Paris, Fayard, 1964.)

RABUT, OLIVIER, O.P., *Dialogue avec Teilhard de Chardin* (Paris, Editions du Cerf, 1958). [Eng. trans., *Dialogue with Teilhard de Chardin* (London, Sheed and Ward, 1961.]

RIDEAU, EMILE, S.J., *La Pensée du Père Teilhard de Chardin* (Paris, Editions du Seuil, 1965).

SMULDERS, PIERRE, S.J., *La Vision de Teilhard de Chardin* (Paris, Desclée de Brouwer, 1964).

TRESMONTANT, CLAUDE, *Introduction à la pensée de Pierre Teilhard de Chardin* (Paris, Editions du Seuil, 1956). [Eng. trans., *Pierre Teilhard de Chardin, His Thought* (Baltimore, Helicon Press, 1959).]

WILDIERS, N. M., O.F.M.CAP., *Teilhard de Chardin* (Paris, Editions Universitaires, 1960).

B *Articles*

D'ARMAGNAC, CHRISTIAN, S.J., 'De Blondel à Teilhard, nature et intériorité', *Archives de Philosophie*, xxi (1958), 298-312.

—'Philosophie de la nature et méthode chez le Père Teilhard de Chardin', *Archives de Philosophie*, xx (1957), 5-41.

—'La Pensée du Père Teilhard de Chardin comme apologétique moderne', *Nouvelle Revue Théologique*, lxxxiv (1962), 598-621.

VON BALTHAZAR, HANS URS, 'Die Spiritualität Teilhards de Chardin', *Wort und Wahrheit*, xvii (1963), 339-50.

BARTHELEMY-MADAULE, MADELEINE, 'Teilhard de Chardin, Marxism, Existentialism: A Confrontation', *International Philosophical Quarterly*, i (1961), 648-67.

BOROS, LADISLAUS, S.J., 'Evolutionismus und Spiritualität', *Der Grosse Entshchluss*, xv (1960), 254-9, 301-3, 346-50, 399-403.

—'Evolution und Metaphysik', *Orientierung*, xxv (1961), 237-41.

BRUNNER, AUGUST, S.J., 'Pierre Teilhard de Chardin', *Stimmen der Zeit*, clxv (1959), 210-22.

BRUNS, J. EDGAR, 'Cosmogenesis and Theology', in *The World of Teilhard*, ed. Robert T. Francoeur (Baltimore, Helicon Press, 1961), 167-85.

DANIELOU, S.J., 'Signification de Teilhard de Chardin', *Etudes*, cccxii (1962), 145-61.

DONCEEL, JOSEPH F., S.J., 'Teilhard de Chardin: Scientist or Philosopher?' *International Philosophical Quarterly*, v (1965), 248-66.

DONNELLY, WILLIAM, 'The Thought of Teilhard de Chardin', *The Clergy Review* xlv (1960), 324-49.

DUBARLE, DOMINIQUE, O.P., 'A propos du "Phénomène humain" du P. Teilhard de Chardin', *La Vie Intellectuelle*, xxvii (1956), 6-25.

FESSARD, GASTON, S.J., 'La Vision religieuse et cosmique de Teilhard de Chardin', *L'Homme devant Dieu*, vol. iii (Paris, Aubier, Montaigne, 1964), 223-48.

FLEMING, T. V., S.J., 'Two Unpublished Letters of Teilhard', *The Heythrop Journal*, vi (1965), 36-45.

FORSTHOEFEL, PAULINUS, S.J., 'Beneath the Microscope', *The World of Teilhard*, ed. Robert T. Francoeur (Baltimore, Helicon Press, 1961), 98-113.

JEANNIERE, ABEL, S.J., 'Approches christologiques', *Essais sur Teilhard de Chardin*, *Recherches et Débats*, Numéro 40 (Paris, Arthème Fayard, 1962), 79-95.

—'L'Avenir de l'humanité d'après Teilhard de Chardin', *Revue de l'Action Populaire*, xii (1962), 5-12.

JOURNET, CHARLES, 'La Vision teilhardienne du monde', *Divinitas*, iii (1959), 330-44.

KONIG, FRANZ CARDINAL, 'Les Taches de l'intellectuel catholique dans le monde d'aujourd'hui', *Union Catholique des Scientifiques Français*, July-August, 1961, 17-18.

KUHN, WOLFGANG, 'Teilhard de Chardin und die Biologie', *Stimmen der Zeit*, clxxii (1963), 246-63.

LE BLOND, J.-M., S.J., 'Consacrer l'effort humain', *Etudes*, ccxcvi (1958), 58-68.

MALEVEZ, LEOPOLD, S.J., 'La Méthode du P. Teilhard de Chardin et la phénoménologie', *Nouvelle Revue Théologique*, lxxxix (1957), 579-99.

MOONEY, CHRISTOPHER F., S.J., 'Blondel and Teilhard de Chardin', *Thought*, xxxvii (1962), 543-62.

MOREL, GEORGE, S.J., 'Karl Marx et le P. Teilhard de Chardin', *Etudes*, ccciv (1960), 80-7.

NORTH, ROBERT, S.J., 'Teilhard and the Problem of Creation', *Theological Studies*, xxiv (1964), 577-601.

D'OUINCE, RENE, S.J., 'Vivre dans la plénitude du Christ', *Christus*, ix (1962), 239-47.

—'L'Epreuve de l'obéissance dans la vie du Père Teilhard de Chardin', *L'Homme devant Dieu*, vol. iii (Paris, Aubier, Montaigne, 1964), 331-46.

PHILIPPE DE LA TRINITE, O.C.D., 'Teilhard de Chardin, synthèse ou confusion?' *Divinitas*, iii (1959), 285-329.

RUSSELL, JOHN L., S.J., 'The Phenomenon of Man', *The Heythrop Journal*, i (1960), 271-84; ii (1961), 3-13.

—'The Principle of Finality in the Philosophy of Aristotle and Teilhard de Chardin', *The Heythrop Journal*, iii (1962), 347-57; iv (1963), 32-41.

RUSSO, FRANCOIS, S.J., 'La Socialisation selon Teilhard de Chardin', *Revue de l'Action Populaire*, xii (1962), 1157-70.

SCHEFFCZYK, LEO, 'Die "Christogénèse" Teilhard de Chardins und der Kosmische Christus bei Paulus', *Tübinger Theoligische Quartalschrift*, cxliii (1963), 136-74.

DE SOLAGES, BRUNO, 'La Pensée chrétienne face à l'évolution', *Bulletin de Littérature Ecclésiastique*, xlviii (1947), ciii-cxvi. [Eng. trans., 'Christianity and Evolution', *Cross Currents*, i (1951), 26-7.]

—'Les Preuves teilhardiennes de Dieu', *L'Homme devant Dieu*, vol. iii (Paris, Aubier, Montaigne, 1964), 125-32.

BIBLIOGRAPHY

TRESMONTANT, CLAUDE, 'Le Père Teilhard de Chardin et la théologie', *Lettre*, (1962), 3-53.

VASS, GEORGE, S.J., 'Teilhard de Chardin and Inward Vision', *The Heythrop Journal*, ii (1961), 237-49.

VOLLERT, CYRIL, S.J., 'Toward Omega: Man in the Vision of Teilhard de Chardin', *The Month*, xxiii (1960), 261-9.

III WORKS CITED ON RELATED SUBJECTS

A Books

ALLO, E. B. *Première épître aux Corinthiens* (Paris, Gabalda, 1934).

AQUINAS, ST. THOMAS. *Opera Omnia*, 25 vol. (Parma, 1852-73).
Summa Theologica, vol. i-iv.
Contra Gentiles, vol. v.
Commentarium in iv Sententiarum, vol. vi-vii.
De Potentia, vol. viii.
De Veritate, vol. ix.
In 1 am ad Timotheum, vol. xiii.
In Boetium de Trinitate, vol. xvii.

VON BALTHAZAR, HANS URS, *Theologie der Geschichte* (Basle, Johannes, 1959). [Eng. trans., *A Theology of History*, (London, Sheed & Ward, 1964).]
—*Das Ganze im Fragment* (Einsiedeln, Benziger, 1964).

BEAUCAMP, EVODE, O.F.M., *La Bible et le sens religieux de l'univers* (Paris, Editions du Cerf, 1959). [Eng. trans., *The Bible and the Universe* (Westminster, Newman Press, 1963).]

BEST, ERNEST, *One Body in Christ*, (London, S.P.C.K., 1955).

BLONDEL, MAURICE, *Une Enigme historique, le 'Vinculum Substantiale' d'après Leibnitz et l'ébauche d'un réalisme supérieur* (Paris, Beauchesne, 1930.)
—*Lettre sur l'apologétique de 1896*, in *Les premiers écrits de Maurice Blondel*, vol. ii (Paris, Presses Universitaires, 1956), 5-95.

BONSIRVEN, JOSEPH, S.J., *L'Evangile de Paul* (Paris, Aubier, Montaigne, 1948).
—*Théologie du Nouveau Testament* (Paris, Aubier, Montaigne, 1951). [Eng. trans., *Theology of the New Testament* (Westminster, Newman Press, 1963).]

BOROS, LADISLAUS, S.J., *Mysterium Mortis, Der Mensch in der Letzten Entscheidung* (Freiburg, Walter, 1962).

BOUILLARD, HENRI, S.J., *Blondel et le Christianisme* (Paris, Editions du Seuil, 1961).

CERFAUX, LUCIEN, *La Théologie de l'Eglise suivant Saint Paul* (Paris, Editions du Cerf, 2è éd., 1948). [Eng. trans., *The Church in the Theology of St. Paul* (New York, Herder and Herder, 1959).]

—*Le Christ dans le Théologie de Saint Paul* (Paris, Editions du Cerf, 1951). [Eng. trans., *Christ in the Theology of Saint Paul* (New York, Herder and Herder, 1959).]

CULLMANN, OSCAR, *Christus und die Zeit* (Zürich, Evangelischer Verlag, 1946). [Eng. trans., *Christ and Time*, 3rd ed. (London, S.C.M. Press, 1962).]

—*La Christologie du Nouveau Testament* (Paris, Neuchatel, 1958).

DENZINGER, HENRICUS, *Enchiridion Symbolorum*, 32nd edition, ed. Adolfus Schönmetzer (Freiburg, Herder, 1963).

DUBARLE, DOMINIQUE, O.P., *Optimisme devant ce monde* (Paris, Editions du Cerf, 1949).

DUBARLE, A.-M., O.P., *Le Péché originel dans l'écriture* (Paris, Editions du Cerf, 1958). [Eng. trans., *The Biblical Doctrine of Original Sin* (London, Chapman & Hall, 1964).]

DUPONT, JACQUES, O.S.B., *Gnosis, La Connaissance religieuse dans les épîtres de Saint Paul* (Bruges, Desclée de Brouwer, 1949).

DE FRAINE, JEAN, S.J., *Adam et son lignage: Etudes sur la notion de 'personalité corporative' dans la Bible* (Bruges, Desclée de Brouwer, 1959).

GALLOWAY, ALLEN D., *The Cosmic Christ* (London, Nisbet, 1951).

GOUHIER, HENRI, *Bergson et le Christ des évangiles* (Paris, Arthème Fayard, 1961).

GROSS, J., *La Divinisation du Chrétien d'après les Pères Grecs* (Paris, Gabalda, 1938).

HENRY, PAUL, S.J., *Philosophie religieuse de l'épître aux Romains* (Paris, 1950, manuscript).

HUBY, JOSEPH, S.J., *Les Epîtres de la captivité* (Paris, Beauchesne, 1935).

KUNG, HANS, *Rechterfertigung* (Einsiedeln, Johannes, 1957). [Eng. trans., *Justification* (New York, Nelson, 1964).]

LEYS, ROGER, S.J., *L'Image de Dieu chez St. Grégoire de Nysse* (Paris, L'Edition Universelle, 1951).

LIGHTFOOT, J. B., *St. Paul's Epistles to the Colossians and to Philemon* (London, Macmillan, 1904).

LIGIER, LOUIS, S.J., *Péché d'Adam et péché du monde*, vol. i (Paris, Aubier, Montaigne, 1960), vol. ii (Paris, Aubier, Montaigne, 1961).

DE LUBAC, HENRI, S.J., *Catholicisme* (Paris, Editions du Cerf, 1937). [Eng. trans., *Catholicism* (London, Longmans, Green, 1950).]

MASCALL, E. L., *Christian Theology and Natural Science* (London, Longmans, Green, 1956).

MALMBERG, FELIX, S.J., *Ein Leib—Ein Geist* (Freiburg, Herder, 1960).

—*Über den Gottmenschen* (Freiburg, Herder, 1960).

MARTELET, GUSTAVE, S.J., *Victoire sur la mort* (Paris, Chronique Sociale, 1962).

MERSCH, EMILE, S.J., *Le Corps mystique du Christ, Etudes de théologie historique*, 2 vol. (Bruges, 3e éd., Desclée de Brouwer, 1951). [Eng. trans., *The Whole Christ* (Milwaukee, Bruce, 1938).]

—*La Théologie du Corps Mystique*, 2 vol. (Bruges, Desclée de Brouwer, 4e éd., 1954). [Eng. trans., *The Theology of the Mystical Body* (St. Louis, Herder, 1952).]

MOROUX, JEAN, *Le Mystère du temps* (Paris, Aubier, Montaigne, 1962). [Eng. trans., *The Mystery of Time* (New York, Desclée, 1964).]

MUSSNER, FRANZ, *Christus, das All und die Kirche* (Trier, Paulinus, 1955).

NEWMAN, JOHN HENRY, *The Idea of a University*, 4th edition (London, Pickering, 1875).

OVERHAGE, PAUL, S.J., and RAHNER, KARL, S.J., *Das Problem der Hominisation* (Freiburg, Herder, 1961).

PEIPER, JOSEF, *Scholastik* (München, Kösel, 1960). [Eng. trans., *Scholasticism* (New York, Pantheon, 1960).]

PIUS XII, *Mystici Corporis Christi, Acta Apostolicae Sedis*, xxxv (1943), 195-248.

—*Humani Generis, Acta Apostolicae Sedis*, xlii (1950), 561-7.

RAHNER, KARL, S.J., *Zur Theologie des Todes* (Freiburg, Herder, 1958). [Eng. trans., *On the Theology of Death* (London, Nelson, 1961).]

—*Über den Schriftinspiration* (Freiburg, Herder, 1959). [Eng. trans., *Inspiration in the Bible* (London, Nelson, 1961).]

—*Sendung und Gnade* (Innsbruck, Tyrolia, 1959). [Eng. trans., *Mission and Grace*, vol. i (London, Sheed & Ward, 1963).]

RICHARD, L., *Le Mystère de la rédemption* (Paris, Desclée, 1959).

ROBINSON, H. WHEELER, *Inspiration and Revelation in the Old Testament* (Oxford, Clarendon Press, 1946).

ROBINSON, J. A. T., *The Body* (London, S.C.M. Press, 1952).

RUST, E. C., *Nature and Man in Biblical Thought* (London, Lutterworth Press, 1953).

SCHLIER, HEINRICH, *Der Brief an die Epheser* (Düsseldorf, 3. Aufl., Patmos, 1962).

THILS, GUSTAVE, *Théologie des réalités terrestres, I Préludes* (Paris, Desclée de Brouwer, 1947), *II Théologie de l'histoire* (Paris, Desclée de Brouwer, 1949).

THORNTON, L. S., *The Incarnate Lord* (London, Longmans, Green, 1928).

TROISFONTAINES, ROGER, S.J., *Je ne meurs pas* (Paris, Editions Universitaires, 1960). [Eng. trans., *I Do Not Die* (New York, Desclée, 1964).]

B *Articles*

AHERN, BARNABAS, C.P., 'The Christian's Union with the Body of Christ in Cor., Gal. and Rom.', *Catholic Biblical Quarterly*, xxiii (1961), 199-209.

ALFARO, JUAN, S.J., 'Natur und Gnade', *Lexikon für Theologie und Kirche*, vol. vii (Freiburg, Herder, 1962), 830-5.

BIBLIOGRAPHY

VON BALTHASAR, HANS URS, 'Eschatologie', *Fragen der Theologie Heute*, ed. J. Feiner, J. Trütch, F. Böckle (Einsiedeln, Benziger, 1957), 403-21.

BENOIT, PIERRE, O.P. 'Corps, Tête et Plérôme dans les épîtres de la captivité', *Revue Biblique*, lxiii (1956), 5-44.

BOISMARD, M. E., O.P., 'Le Retour du Christ', *Lumière et Vie*, ii (1953), 53-76.

BONE, EDOUARD, S.J., 'Polygénisme et polyphylétisme', *Archives de Philosophie*, xxiii (1960), 99-141.

BOROS, LADISLAUS, S.J., 'Meditationen über die Eucharistie', *Orientierung*, xxvii (1963), 117-19, 134-6.

BOUILLARD, HENRI, S.J., 'L'Idée de surnaturel et le mystère chrétien', *L'Homme devant Dieu*, vol. iii (Paris, Aubier, Montaigne, 1964), 153-6.

BOUYER, LOUIS, 'Les Deux économies du gouvernement divin, Satan et le Christ', *Initiation Théologique*, ed. A.-M. Henry, O.P., vol. ii (Paris, Editions du Cerf, 1952), 503-35. [Eng. trans., *God and His Creation* (Chicago, Fides, 1955), 466-96.]

BRINKMANN, B., 'Die kosmische Stellung des Gottmenschen in Paulinischer Sicht', *Wissenschaft und Weisheit*, xiii (1950), 6-33.

DE BROGLIE, GUY, S.J., 'De la place du surnaturel dans la philosophie de Saint-Thomas', *Recherches de Science Religieuse*, xiv (1924), 193-245.

CONGAR, YVES, O.P., 'Dogme Christologique et Ecclésiologie', *Das Konzil von Chalkedon*, ed. by A. Grillmeier, S.J., and H. Bacht, S.J., vol. iii (Würzburg, Echter, 1954), 239-68.

—'Sur l'inclusion de l'humanité dans le Christ', *Revue de Sciences Philosophiques et Théologiques*, xxv (1936), 489-95.

DAVID, JAKOB, 'Theologie der irdischen Wirklichkeiten', *Fragen der Theologie Heute*, ed. by J. Feiner, J. Trütsch, and F. Böckle (Einsiedeln, Benziger, 1960), 549-68.

DUBARLE, DOMINIQUE, O.P., 'L'Homme et la fin de l'humanité', *Lumière et Vie*, ii (1953), 24-38.

—'L'Entreprise scientifique moderne et sa mise en accusation religieuse', *Signes du Temps*, i (1960) 9-12.

—'Concept de la matiére et discussions sur le matérialisme', *Science et Matérialisme, Recherches et Débats, Numéro 41* (Paris, 1962), 37-70.

DUMONT, C., S.J., 'La Prédication du péché originel', *Nouvelle Revue Théolgique*, lxxxiii (1961), 113-34.

DURRWELL, F. X., C.SS.R., 'Le Christ, premier et dernier', *Bible et Vie Chrétienne*, ix (1963), 16-28.

ERBRICH, P., S.J., 'Mysticher oder Auferstandener Leib Christi', *Orientierung*, xxiii (1959), 193-5, 204-7.

EWING, J. FRANKLIN, S.J., 'Human Evolution-1956', *Anthropological Quarterly*, xxix (1956), 91-139.

BIBLIOGRAPHY

FEUILLET, ANDRE, 'La Synthèse eschatologique de Saint-Matthieu (xxiv-xxv)', *Revue Biblique*, lvi (1949), 340-64; lvii (1950), 62-91, 180-211.

—'L'Eglise plérôme du Christ d'aprés Eph.', *Nouvelle Revue Théologique*, lxxviii (1956), 446-72, 596-610.

—'Le Temps de l'Eglise d'après le quatrième Evangile et l'Apocalypse', *La Maison-Dieu*, lxv (1961), 60-79.

FRANSEN, PETER, S.J., 'Three Ways of Dogmatic Thought', *The Heythrop Journal*, iv (1963), 3-24.

GELIN, A., 'Jours de Yahvé et jour de Yahvé', *Lumière et Vie*, ii (1953), 39-52.

GRILLMEIER, A., S.J., 'Zum Christusbild der Heutigen Katholischen Theologie', *Fragen der Theologie Heute*, ed. J. Feiner, J. Trütch, F. Böckle (Einsiedeln, Benziger, 1957), 265-300.

HAVET, J., 'La Doctrine Paulinienne du "Corps du Christ", essai de mise au point', *Littérature et théologie Paulinienne* (Louvain, Desclée, 1960,) 186-216.

HENRY, PAUL, S.J., 'Kénose', *Dictionnaire de la Bible, Supplément*, vol. v (Paris, 1950), 7-161.

HURZELER, JOHANNES, 'Evolution und Monogenismus/Polygenismus', *Orientierung*, xxviii (1964), 196-7.

ISAYE, G., S.J., 'L'Unité de l'opération divine dans les écrits de Saint Grégoire de Nysse', *Recherches de Science Religieuse*, xxvii (1937), 422-39.

LAMARCHE, PAUL, S.J., 'L'Hymne de l'épître aux Philippiens et le kénose du Christ', *L'Homme devant Dieu*, vol. i, (Paris, Aubier, Montaigne, 1964), 147-58.

LEGRAND, LUCIEN, 'La Création, triomphe cosmique de Yahvé', *Nouvelle Revue Théologique*, lxxxiii (1961), 449-70.

LYONNET, STANISLAUS, S.J., 'Le Péché originel et l'exégèse de Rom. 5:12-14', *Recherches de Science Religieuse*, xliv (1956), 63-84.

—'La Rédemption de l'univers', *Lumière et Vie*, ix (1960), 41-62.

MALEVEZ, LEOPOLD, S.J., 'L'Eglise dans le Christ', *Recherches de Science Religieuse*, xxv (1935), 257-91, 418-43.

—'L'Esprit et le désir de Dieu', *Nouvelle Revue Théologique*, lxix (1947), 3-31.

—'La Vision chrétienne de l'histoire', *Nouvelle Revue Théologique*, lxxi (1949), 113-34, 244-64.

DE MONTCHEUIL, YVES, S.J., 'Les Problèmes du "Vinculum" Leibnitzien d'après M. Blondel', *Mélanges Théologiques* (Paris, Aubier, Montaigne, 1946).

—'L' Unité du sacrifice et du sacrement dans l'Eucharistie', *Mélanges Théoligiques* (Paris, Aubier, Montaigne, 1946), 49-70.

MOONEY, CHRISTOPHER F., S.J., 'Paul's Vision of the Church in "Ephesians"', *Scripture*, xv (1963), 33-43.

PHILIPS, G., 'Deux tendances dans la théologie contemporaine,' *Nouvelle Revue Théologique*, lxxxv (1963), 225-38.

275

RAHNER, KARL, S.J., 'Probleme der Christologie von Heute', *Schriften zur Theologie*, vol i (Einsiedeln, Benziger, 1954), 169-222. [Eng. trans., *Theological Investigations*, vol. i (London, Darton, Longman & Todd, 1960), 149-200.]

—'Theologisches zum Monogenismus', *Schriften zur Theologie*, vol. i (Einsiedeln, Benziger, 1954), 265-71. [Eng. trans., *Theological Investigations* vol. i (London, Darton, Longman & Todd, 1961), 240-7.]

—'Über das Verhältnis von Natur und Gnade', *Schriften zur Theologie*, vol. i (Einsiedeln, Benziger, 1954), 323-45. [Eng. trans., *Theological Investigations*, vol. i (London, Darton, Longman & Todd, 1961), 297-317.]

—'Die Kirche der Heiligen', *Schriften zur Theologie*, vol. iii (Einsiedeln, Benziger, 1956), 111-26.

—'Die Christologie innerhalb einer evolutiven Weltanschauung', *Schriften zur Theologie*, vol. v (Einsiedeln, Benziger, 1962), 183-221.

—'Natur und Gnade', *Fragen der Theologie heute* (Einsiedeln, 1960), 209-30. [Eng. trans., in *Nature and Grace* (London, Sheed & Ward, 1963), 3-50.]

RAMOND, P., O.F.M.CAP., 'Duns Scot', *Dictionnaire de théologie catholique*, vol. iv (Paris, 1911), 1865-1947.

RATZINGER, JOSEPH, 'Theologia Perennis?' *Wort und Wahrheit*, xv (1960), 179-88.

RAWLINSON, A. E. J., 'Corpus Christi', *Mysterium Christi*, ed. G. Bell and A. Deissmann (Berlin, Weidmann, 1931), 275-96.

RIMAUD, JEAN, S.J., 'Vie spirituelle et philosophie: Maurice Blondel', *Christus*, ix (1962), 272-88.

ROBINSON, H. WHEELER, 'The Hebrew Concept of the Corporate Personality', *Werden und Wesen des Alten Testaments*, ed. J. Hempel (Berlin, Töpelmann, 1936), 58-69.

SAGNARD, F.M.M., O.P., 'A propos de I Cor. viii, 6', *Ephemerides Theologicae Louvanienses*, xxvi (1950), 54-8.

SCHEFFCZYK, LEO, 'Die Idee der Einheit von Schöpfung und Erlösung', *Tübinger Theologische Quartalschrift*, cxl (1960), 19-37.

SCHLIER, HEINRICH, 'Kephlē, Anakephalaioomai', *Theologisches Wörterbuch zum Neuen Testament*, ed. Gerhard Kittel, vol. iii (Stuttgart, Kohlhammer, 1938), 672-82.

—'Die Kirche nach dem Briefe and die Epheser', *Die Zeit der Kirche* (Freiburg, Herder, 1956), 159-86.

SCHOONENBERG, P., S.J., 'Erbsünde und Sünde der Welt', *Orientierung*, xxvi (1962), 65-9.

VANNESTE, A., 'La Préhistoire du décret du Concile de Trente sur le péché originel', *Nouvelle Revue Théologique*, lxxxvi (1964), 355-68, 490-510.

VIARD, A., O.P., 'Expectatio Creaturae, (Rom. viii, 19-22)', *Revue Biblique*, lix (1952), 337-54.

VOLLERT, CYRIL, S.J., 'Human Evolution and Theological Implications', *Proceedings, Catholic Theological Society of America*, vi (1951), 122-45.

WARNACH, VICTOR, O.S.B., 'Kirche und Kosmos', *Enkainia*, ed. Hilarius Emonds, O.S.B. (Düsseldorf, Patmos, 1956), 170-205.

ZAPELENA, TH., 'Vos Estis Corpus Christi', *Verbum Domini*, xxxvii (1959), 78-95, 162-70.

Christian life, 184; hominization of, 111, 182-3; joy in death, 112; and original sin, 138-9; overcoming death, *see* death of Christ; as radical sacrifice of egoism, 116; Teilhard's experience of, 15-16; total death, 19-20, 25, 26, 54. *See* death of Christ

death of Christ, *114-45*; 63, 104-6; conquers human death, 115-16; Teilhard's view contrasted with Dun Scotus', 121-2. *See* redemption

despair, 112, 113

destiny, 26

detachment, 28-30, 118, 154

determinism, 37, 42, 104, 123-4, 127. *See* freedom

diminishments, 113, 116, 119, 127. *See* evil; death of Christ

disgust, 15-20

disorder, 108-9, 126

disunion, 126, 135

divine, *see* grace; Omega; supernatural

Divine Milieu, The, 14, 20, 25, 80, 81, 83, 131, 151

divine Milieu; *def.*, 80; 32, 79, 84, 100, 118, 129, 154; as Centre, 80; and Eucharist, 84; and Pleroma, 152; use as synonym for presence of Christ and person of Christ, 80

divinization, 82, 114, 193, 259; of hominization, 62; of human love, 29

dogma, 63, 69

dualism; between matter and consciousness, 38; spiritual, 30

duration, 50, 80-1

earth, 44, 193. *See* New Earth

Eastern religions, *see* religion

effort, human, 132, 152; Christian lack of interest in, 6; Christian value of, 21, 35, 150-1; completed by faith, 208; contempt of, 15; and Cross, 118; and detachment, 154; eternalization of, 22, 27; must have chance to succeed, 18; has positive as well as moral value, 29; and Pleroma, 151; presupposes an absolute, 19, 54, 119; and suffering, 134. *See* action

élan, 18, 19, 25, 27, 31, 119

Element, universal, 79, 80, 86, 178

élu, see chosen part

energy, 24, 38-40, 82; all e. is psychic, 38; Christ's love as, 26; divine, 86; of Eucharist, 83; love-energy, 54, 68, 125, 153, 154. *See* radial energy

epistemology, *see* methodology

Eucharist, *81-7*; 23, 26, 70, 71, 92, 236, 237; Blessed Sacrament, 81; as Centre, 81, 84; and Christogenesis, 86, 162; cult of, 83; energy of, 83; Eucharistic Christ controls universe, 83; Eucharistic transformation of man and material world, 84; expression of divine energy, 86; and Incarnation, 162; as individual realization of Incarnation, 82, 83; mode of omnipresence, 84, 86; physical presence of Christ in, 82-4; and redemption, 118; sanctifies matter, 83; as understood by St. Paul, 91

evil, physical, *104-45*; and creative union, 252; of death, 109-12, *see* death; of disorder and failure, 108-9; evil neutralized (critique), 204, 208; evil spirits, 130; and evolution, 107-22, 134; excess of, 130; God's existence and problem of, *see* God; of growth, 107; manifested in obscurity of faith, 145; and multiplicity, 108, 109-10; overcoming of, *see* death of Christ; passivity toward, 119; of suffering, 113-14; Teilhard's sensitivity to, 113. *See* death of Christ, moral evil, original sin

evolution; *def.*, 206; and attraction from above, 27; biological, 39, 40-2; Catholic Church's position on, 202; and charity, 153; Christ, focus of, 25; and Christogenesis, 160-88; and Church, 154-68; and creation, 173; critical points of, 39, 40, 41, 111, 182; dependent on Christ, 26, 66, 76, 103, 177, 206; deterministic, 42; and efficient causality, 172; evolutionism (critique), 64, 199-202; and freedom, 18; God, cause of, 5; and Incarnation, 160; includes anthropogenesis, 5; irreversible, 41; and love, 123-45, 162; of man, 40-8; of man and Christian Revelation, 57-66; of man

reason, *see* concordism; methodology
redemption, *104-45*; 146, 168, 176-7;
cosmic character of, 136, 143; and
creation, 76, 102, 147, 148; and
Eucharist, 118; and *genèse*, 119; and
Incarnation, 122, 203; in St. Paul, 95-
6, 97; primacy of re-creation over
reparation, 105-6, 142; as reparation
and atonement, 105; reparation for
sin minimized (critique), 122-45, 203;
suffering makes reparation for moral
evil, 118, 125
reflection; collective act of, *see* Omega;
as critical point in evolution, 40. *See*
thought
religion; Eastern, 180, 240, 256; history
of, 155. *See* Catholic Church;
Christianity
reparation; for sin minimized (critique), 122-45, 203. *See* redemption
resignation, 119
responsibility; of Christian for cosmos,
149; of man for evolutionary progress, 18, 50, 124; and original sin,
137. *See* freedom
Resurrection, 61, 63, 73, 90, 96, 104-6,
114-45, 147, 148, 170; of the body,
85, 96, 149
revelation; Christian r. and evolution
of man, 57-66; and creative union,
171; gratuity of Christian r., 60. *See*
concordism; Paul, St.
reversal, 33, 111, 184, 185. *See* transformation
risk, *see* theological risk

sacraments, 86
sacred; and profane distinction minimized (critique), 208-9
Sacred Heart of Christ, 24, 73, 76;
cult of, 27-8, 137
salvation, 63, 85, 96, 121, 135, 146,
154. *See* redemption
sanctification; of human endeavour,
152; of man, 69; of matter, 85, 117;
of universe, 239
sanctity, 75; made dependent on
evolution (critique), 155-6; and renunciation, 29; and work, 150
scholasticism, *see* Thomism

science, 37, 149; and revelation, 13,
58-61, 191; Teilhard's views as discussed by scientists, 224
Scotus, Duns, 121-2
scripture, 213; New Testament, 72,
119, 130, 185-6; Old Testament, 91,
97. *See* Paul, St.
sex, 52, 227
shut-in, 16-19, 219. *See* issue
sin, *122-45*; 105, 127, 205; as limitation
of love energy, 125; mystery of, 128;
and progress, 134; statistical aspect of,
142; reparation for sin minimized
(critique), 106, 122-45, 203; sin de-
personalized (critique), 134-5, 142,
143-5, 208. *See* moral evil; original
sin
Smulders, Pierre, 222, 228, 243, 246,
252
social, 43
socialization, 43-6, 67
soul, 37, 70, 78, 102, 111, 112, 151. *See*
immortality
space-time, *49-51*; 44, 45, 54, 80, 183,
249; and Jesus, 63; and modern
anxiety, 17; and Omega, 54
spirit, 42, 73, 119; contains matter, 117;
growth in s. depends on deficiency in
matter, 114-17, 125; matter directed
towards, 151; spiritual contact implies
bodily contact, 110; spiritualization,
45; unity between matter and, 30.
See Holy Spirit
states of life, 29, 150
Stoicism, 97
suffering, 29, 95, 125, 134; aids
humanization and divinization of
universe, 114; Christification of, 114;
compensation for moral evil, 118,
125; demanded by progress, 109; evil
of, 113-14; to be fought, 114; overcoming evil of, *see* death of Christ;
and resignation, 119; transformed by
Christian message, 113-14
super-Christ, 178
super-humanity, 47, 256
superman, 46
supernatural; act of faith, 58, 68, 163-4;
envelops natural, 206; gratuity of, 59,
74-5, 103, 176, 207; gratuity of s.